Canada and the Cold War

Reg Whitaker and Steve Hewitt

A Bomarc missile in the early 1960s.

James Lorimer & Company Ltd., Publishers
Toronto, Ontario

James Lorimer & Company Ltd. acknowledges the support of the Ontario Arts Council. We acknowledge the support of the Government of Canada through the Book Publishing Industry Development Program (BPIDP) for our publishing activities. We acknowledge the support of the Canada Council for the Arts for our publishing program. We acknowledge the support of the Government of Ontario through the Ontario Media Development Corporation's Ontario Book Initiative.

ONTARIO ARTS COUNCIL
CONSEIL DES ARTS DE L'ONTARIO

The Canada Council | Le Conseil des Arts
for the Arts | du Canada

National Library of Canada Cataloguing in Publication

Whitaker, Reginald, 1943-
    Canada and the Cold War / Reg Whitaker and Steve Hewitt.

ISBN 1-55028-769-9

    1. Espionage—Canada—History—20th century. 2. Canada—Foreign
relations—1945- 3. Cold War. I. Hewitt, Steve II. Title.

FC602.W47 2002   327.12'0971   C2002-904278-X
F1034.2.W47 2002

Page Design: Gwen North
Cover design: Nick Shinn

James Lorimer & Company Ltd.,
Publishers
35 Britain Street
Toronto, Ontario
M5A 1R7
www.lorimer.ca

Distributed in the U.S. by
Casemate
2114 Darby Road, 2nd floor
Havertown, PA
19083

Printed and bound in Canada

Table of Contents

Hiroshima in 1959.

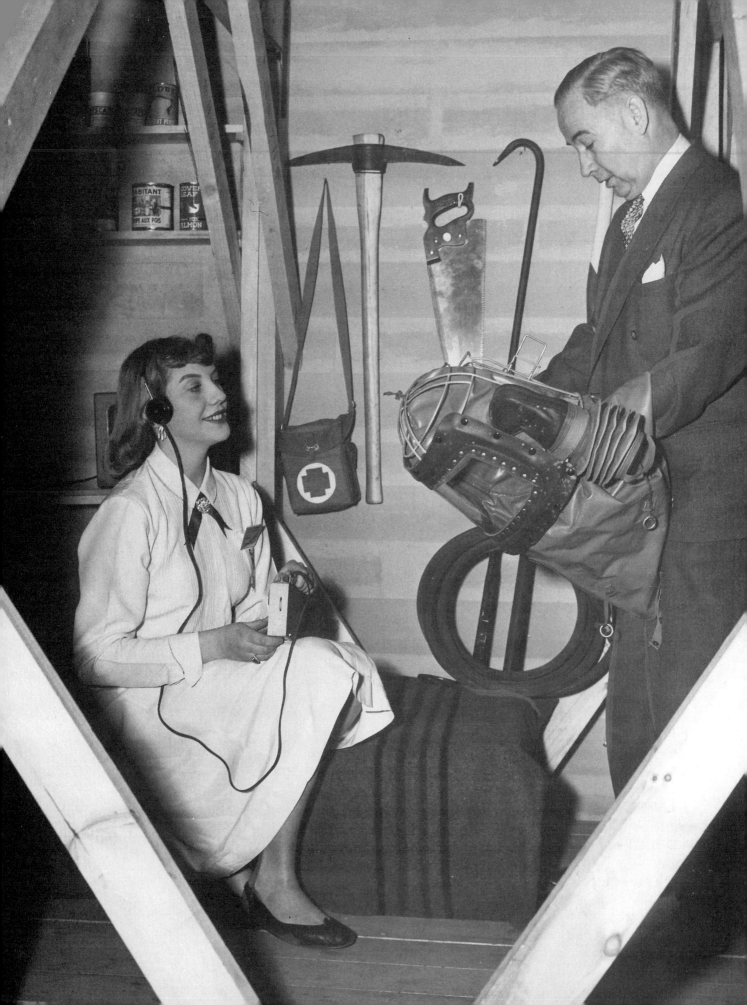

Introduction

Canada's first underground bomb shelter, 1955.

Why write a book on Canada and the Cold War? One answer to this question goes back to a moment in late 1989. The Communist regimes of Eastern Europe are toppling one after another as the world watches, astonished. On television, there are amazing scenes. People are dancing on the Berlin Wall. A nine-year-old son asks his father (one of the authors): "So, Dad, what's the big deal about this Berlin Wall anyway?" The answer to this innocent question turns out to be both simple and complex. And it entails a journey back in time.

The Cold War was one of the most important events in shaping Canada in the twentieth century. The two world wars were more dramatic, and tragic, in their impact, but they were both mercifully of relatively short duration, four and six years respectively. The Cold War endured for more than four decades, from the latter half of the 1940s to the end of the 1980s. Its effects on Canadian society and politics were far ranging and long lasting. Although Canada played only a relatively minor military role in one bloody local Cold

(opposite): Testing nuclear fallout gear, 1952.

War conflict in Korea from 1950 to 1953, Cold War thinking and Cold War assumptions shaped successive generations of Canadians, both in support and in convictions. In a way that succeeding generations will find difficult to comprehend, the Cold War was, for those who grew up and lived within it, an all encompassing experience, the very air that we breathed.

The Cold War was much more than an international alignment in which a Western bloc of nuclear-armed states led by the United States confronted another Eastern bloc of nuclear-armed states led by the USSR. It was a war of intelligence, of spy versus spy, the CIA versus KGB. It was a war of loyalty versus disloyalty, patriotism versus subversion. It was an ideological and cultural clash between capitalism and Communism, imperialism and socialism, freedom and totalitarianism, democracy and dictatorship, godliness and atheism, and so on. It did not take long for cynicism to grow on both sides about the ideological stakes, but there were always true believers, Cold Warriors to carry on the crusade. Ideological crusades have a way of permeating all aspects of life, leaving nothing untouched. The Cold War left its mark everywhere in Canada, even on those people and institutions that scarcely gave a conscious thought to the Cold War on a daily basis.

We may have forgotten much about the Cold War in the years since 1989, and young people who did not grow up under its shadow may be genuinely puzzled about an era that must now seem as remote as the medieval wars of religion. And yet history has a way of suddenly biting back, just when you think it has relaxed its grip. On September 11, 2001, a dozen years after the fall of the Berlin Wall, terrorist attacks brought down the twin towers of the World Trade Center in New York at the cost of thousands of lives. Suddenly, at the dawn of the millennium, the world was seeing a surrealistic re-run of an old movie of the late 1940s. The U.S. was again calling the free world to a long struggle with an enemy that strikes both from without and from within, an enemy that poses a threat to national security that is at once military and ideological. Once again the cry went out that, if we were not prepared, vigilant, and strong, death could rain down from the skies, in bolts from the blue. Or insidious Fifth Columnists could sneak up on us from behind. Once again, soldiers are dispatched to distant battlefields in defence of collective security. Once again, emergency legislation authorizes the "temporary" suspension of some rights in the name of national security and public safety. Once again, the air is rife with rumours of treasonous plots and conspiracies, and the search for scapegoats for letting the attacks happen.

The older among us may shrug: "Been there, done that, got the T-shirt." The younger may miss the historical allusions and imagine that today's events are without precedent. Both could profit from reviewing some history. This is especially the case for Canadians, for whom the Cold War was always felt at one remove, as it were. There is a huge literature on America and the Cold War, as befits the hegemonic power that directed the Western bloc throughout the Cold War. There is a relatively sparse literature on Canada and the Cold War. Each of the two authors have contributed to this Canadian Cold War literature. One of us is a political scientist and the other an historian.

Here, we would like to tell some of the fascinating stories to a wider audience of Canadians interested in knowing where we have come from, perhaps to better understand where we are going.

Inevitably, we have had to be arbitrary in choosing which subjects to write about, and which to set aside for the purposes of this book. We have tried to touch on the most important themes, although some receive more emphasis than others. We have also tried to tell stories that are interesting in themselves, and present personalities of the era that are vivid and memorable.

We have divided the book into decades, from the 1940s through the 1980s, with particular topics within these decades (although in many cases, the stories inevitably spill over more than one decade). We briefly introduce each decade, and offer a timeline to orient readers chronologically. For those whose appetite has been whetted, we conclude with a list of additional readings.

A Canadian peace rally in the early 1960s.

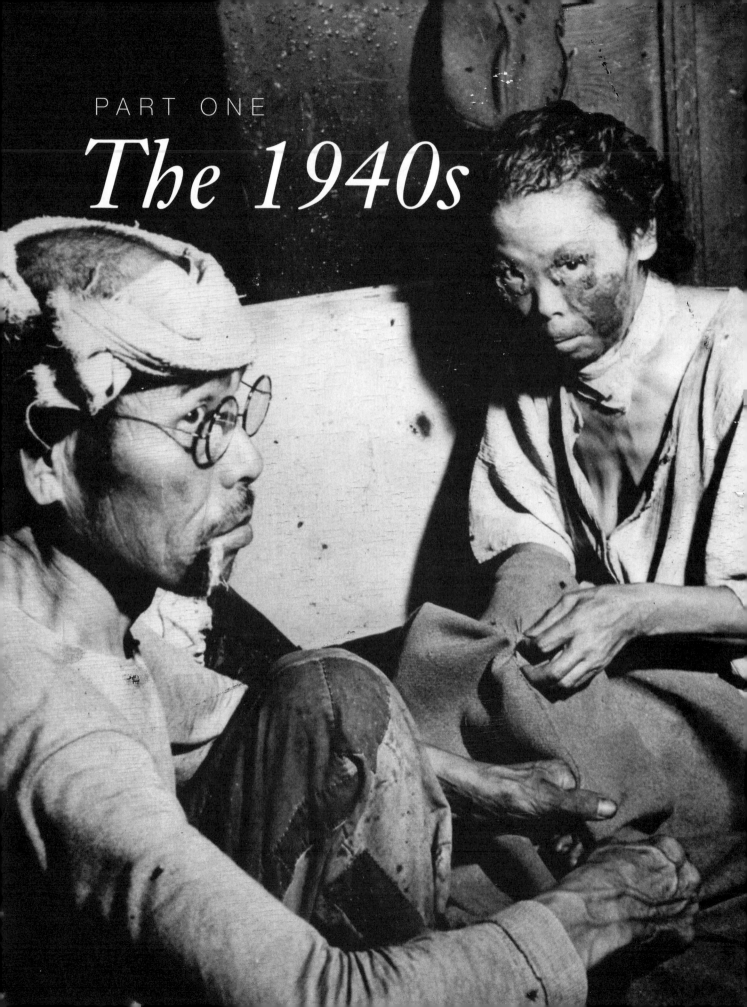

PART ONE

The 1940s

The 1940s was perhaps the most turbulent decade for Canada in the twentieth century. The decade began with Canada and the Commonwealth standing alone alongside Britain, with the Nazi Wehrmacht poised on the coast of France and Hitler's Luftwaffe bombing London. Halfway through the decade, the Axis powers were defeated at the cost of millions of lives and the use of a terrifying new weapon of mass destruction, the atomic bomb, on Japan.

By the end of the decade, the world was entering a new phase of international hostility with the Western states arrayed against the Communist bloc. This included all of Eastern Europe, led by the Soviet dictator and former wartime ally Josef Stalin. The world's most populous country, China, had just fallen to the Communists. "Red scares" swept through Western countries, while bloody purges shook the Soviet bloc. With both sides preaching ideological crusades against each other, and both armed with nuclear weapons, the fate of the earth seemed to hang in the balance, and would do so for four long decades.

The Second World War was barely over when Canada found itself at the very epicentre of a new conflict. Igor Gouzenko, a cipher clerk in the Soviet Embassy in Ottawa, defected in late 1945. He brought with him evidence of Soviet espionage against the Canadian state. When the news broke publicly six months later, it became an international sensation. Even if it had wanted to, Canada could not return to its pre-war isolationism. By the end of the decade, Canada was an original signatory to the North Atlantic Treaty Organization (NATO), a participant in a military alliance against the Soviet bloc.

The late 1940s were critical in setting the tone for the Cold War decades to follow. In government, in political parties, in the press, in business, in trade unions, in churches and other associations across the land, and in the minds of ordinary Canadians, it was decided that Canada had come out of one war only to enter a even stranger peacetime conflict. This conflict could not be allowed to become another shooting war, for the consequences in the atomic age were too dire to contemplate. Yet the war would be waged on all other fronts.

As part of this new "cold" war, Canadians learned to become suspicious of

Alger Hiss, who played a pivotal role in building the United Nations, testifying before the House Un-American Activities Committee, August 5, 1948.

(opposite): A victim of the atomic bomb dropped on Hiroshima in August, 1945, photographed 14 years later.

one another, to look for Stalin's Fifth Columnists operating undercover. In the late 1940s, "Communism" became a heresy and "Communists," heretics. Democracy was redefined as a privilege for those who qualified. In some ways, then and later, Canadians were unaware of this process for they were mesmerized by the sensational spectacle of the witch hunting and McCarthyism to the south in the United States. Surely Canadians were more liberal, tolerant, and level-headed than their excitable, evangelistic neighbours. They may have been, but Canadians nonetheless went down the same path during this period.

Government set rules to screen out Communists and Communist sympathizers from government and defence employment, and from among immigrants and refugees to Canada. Communist unions and Communist trade union officials were purged from the mainstream union movement. While the U.S. House Committee on Un-American Activities embarked on a highly publicized witch-hunting rampage in Hollywood in 1947, a quiet but deadly purge of left-wingers was carried out at the National Film Board of Canada in 1949. There was never a Committee on Un-Canadian Activities — indeed the idea seems somewhat laughable — but the Royal Canadian Mounted Police (RCMP), that quintessential symbol of Canadianism, were

Economist Victor Perlo, one of many left-wing Americans brought before the House Un-American Activities Committee, testifying on August 8, 1948.

fanning out throughout Canadian society to police Canadian politics, and to enforce a new right-thinking orthodoxy.

In the late 1940s, the new battle lines were drawn, and there were still significant numbers of Canadians who resisted the new orthodoxy. The Cold War triumphed, but not without struggles. Trade unions had long been a target for Communist organizers. In the late 1940s, they became a battlefield, literally such on the waterfront, where a gangster American union was imported to smash a Communist seamen's union. Blood flowed, but by the end of the decade, the Communists had been routed. Quieter, more genteel, battles were waged elsewhere, but everywhere the results were the same. In the microcosm of the Cold War waged on Canadian soil, the verdict was swift and decisive: Communism was the loser, by a knockout in the first round.

It is easy to see this in retrospect, but in reality, it took a long time for the results to sink in. The 1940s were a watershed decade, when the shape of the post-war era was up for grabs, with very high stakes. At the time, there was high drama, and an almost desperate sense of commitment on all sides. This was a larger-than-life decade, and it would be followed by a decade characterized by a retreat from public life, a search for security, and rest from seemingly endless turbulence.

Igor Gouzenko

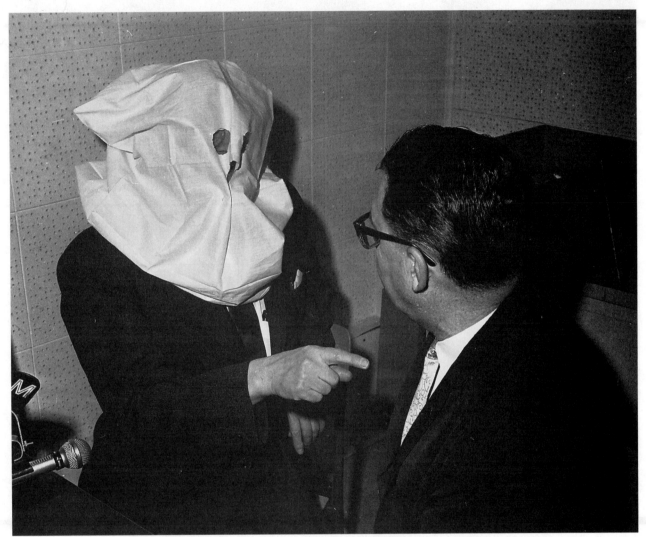

Igor Gouzenko, appearing as
Canadians would come to know him,
at Toronto radio station CFGM on
April 3, 1968.

The Cold War held the world in its grip for more than four decades
of international conflict. From the 1940s through the 1980s, the two
great superpowers, the United States and the Soviet Union, their
armed forces and their military blocs, the North Atlantic Treaty Organization
and the Warsaw Pact, faced off around the globe, and the world continually
teetered on the brink of nuclear apocalypse. The entire world was held ran-
som by these two competitors who fought one another politically,
economically, diplomatically, occasionally by proxy in ground wars, and in
intelligence wars between America's Central Intelligence Agency and the
Soviet KGB. The Cold War even extended into space, as Soviets and
Americans raced to land the first man on the moon.

The Cold War dominated international relations for two generations. Yet the first public notice of the prolonged conflict that would follow the Second World War came, not in one of the hotspots of East-West competition that would later dominate the news, but in Canada — in Canada's sleepy, dull little capital of Ottawa.

It began far away from public notice, on a warm night on September 5, 1945, just three weeks after Japan's surrender following the atomic bombing of Hiroshima and Nagasaki and the final end of the war. An obscure cipher clerk in the Soviet Embassy in Ottawa, Igor Gouzenko, was working late. In reality, he was feverishly amassing documents incriminating the USSR in organizing a Canadian spy ring. Having stuffed a hundred or so documents inside his shirt, Gouzenko fled the embassy and entered the offices of the *Ottawa Journal*, where he attempted, in agitated and heavily accented English, to convince a baffled night editor that he had a story of espionage and betrayal that should earn him asylum in Canada from Stalin's Russia. He was turned away and advised to call on the RCMP.

IGOR GOUZENKO

MEMORANDUM

TRUDEAU, A POTENTIAL CANADIAN CASTRO

Because Canadian and U.S. press, radio and television largely ignored the past activities and writings of Trudeau, the public is not aware of a real possibility that on the 6th of April, 1968, the next Prime Minister of Canada might be a self-admitted radical socialist, and Canada might with ever increasing pace turn into a second Cuba. The situation is already pregnant with a multiple threat to Canadian freedom.

The present Minister of Justice, Pierre Elliot Trudeau, was elected to Parliament only in 1965. Before this he was professor at the University of Montreal; he was the founder of a radical left magazine, Cite Libre. He is careful not to call himself a communist, but as a matter of record, he was once barred from the United States as a communist. Below is the clipping from the Toronto Daily Star, dated February 16, 1968:

In another revelation, he admitted he was once blacklisted by U.S. immigration authorities because they suspected he was a Communist.

Yet in spite of this background, shortly after Trudeau was elected to Parliament in 1965, Prime Minister Pearson appointed him his Parliamentary Secretary, and then made him, of all things, the Minister of Justice.

Pearson now supports Trudeau in the leadership race in obvious preference to other candidates. Press, radio and television are giving Trudeau unprecedented publicity, building him up as an intellectual, ignoring the fact that many of his so-called new ideas are borrowed from the outworn, reactionary writings of Lenin and Mao.

The Liberal Convention will choose not just a new leader, but a new Prime Minister. The next Prime Minister, therefore, would be elected not by the Canadian people at a general election but by several hundred delegates at the convention. The responsibility of the delegates, therefore, takes truly a historic proportion.

(left): An advertisement published by Igor Gouzenko in the late 1960s.

Gouzenko and his wife, Svetlana, and their infant son thus began a brief odyssey that has since entered into Canadian mythology. Turned away by the Justice Department, the Gouzenkos furtively scurried around Ottawa before returning to their apartment building where they moved in temporarily with a neighbour. That evening, four heavies from the Soviet Embassy broke into the Gouzenko apartment and began ransacking it, looking for the purloined documents. A Royal Canadian Mounted Police (RCMP) watch team across the street, which had been tailing the Gouzenkos, apprehended the Soviets in the act. Although the Soviets were let go, citing diplomatic immunity, the Gouzenkos were quickly taken into protection. The first major Soviet defection of the post-war era had taken place — in Ottawa.

At first, this unusual new Canadian was kept under the tightest of wraps. He and his family were whisked away to a safe location for debriefing. Top counter-intelligence officials from the United Kingdom and the U.S. were

*A home briefly occupied by the
Gouzenkos after their defection.*

*Igor Gouzenko at the time of his
defection.*

flown in to pick up all that they could about the Soviet Union's espionage operations against its former wartime allies. Prime Minister Mackenzie King and senior advisors travelled to Washington and London to inform the U.S. president and the British prime minister of the situation that Gouzenko had uncovered. And all the while, the government was carefully assessing the extent of the damage that might have been done. The Mounties were piecing together a picture of the espionage operation, while keeping close watch on all the suspects to which Gouzenko's evidence pointed, and waiting for the order to close in.

That order took some time. At a meeting between the Canadian, American, and British leaders, a secret memorandum was drawn up, sketching out a strategy to blow the whistle on the Soviets. But the international ramifications were very serious, especially since the wartime alliance was in the process of breaking down in the aftermath of victory. And there was the chance that close surveillance of the suspects might offer further leads. At one point, Mackenzie King briefly contemplated using the information to bring pressure to bear on the Soviets to change their ways, but was persuaded not to pursue such a quixotic initiative. Over six months later, a mysterious leak to an American journalist finally precipitated action. At this point, the government struck, rounding up suspects in pre-dawn raids, and taking them away for interrogation to the RCMP barracks in Ottawa, followed soon by the secret proceedings of a Royal Commission of Inquiry (see the section on The Kellock-Taschereau Commission).

When the news broke of the Canadian arrests on February 15, 1946, it was a worldwide sensation, and Igor Gouzenko became an instant international celebrity. Although that celebrity faded with the years as the Cold War accumulated more defectors and spy scandals, Gouzenko's place in Canadian history has remained secure. He was someone who made Canadians feel important. In part as well, Gouzenko's image was carefully crafted. Numerous newspaper and magazine articles in Canada and abroad extolled the man who had struck a blow for the free world. He published a bestselling autobiography, *This Was My Choice*, co-authored by a Montreal sports writer. Later he published a novel about Soviet life, *The Fall of a Titan*, that was awarded the Governor General's Prize for fiction — more a tribute to the Cold War politics of the 1950s than to its literary merits. In 1949, Gouzenko received the ultimate accolade of celebrity when his story became the subject of the Hollywood film, *The Iron Curtain*, which improbably cast the dapper Dana Andrews as Gouzenko and the glamorous Jean Tierney as Svetlana. In Canada, his image was indelibly confirmed in the 1950s when he came out of hiding wearing a bag over his head. This was supposedly to baffle Soviet assassins whom Gouzenko was convinced had been sent to eliminate him. Whether this was true or not, the bag over the head was a brilliant piece of imagery.

Gouzenko in his later years.

Behind the scenes, Gouzenko was less a hero than a persistent nuisance to the Canadian government, which had offered him refuge and protection. He made constant demands upon the Canadian taxpayer for support for himself and his growing family. He deeply distrusted the Mounties assigned to his protection, suspecting them of being Soviet agents. The Mounties returned the favour in growing exasperation at his demands and complaints. Soon he and his family were taken off the Mounties' hands, given new identities, and moved to a series of communities away from the Ottawa spotlight. Like other defectors after him, Gouzenko tried to keep his value alive long after all useful intelligence had been wrung out of him. This brought him into association with right-wingers, who made Gouzenko an icon of anti-Communism. In the mid-1950s, the witch-hunting U.S. House Committee on Un-American Activities came to Ottawa to interview Gouzenko about Communist subversion in North America. This might have provoked an international incident, but trouble was averted by strict rules imposed by Canada on the meeting, and by the evident fact that Gouzenko's information had long since dried up.

In the 1960s and 1970s, Gouzenko took to launching lawsuits against anyone who wrote about him, thus enforcing a kind of chill on anyone who tried to impose upon his self-constructed image. This was perhaps an odd way to celebrate freedom of expression in the West, which he had chosen over totalitarian repression.

Igor Gouzenko died in 1982. In 2002, the government of Canada officially declared Gouzenko's defection an event of National Historic Significance. He will always be a part of Canadian mythology.

The Kellock-Taschereau Royal Commission: Canada's "Star Chamber"?

The Communist Party of Canada executive during the 1940s.

Canadians like to think of their country as a liberal, tolerant society that follows the rule of law and protects the rights of its citizens from arbitrary actions of government. In the early Cold War era, Canadians looked askance at their southern neighbour, which, in the late 1940s and early 1950s, went on an anti-Communist witch-hunting rampage. The House Committee on Un-American Activities, the Senate Internal Security Subcommittee, and Senator Joseph McCarthy made daily headlines publicly accusing Americans of disloyalty and treason. "McCarthyism" became an epithet for the ugly intolerance of difference that disgraced a liberal democracy such as that of the United States. Canadians smugly believed themselves to be immune from such excesses.

In 1946, at the very outset of the Cold War, Canada faced the threat of Soviet espionage and the alarming willingness of some Canadians to betray their country on behalf of a foreign ideology. It did so without the benefit of any models of how it should handle such a crisis. In this situation, the Canadian government reacted with the firmest of hands, and with little regard for such niceties as civil liberties, or the rule of law. A secret order in council known to only three members of Cabinet directed an extraordinary investigation under the draconian authority of the War Measures Act, even though the war had already ended. There were pre-dawn raids to detain and interrogate suspects without charge, without bail or habeas corpus, and without legal representation. A secret tribunal demanded that detainees answer all questions put to them without protection against self-incrimination. At the end of this process, the government publicly named some two dozen Canadians, mainly public servants, and including a Member of Parliament, as traitors to their country, and then sent them to trial. Only half of those charged were ever convicted, all on the basis of self-incrimination. Even those released were barred from government employment. Canadians might sneer at American McCarthyism in this era, but in this case, Canada outdid the Americans in placing national security above individual rights.

In some ways, this story does not accord with Canadians' self-image as being part of a society in which individual rights are protected and cherished. In other ways, however, it is in keeping with an older Canadian tradition, that of deference to the Crown and authority, a Canada of "peace, order, and good government" in which the red-coated RCMP are a leading national symbol.

Igor Gouzenko was debriefed for six months after his defection in September 1945. Meanwhile, the government was wrestling with the problem of what to do with the information that he revealed about the Soviet spy scandal. In consultation with the Americans and the British, a decision was made not to open with legal charges, but to detain the suspects and bring them secretly before a commission of inquiry. This method would, their government believed, be more likely to bring out the full facts, without the procedural checks and balances inherent in the trial process.

A Royal Commission was struck, headed by two Supreme Court justices, Mr. Justice Lindsay Kellock and Mr. Justice Robert Taschereau. Counsel for the commission was the president of the Canadian Bar Association, E.K. Williams. The authority for the commission's deliberations was derived from the War Measures Act.

When the suspects were taken by the RCMP from their cells and brought before the commissioners, they were on their own and faced the full majesty of the Crown and the legal establishment. Not surprisingly, some broke down and quickly confessed that they had knowingly passed classified information to the Soviet Union. Some tried to justify their actions as helping a wartime ally, but the Commissioners had no interest in their explanations. Each one who did confess was subsequently convicted in court on the basis of their own words. Among these were Raymond Boyer, a McGill University scientist working in defence research; Emma Woikin, a cipher clerk in External Affairs; and Kathleen Willsher, a secretary in the British High Commission.

Others were less cooperative. The commission did nothing to apprise its witnesses of the protection that Parliament had provided Canadians against self-incrimination. Instead, they were told that they had no choice but to answer everything put to them. Some nevertheless resisted. The case of one detainee, Queen's University mathematician Israel Halperin, who appears to have in fact been innocent of espionage, highlighted the Kafkaesque nature of the proceedings. Ordered to be sworn in as a witness, after five weeks of incommunicado interrogation at the RCMP barracks, Halperin fired back: "Before you swear me, would you mind telling me who you are?" "Well," answered Mr. Justice Taschereau, "we are the Royal Commission appointed by the government to investigate certain matters." "Are you empowered to use physical intimidation?" asked Halperin. "Not physical intimidation, but we have the power to punish you if you do not answer," insisted Taschereau. Halperin then turned and tried to leave the room, but was forcibly returned to the witness box. He was subsequently named as a spy in the commission's report, charged with espionage, but released when the Crown case collapsed entirely in court. Despite his exoneration, Halperin later came very close to losing his position at Queen's as a result of being public smeared by his own government.

Some of the biggest fish caught in Gouzenko's net were never brought before the commission. The British scientist Alan Nunn May, who had worked on the Canadian side of wartime Allied defence research, was arrested in Britain, brought before the Old Bailey in London, and sentenced to ten years imprisonment. Although the press made much ado about Canadian "atom bomb spies," Nunn May was actually the only link to atomic espionage, and in his case, the link was rather tenuous. The Russians had indeed deeply penetrated the Manhattan Project that developed the first atomic bomb at Los Alamos, New Mexico, but the real atom spies were not in Canada, which was quite peripheral to the top secret project.

Implicated in the Canadian spy ring was Fred Rose, the only Communist ever elected under the party banner to the House of Commons. Convicted, Rose served a sentence and was then deported to his native Poland. Also charged was the Communist Party's national organizer, Sam Carr, who briefly fled the country but later returned to face a prison term. The Canadian Communist Party never recovered from this public relations disaster. From this time on, the party's image of slavish devotion to the Soviet Union was confirmed.

According to the commission's report, the reason why Canadian public servants had betrayed the secrets entrusted to them was their devotion to Communism. The commission informed its readers that Communism was not just another political program like liberalism or conservatism. It was an insidious doctrine that infected its followers' moral fibre. It instilled the notion that there was a higher loyalty to the homeland of Communism, the Soviet Union. The Kellock-Taschereau Commission thus did what the anti-Communist crusaders were doing in the United States: they linked the threat of Soviet espionage to the internal threat of Communist subversion. This was a crucial point in the opening of the Cold War — the enemy without was linked to the enemy within. There may have been no House Committee on Un-Canadian Activities, but an official witch hunt against "Communists" was launched with this commission. Canadian public opinion, it seems, largely

The Canadian Communist Party executive.

approved of the commission and its methods. Only a few protests from civil libertarians were heard and dismissed by the government, which cited the need to protect national security.

Why did the government proceed in such a draconian and authoritarian manner, with so little regard for individual rights? Canada had just come through a war in which real or alleged enemy "fifth columnists" had been dealt with sternly. In some cases, excesses later led to official embarrassment and apologies, as with the relocation of the entire Japanese-Canadian population on the West Coast to camps in the interior. The same mentality was carried over into a "peacetime" that quickly turned into a "cold" war. It must be recalled that Canada in the 1940s had no Charter of Rights and Freedoms entrenched in its Constitution. Indeed, this charter only came four decades later.

Canada was also anxious that the revelations of Soviet espionage not torpedo the prospects for post-war amity between the wartime allies. In early 1946, when the Gouzenko inquiry unfolded, the wartime alliance had not yet broken down into hostile camps, although many warning signs were already present. Canada was very uncomfortable about taking any lead role in East-West relations. Mackenzie King was a very cautious politician, especially when it came to foreign affairs, in which Canada had always taken a deferential position toward Britain, and now increasingly toward the United States, as it assumed the mantle of Western leadership. The spy scandal vaulted an unprepared Canada into a highly exposed position. King was afraid that any wrong moves could precipitate an international crisis of which he wanted no part. The commission systematically downplayed any anti-Soviet implications, while playing up the domestic implications of Communism. By maintaining this "spin" on the story, the government hoped to leave the big decisions about international relations to their senior partners.

The government also sought to control the domestic ramifications of labelling Communists as subversives. Neither the Liberal Cabinet nor the

RCMP wanted to see unpredictable and potentially chaotic public witch hunts in Canada. The Canadian style of waging Cold War was to keep the reins firmly in official hands and to discourage freelance accusations of disloyalty and any spreading of anti-Communist panic about traitors in our midst.

The Royal Commission report was an international bestseller, somewhat to the embarrassment of the government that sponsored it. Although there were a number of sensationalist journalistic knock-offs of the report, especially in the American press, the official report was an unlikely bestseller. Staid and purposefully dull in presentation, with hundreds of pages of detailed print unrelieved by photographs, it bore the resolutely boring and deliberately obscure title *The Report of the Royal Commission to Investigate the Facts Relating to and Circumstances Surrounding the Communication by Public Officials and Others in Positions of Trust of Secret and Confidential Information to Agents of a Foreign Power* — not exactly a title to attract impulse buyers.

When Hollywood descended on Ottawa to film a fictionalized (and romanticized) version of Gouzenko's story (*The Iron Curtain*), they set up their cameras in the foyer of the House of Commons. Louis St. Laurent, Justice Minister and soon-to-be prime minister, walked in, aghast at the spectacle. St. Laurent ordered the crew off Parliament Hill, never to return. The Liberal government could not, of course, entirely control the spin that others wanted to put on the Canadian spy scandal, but they were determined to maximize the control they could exercise, especially within Canada. Questions of loyalty and treason, and subversive fifth columns working on behalf of foreign enemies, were highly explosive in a liberal democratic society. The Royal Commission was the chosen instrument to maintain an old Canadian tradition of order and deference to authority, while at the same time alerting Canadians to the existence of a new threat to their security. As a result, the rights of those suspected of compliance with the foreign enemy were jettisoned, but the government, by and large, did maintain control of the situation.

A quarter of a century later, another security crisis engulfed Canada when the terrorist group Front de Libération du Québec (FLQ) kidnapped a British diplomat, and kidnapped and murdered a Quebec Cabinet Minister. Once again, the government invoked the War Measures Act and detained scores of suspects without bail or legal representation. The October 1970 Crisis was different from the spy crisis of 1945-46, but the government's reaction was similar: maximum force, and minimum respect for individual rights and liberties. The War Measures Act was later repealed, but following the September 11, 2001 terrorist attacks on the World Trade Center and the Pentagon, Canada swiftly passed new draconian anti-terrorist legislation that, among other things, provides for preventive arrest and investigative hearings in which witnesses are compelled to answer questions, on pain of imprisonment. This has become, it would seem, something of a Canadian tradition.

The Security Panel: Nerve Centre of Ottawa's Cold War

President Roosevelt and Mackenzie King, April 25, 1940. The close relationship between Canada and U.S. during World War II was one of the reasons for the creation of the Security Panel.

Following the revelations of the Gouzenko affair and the onset of the Cold War in 1946, Ottawa set about designing administrative machinery to safeguard government security.

In the United States of the late 1940s, Cold War security issues became a political football with everyone — congressmen and senators, Federal Bureau of Investigation director J. Edgar Hoover, lawyers, journalists, get-rich-quick entrepreneurs — trying to get a piece of the publicity by exposing "Communists" in high (and low) places. The result was witch hunts, headlines, and political turmoil.

The Liberal government of Mackenzie King and its senior civil servants wanted to keep control over the issue of Communist infiltration. Public witch hunts were bad for liberal democracy — and bad for the government in power. Ottawa had little experience with such matters, but the government was determined to get it right. It chose to follow the British model, rather than the American, something it still tended to do in those days. A single interdepartmental body was recommended to coordinate and advise the Cabinet on all aspects of the government's internal security. In May 1946, the Security Panel was created, chaired by the Cabinet Secretary (the senior civil servant), with senior representatives from the Joint Chiefs of Defence Staff, the Royal Canadian Mounted Police (RCMP), and External Affairs.

The panel's first order of business was to devise a screening program for the civil service. Guidelines were drawn up and the RCMP was tasked to screen out Communists among bureaucrats with access to classified information. Soon tens of thousands each year were subjected to investigations of their past, their relatives and associates, their personal habits, and their political beliefs. Nor did it stop with the civil service. Workers in defence industries were soon added, and even seamen on the Great Lakes (this at the demand of the Americans, who wanted to keep Communists out of American ports). Also, in the late 1940s, the panel oversaw the extension of security screening to immigrants and refugees coming into Canada, and to applicants for Canadian citizenship.

The RCMP did the legwork and provided the security evaluations. Final decisions on civil servants were always to be made by Cabinet Ministers. The Security Panel's job was to oversee, coordinate, and advise, but inevitably it was where major policy decisions were actually made. Busy and less knowledgeable Ministers could only take sporadic notice, while the bureaucrats provided continuity. In the early 1950s, the panel was reorganized into two bodies, one for routine administration and the other for consideration of policy questions. An outside expert, Peter Dwyer, left a career in British intelligence (he is believed to have been instrumental in unmasking Soviet atomic spy Klaus Fuchs) to preside over both panels as permanent secretary. Later, Dwyer retired from security and became a key figure in Ottawa's cultural bureaucracy with the fledgling Canada Council for the Arts.

The Security Panel provided something else that was very valuable to the government. They kept security issues out of the limelight. When individuals were denied clearance, they were not told that security was the reason. No independent appeal process was allowed. For many years, even the Cabinet directive that established the government's security guidelines remained secret. The anti-Communist purge in Ottawa took place quietly, behind closed doors. No one outside of a small circle in government even knew of the existence of the Security Panel. Yet here the mandarins of the public service, Arnold Heeney, Norman Robertson, Gordon Robertson and Robert Bryce, set policy that had consequences for tens of thousands of Canadians. It was only decades later, in the 1970s and 1980s, that declassified documents and the recollections of participants opened up a corner of this secret page in Canada's Cold War history.

Even now, the effects of the Security Panel on Canadian society are difficult to assess. Keeping the explosive issue of Communist espionage and
subversion out of the hands of partisan politicians and groups with ideological
axes to grind was undoubtedly a good thing for Canadian democracy. To see
why, Canadians need only look at the example of McCarthy-era America. On
the other hand, there was an anti-Communist purge in Canada, but here,
there was little or no opportunity for those affected to fight back.

Years later, Brooke Claxton, who had been Defence Minister during the
Korean War, suggested to Dean Acheson, who had been U.S. Secretary of
State during the same period, that the Canadian way of controlling security
was much preferable to the American way: "There is a good deal to be said
for the view that it was the publicity given to your cases and to the manner of
dealing with them which created the turmoil. Under our system McCarthy
had no place to go and as I say I never heard of an unjust result." If there
were unjust results, of course, no one under the Canadian system would even
have heard of them, not even Cabinet Ministers.

Cold War Immigration

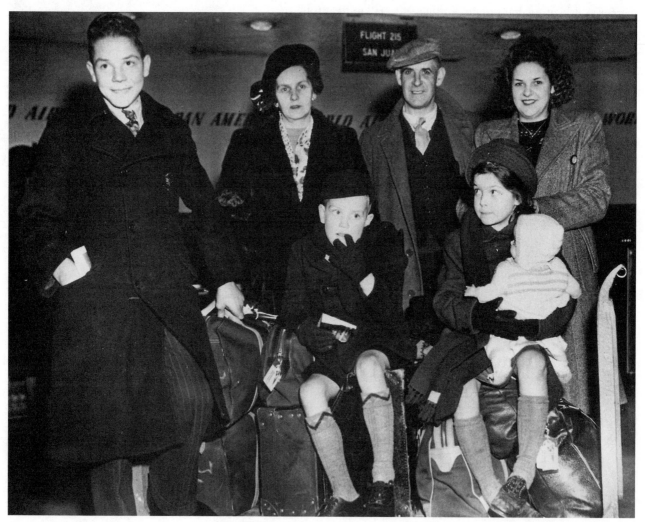

Postwar immigrants arriving, December 9, 1947.

The Cold War coincided with large-scale immigration and refugee movements into Canada. Post-war immigration changed the face of Canada forever. What is less well known is the impact that the Cold War had on who got into Canada, who stayed, who was deported, and the acceptable and unacceptable politics of New Canadians.

As usual, the U.S. imposed Cold War rules on immigration in the full glare of publicity and debate. Just as typically, Canada acted silently, behind the scenes, and took every precaution against publicity. In 1952, the U.S. passed anti-Communist immigration legislation, the McCarran-Walter Act, which stood for decades. Canada acted instead by administrative fiat, with bureaucrats — unaccountable to Parliament or the public — applying secret rules.

It began in the late 1940s, when the first waves of displaced persons were seeking refuge from a war-ravaged Europe. Accepting refugees was sound policy, economically, morally, and politically. The post-war European immigrants selected by Canada contributed greatly to the prosperity of the 1950s. It so happened that it was also good Cold War politics: many who had suffered under the Nazis now sought to flee the scarcely less brutal rule of the Soviets as they took over Eastern Europe. The contrast between free societies that were open to newcomers and the police states of the East that kept people prisoner behind the "Iron Curtain" could not have been more striking. Refugee politics offered propaganda victories to the West in the global ideological contest between the two systems.

Behind the scenes, however, Canadian security people were worried. What if the Communists planted agents and sympathizers among the hordes of applicants? What about countries with large Communist movements, such as Italy and France? How could Communists be screened out without rousing protests from ethnic communities in Canada that might be adversely affected?

The answer was to execute, in utmost secrecy, administrative rules that designated prohibited entry to those with suspicious political pasts or associations. To gather the intelligence on which this screening would be based, RCMP officers were sent abroad incognito to visa posts, under cover as regular immigration officers. They liaised with local police and security forces, and had access to the databases maintained by American and British intelligence. This was a window on the world for the RCMP, and they made good use of it to establish close links with their counterparts abroad. For any immigrants or refugees who somehow slipped through the net at entry, there was a second round of investigation when they applied for citizenship. One way or another, huge numbers of post-war New Canadians were politically vetted by the police with very little public notice.

It is always a fear of people in open societies that some newcomers who enter will misuse their access to undermine free institutions (in the early twenty-first century, Canadians are well aware of the threat of terrorists). Canadians generally did not want Communists slipping into the country who might act as covert agents of the Soviet Union. The government indicated that it was vigilant about this problem, but it offered very few details. That seemed to satisfy public opinion through the 1960s, but eventually a number of problems began to surface.

It is clear that Cold War immigration security imposed double standards. This was evident in the unequal incidence of the screening of applicants from different countries of origin. Those from countries with large Communist movements, such as Italy, France, and Greece, were screened more closely and more often barred from entry than were those from countries with few Communists. In the case of France, an official policy that placed French immigrants on the same favoured basis as British applicants was secretly undermined by the application of security guidelines.

One by-product of the Cold War mentality was the entry of Nazis, including some who later proved to be in the category of "war criminals," and of

War brides sailing for North America.

Baby Killers Are NOT Welcome Here!

The letter we reproduce below speaks for itself. Here a Yugoslav woman, a collaborationist, boasts of the fact that she has been killing innocent children "like chickens", and promises to do so again if given an opportunity.

Is this the type of immigrant Canada needs? Is this why sons of Canada went to lay down their lives to defeat our enemy only to win the war and open our doors to our enemies and their collaborators? We, together with all democratic Canadians say emphatically no!

We urge upon the Canadian government to immediately institute an enquiry into the case of Vera Potkonjak and to rid Canada of a war criminal. We appeal to all liberty-loving Canadians to join with us in urging action by the Canadian authorities in the case of Vera Potkonjak.

Pamphlet warning of the dangers posed by eastern European immigrants.

wartime collaborators with the Axis occupation. Some of these entered more or less by accident, simply because the attention of the immigration security screeners was focused firmly on Communism, rather than Fascism. In other cases, there is evidence of more sinister complicity in bringing in "anti-Communists" while turning a blind eye to their unsavoury pasts. In post-war Europe, there were "ratlines" organized by Western intelligence and even by the Vatican to bring out some with ugly Nazi records who might prove valuable in the Cold War against the new adversary. Jewish Canadians, who had witnessed overt discrimination against Jewish refugees from the Nazis in the late 1930s, were incensed when former members of a Ukrainian Waffen SS Division were allowed to enter. Later, in the 1980s, the numbers of war criminals living in Canada became a public scandal and led to an official commission of inquiry under Mr. Justice Deschênes. The issue still festers today.

Another double standard gained public notoriety in the 1970s. Canadian screening had always welcomed refugees from Communism. Following the bloody repression of the Hungarian Revolt in 1956, Canada took in some 37,000 Hungarian refugees. Similar generosity was shown to those who fled Czechoslovakia after the "Prague Spring" of 1968 was crushed. As late as 1979, Canada took in over 60,000 Indo-Chinese "boat people" fleeing Communism and war [see chapter on Boat People]. The double standard became evident when General Augusto Pinochet unleashed a right-wing military coup against the democratically elected Socialist-Communist government of Salvador Allende in Chile in 1975. Although supporters of the Allende government were being rounded up and tortured and murdered, Canada was slow and reluctant to offer refuge. Similar double standards were evident in the 1980s with regard to refugees from political conflicts in Central America.

Not content to simply screen immigration and citizenship applicants, Canada went further to police immigrant groups, encouraging anti-Communism and discouraging (and sometimes punishing) pro-Communism. Many ethnic groups were untouched by this, as Communism was not part of their background, but in others, there were bitter divisions between left- and right-wing factions. When this happened, as for instance among Ukrainian Canadians, the state was not neutral but intervened actively on one side against the other. Pro-Communist ethnic associations were the objects of RCMP surveillance and were denied access to representation with government, regularly denounced from on high; and saw their adherents barred from entry, denied citizenship, and sometimes deported. At the same time, they could see their anti-Communist rivals feted and funded by governments, and offered symbolic representation in government counsels.

It is hardly surprising that, under such circumstances, few New Canadians chose to brave official disapproval and actively espouse left-wing politics. Of course, the anti-Communism of refugees from Eastern Europe was genuine and would have been there even without official encouragement. But the partisan intervention of Ottawa in the political policing of immigrant communities was perhaps not the best lesson in democratic citizenship, especially for communities that contained deep internal divisions.

John Leopold

John Leopold, head of the RCMP's intelligence wing during the onset of the Cold War.

One of the early heroes of the Canadian Cold War looked miscast. John Leopold was a balding and jowly Central European who spoke accented English — the exact opposite of the Mountie image held by a heavily prejudiced nation. Leopold's ethnicity was trumped by his career in the Royal Canadian Mounted Police. Under ordinary circumstances, a career with arguably the world's most famous police force would have been out of the question. The RCMP spied on Eastern Europeans; they did not hire them as policemen. What's more, Leopold did not meet height requirements, nor was he even a Canadian citizen when he signed on with the Mounted Police in 1917. What he did possess were skills that state security demanded in the early Cold War when ethnicity was openly equated with radicalism. Fluent in several languages, the new Mountie's unique appearance allowed him to infiltrate groups deemed subversive. He looked so unlike a policeman that he would later be regularly challenged by the guards at the RCMP's head-quarters in Ottawa to provide identification before he could enter the building.

Johan (John) Leopold was born in 1890 in rural Bohemia (today part of

John Leopold in his RCMP uniform.

the Czech Republic). His chosen career in the old country, which might explain the roots of his strong anti-Communism, had been that of an agriculturist and forester. After graduating from college, he had spent time managing an estate. His pre-Mountie career in Canada, to which he immigrated in 1912 or 1913, also involved agriculture. In 1914, he took out a homestead in a region of Alberta that was not conducive to farming success.

Leopold first attained nationwide fame in 1931 when he emerged from the shadows to testify in his full RCMP uniform in front of a packed Toronto courtroom. His testimony would be pivotal in helping to convict several senior members of the Communist Party of Canada, including party leader Tim Buck, who had been arrested on sedition charges under Section 98 of the Criminal Code. Leopold recounted in detail his secret life in the 1920s when, under the guise of a Regina housepainter named Jack Esselwein, he had spent years infiltrating and reporting to the police on the fledgling Communist Party of Canada. This undercover work ended in 1928 when the Communist Party expelled him after being supplied with evidence of his real identity by a Eastern European friend of Leopold's.

After his public exposure as a Mounted Police spy, Leopold's career and life went awry. Drinking binges, a case of syphilis, and a demotion in rank plagued him in the 1930s. Only the fear of providing the Communists with a public relations victory saved him from being fired. From out of the mess he rebuilt his reputation, and quickly became the force's expert on Communism, offering analysis on whether a diverse list of groups and associations across the nation were being manipulated by Communists.

These skills positioned him perfectly for the post-Second World War era and the emergence of the modern Cold War. As head of the RCMP's fledgling intelligence wing between 1945 and 1947, the now veteran Mounted Policeman dealt with the defection of Soviet Embassy clerk Igor Gouzenko [see chapter on Gouzenko], and the implications of his documents and testimony for Canadian security. When the RCMP's intelligence service expanded in 1947, Leopold, now a senior member of the police, remained the point man on any matters related to research into Communist subversion. Memos and reports on Communism from Mounties across Canada were directed to him at headquarters in Ottawa. In turn, Leopold continued to offer the definitive word on Communist intentions, while at the same time issuing his own instructions directed at professionalizing the RCMP's domestic spy operations.

By 1952, the old spy's career had come to an end. That retirement ended six years later with his death from heart failure. A few lines from the *Ottawa Journal* served as a fitting epitaph for one of Canada's original Cold Warriors:

He looked neither like a Mountie nor an undercover agent. ... [H]e regarded life with eternal good cheer except when communism was mentioned. On that he was deadly serious. It was a menace to which he dedicated his life.

Tim Buck

Tim Buck, January 17, 1958.

Tim Buck was never really alone. Wherever he went, the General Secretary of the Communist Party of Canada from 1929 to 1962 had secret shadows. Members of the Royal Canadian Mounted Police, their informants, and their listening devices combined to literally watch his every step.

This prime police target was born in Suffolk, England, in 1891. The son of an innkeeper and soap maker, the young Buck followed a proletarian path by apprenticing as a machinist. At the age of nineteen, he left his homeland for a new beginning in Canada. He established himself in Toronto before spending time in Saskatchewan and the United States.

During the First World War, Buck began his apprenticeship for his life's work: pursuing revolution. It started with his reading material, consisting of various works of Karl Marx, followed by the making of connections with others of similar political leanings. Besides being skilled with his hands, the young immigrant discovered he had an aptitude for organizing and speaking. He and a small group of skilled workers eventually became committed Bolsheviks. With the support and encouragement of American Communists and the Soviet Union, the decision was made to form the Communist Party

of Canada (CPC), and in June 1921, twenty-two delegates gathered in a barn outside of Guelph, Ontario, to organize it. Although Buck would later claim to be among that number — perhaps to prove his central importance to the CPC — that claim cannot be substantiated.

Even if he was not there at the beginning, by the end of the 1920s Buck would emerge as the most important Communist in Canada. Through deft maneuvering to quickly parrot the shifting policy and doctrinal stances emanating from Stalin through the Communist International, Buck, with the aid of pressure from American Communists, was elected leader by delegates at a 1929 party conference. He would hold the position until 1962.

At the helm of what a colleague later called "Tim Buck's party," its namesake experienced first-hand the achievements and turmoil of his organization. In 1931, the Communist leader was arrested and imprisoned under Section 98 of the Criminal Code. His profile and the exaggerated rhetoric surrounding his leadership only grew with his 1934 release from the Kingston penitentiary, where a guard had nearly murdered him during a 1932 prison riot. With a massive portrait of Stalin forming the backdrop, he addressed a boisterous crowd at Maple Leaf Gardens.

The Second World War and its immediate aftermath brought new challenges for Buck and his party. He hid in the United States to avoid internment after the CPC was prohibited in June 1940 over its vocal opposition to Canada's participation in the war, opposition sparked by the Soviet Union's 1939 non-aggression pact with Nazi Germany. Then, with the invasion of the Soviet Union in 1941, the CPC (renamed the Labour Progressive Party [LPP] in 1943) changed course to support the conflict, leading to the restoration of the party and to increased public support; it elected members to provincial legislatures and its first federal member to Parliament.

Wartime success proved illusory. As the slaughter ended, a Soviet embassy clerk made a fateful decision to deposit top secret documents with the Government of Canada. The subsequent spy scandal damaged the party since it reinforced the contentions of critics that Communists represented a fifth

Communist Party members demonstrating in Toronto, 1948.

column within Canadian society; it also drove over a thousand people from the LPP. Equally destructive, however, for the Communist cause was that the Canadian government and other anti-Communists launched a campaign — little different from the spirit of McCarthyism active in the United States — to strip the party of its influence. Communists were driven out of unions and Communist unions were forced out of larger labour organizations. Those holding elected office suffered defeat at the polls.

For Buck, however, 1956 marked a career low point. He and other officials attended the 20th congress of the Communist Party of the Soviet Union in February, but they were excluded when Nikita Khrushchev launched into a stinging denunciation of Stalin and Stalinism. Rumours of his speech soon spread, but a version of it did not appear in the West until June 1956. Buck was outraged at not having had a preview. In his party, which was already experiencing growing discontent over reports of anti-Semitism in the Soviet Union, dissension erupted. At a meeting of senior LPP members in October, critics of Buck's leadership openly chastised him. The criticism of his leadership stunned the sixty-five-year-old Buck, who confessed publicly to regret (and to be surprised) that a "cult of the individual" had developed around him. Acting out of a desire for party unity, his allies stepped forward to offer support and his tenure as leader continued. Many of his critics quit or were driven from the party. They were followed out the door by thousands of disil-

Tim Buck and Ho Chi Minh.

A pamphlet written by Tim Buck.

lusioned members, their numbers enlarged even more by the Soviet Union's military intervention in Hungary in the fall of 1956. To encourage further divisions, the RCMP Security Service distributed to party members a phony letter about Khrushchev's revelations, supposedly written by another LPP member.

Buck had survived, but he now presided over a smaller and even more marginalized organization. He lasted until January 1962, when he retired to an honorary position in the party and his activities continued to be monitored by Canada's secret service. Only death in 1973 freed him from his perpetual watchdogs.

Tim Buck with Leslie Morris, his successor, in 1964.

George Drew: Canada's Joe McCarthy Self-Destructs

George Drew with supporters in 1956.

A s the Cold War settled in on Canadian society in the late 1940s and early 1950s, the Liberal government's aversion to American-style McCarthyism was plain for all to see. As an established governing party (the Liberals remained in office from 1935 to 1957), the Liberals wanted no part of the kind of loyalty politics practised in the United States, where the Democrats — the equivalent in many ways of the Canadian Liberals — were ambushed by Republican witch hunters who pointed accusing fingers at the administrations of Harry Truman and Franklin Roosevelt for being "soft on Communism." In the 1952 presidential election, Senator Joe McCarthy charged the Democrats with "twenty years of treason." The Democrats were driven from the White House in 1952 in an ugly campaign rife with charges of disloyalty and treason, while American soldiers fought Communists in Korea.

The Liberals had no intention of succumbing to such a campaign, and were easily re-elected in 1953. When they were finally defeated by the Progressive Conservatives under John Diefenbaker in 1957, their conduct

George Drew with John Diefenbaker, his successor as Tory leader, in 1956.

Next to the Iroquois engine, part of the Avro Arrow program later cancelled by the Diefenbaker government, August 26, 1957.

during the Cold War was not an issue. However, they did not survive the early Cold War years without challenge. There were would-be Joe McCarthys in Canada, ready to exploit fears of the "enemy within" for partisan gain. The leader of the small, western-based Social Credit Party, Solon Low, sometimes reached for the McCarthyite card, but he had limited influence. Potentially more important, and to the Liberals, more dangerous, was George Drew, leader of the official Conservative opposition for the 1949 and 1953 elections. Drew tried, repeatedly, to sound McCarthyite alarms about Communist subversion and Liberal complicity. Again and again, he failed.

George Drew was a florid, blustering old-school Ontario Tory. A First World War veteran who had been seriously wounded in action, he went on to a career in law and politics in the inter-war years. Elected leader of the Ontario Conservative Party in 1938, he led the Tories to victory in 1943, laying the foundation for a forty-three year Tory dynasty in that province. In 1948, he entered federal politics as the national Conservative leader, but suffered two devastating defeats at the hands of Liberals in 1949 and 1953, finally retiring in 1956. He represented a right-wing, pro-British, Upper Canadian conservatism, in contrast to the prairie populism of his successor, John Diefenbaker. His anti-Communism was visceral and outspoken. As a fervently partisan Tory, he had no hesitation in trying to capitalize on the Communist issue to undermine the Grits. Unfortunately for Drew, his grenades kept exploding in his own face.

George Drew on the campaign trail.

Drew with Winston Churchill in 1958.

Drew was particularly keen to use the law to crush the Communists, and could not understand why the Liberals were reluctant to do so. The liberal scruples of the Ottawa establishment, concerned that democracy would be undermined by excessive repression, drove Drew to frustration. He wanted the discredited Section 98 of the Criminal Code, repealed by the Liberals in the late 1930s, reintroduced and strengthened. This section had made advocating "seditious" ideas a criminal offence, and had been used to outlaw the Communists and bring its leaders to trial in the early 1930s. It had been used frequently by the former Tory Prime Minister R.B. Bennett, who had boasted that he would bring down "the iron heel of repression" on radicals. Not even the anti-Communist Chamber of Commerce was ready to follow Drew back down that road.

George Drew wins his seat in the 1948 election, but is unable to defeat the Liberals.

In 1950, Drew introduced a motion in the House of Commons to outlaw "communist and similar activities." The loose wording of the motion and the idea of banning a political party were too much even for Solon Low, who had once advocated the creation of a House Committee on Un-Canadian Activities. You don't ban "states of mind," Low cautioned. Worse, the Royal Canadian Mounted Police, whom Drew thought he was championing, told him to back off. The usually tight-lipped Mounties told the right-wing *Toronto Telegram* that they would prefer to keep the Communists "out in the open as much as possible."

Drew also tried to draw attention to "Communists" in government. The Liberals stonewalled, citing their own record in rooting out Reds in the Gouzenko affair and instituting security screening in the public service. To bandy names about, they argued, would not only mean that the reputations of individuals would be smeared, but the serious business of protecting national security would be undermined for cheap politics.

Drew's anti-Communist campaign also suffered from his inability to link up with his natural allies, the anti-Communist Roman Catholics in francoph-

Drew at a Progressive Conservative party dinner, 1949.

one Quebec, where Premier Maurice Duplessis was as demagogic an enemy of Communism as Joe McCarthy or J. Edgar Hoover [see chapter on Duplessis]. Duplessis' party, the Union Nationale, was a nationalist variant of the old Quebec bleus, who might have joined forces with their Ontario-based counterparts. But Drew also represented the anti-Catholic, anti-Quebec strain of the Protestant Ontario Tories, wrapped in the Union Jack. Memories were still fresh of the conscription crisis during the war, when Anglo Tories such as Drew thundered about imposing military service on an unwilling Quebec. As premier of Ontario, Drew had organized a special assisted airlift of immigrants from Britain to bring the proper "British stock" into Canada. Clearly, the twain would never meet.

Canada's would-be Joe McCarthy self-destructed. The Liberals successfully managed and contained the Communist issue.

George Drew, April 8, 1953.

M.J. Coldwell: Social Democratic Cold Warrior

M.J. Coldwell speaking in Toronto during the 1958 election.

One of the most important figures on the Canadian left, M.J. Coldwell was born in England in 1888, and immigrated to Canada as a schoolteacher in 1910. Settling in Saskatchewan, he became active in teachers' organizations in the 1920s and became an alderman in Regina with close links to the farmer and socialist movements of the time. In 1932, he was made leader of the Saskatchewan Farmer-Labour Party that arose in response to the Great Depression. He then became part of the Co-operative Commonwealth Federation (CCF) — the forerunner to the New Democrat Party (NDP). As provincial CCF leader, Coldwell unsuccessfully contested the 1934 Saskatchewan election. In 1935, he was elected CCF Member of Parliament (MP) for Rosetown-Biggar, beginning a long career in federal politics. He soon became a prominent parliamentary campaigner for socialist causes.

Coldwell supporting Canadian troops during World War II.

In September 1939, at the outset of hostilities with Nazi Germany, the revered CCF leader, Reverend J.S. Woodsworth, stuck to his pacifist principles and refused to support a unanimous declaration of war by Canada. Coldwell, as well as the majority of the CCF caucus, broke with their leader, and offered full support to the war effort. Upon Woodsworth's death in 1942, Coldwell succeeded to the CCF national leadership, a post he would hold for eighteen years. In 1945, he was named as a Canadian delegate to the founding of the United Nations, in which he confirmed his belief in bipartisan support for collective security.

In 1944, the Saskatchewan CCF, under Tommy Douglas, swept to office, becoming the first socialist government in North America. In the late war years, the CCF seemed, however, on the brink of an upsurge of national support. It failed to become a national contender for office and remained a third party. Part of the reason for this was the canny capacity of the governing Liberals to steal CCF support by moving far enough to the left on issues such as the welfare state. But part of the explanation was the hostile climate for left-wing ideas that was fostered by the new anti-Communist orthodoxy that quickly developed in the late 1940s. No matter how hard the social democrats of the CCF tried to distance themselves from Communism, they were inevitably tarred with the same brush.

As CCF leader, Coldwell was insistent that the party unconditionally support the Western alliance. This was mainly out of principle: Coldwell was strongly anti-Communist, convinced that the Soviet Union was a brutal tyranny and that Canadian Communists were the real enemies of democratic socialism. It could also be seen as politically prudent: the Cold War being generally popular with Canadians in the 1940s and 1950s, it was useful to show that CCFers were loyal and trustworthy allies in the struggle against totalitarianism.

The conversion of the CCF to outright support of military security and a tough line against the Soviet bloc around the globe was an important factor in

Coldwell in 1935. He would be elected to Parliament later that year.

the successful creation of a Cold War consensus. The Communists were discredited as a political force in Canada by Igor Gouzenko's revelations. As the only Communist elected as MP under the party banner, Fred Rose had been convicted of espionage, clearing the field for the CCF to command the left-of-centre on the political stage. On issues such as the Marshall Plan and North Atlantic Treaty Organization (NATO), there were elements of opposition on the non-Communist as well as Communist left. The CCF leadership, in the party and in the trade unions, proved instrumental in heading off such opposition and consolidating a wide Cold War consensus.

This consensus was not arrived at freely. After debate, Coldwell and the CCF leadership, including another principled anti-Communist, National Secretary David Lewis, enforced adherence to the official party line with as much rigour as their Communist antagonists. Dissenters were given the choice of recanting their heresy, or being expelled from the party or from their trade unions. Even some sitting CCF members of legislatures in Ontario, British Columbia and Manitoba were forced out. In the politics of loyalty and disloyalty, there were no prisoners taken.

Coldwell and Lewis could not, it seems, credit critics on their left as sincere but misguided. Instead they were depicted as either the dupes or the tools of the Communists, ironically paralleling the smears of the right against the CCF itself.

Nothing that the CCF leaders such as Coldwell did to purge their ranks of Communists or "fellow travellers" was enough to cleanse the CCF of its "pink" reputation in the eyes of more conservative Cold Warriors. Through its support, the CCF had done a lot for the Cold War, but the Cold War did nothing for the CCF. The mainstream of Canadian voters remained suspicious of the party. The first decade of the Cold War saw a steady decline of the CCF from its momentary high point at the end of the war. Coldwell led his party through five unsuccessful national elections. Finally, in the Diefenbaker landslide of 1958, the CCF was reduced to a fringe, and Coldwell lost his own seat after twenty-three years. Two years later, he retired from the leadership, and in 1961, the CCF itself passed from the scene and was replaced by the New Democratic Party.

Coldwell himself did receive some belated honours from the government of Canada. In 1964, he was appointed a privy councilor, a title normally bestowed on Cabinet Ministers. In 1967, he was made a Companion of the Order of Canada.

In the late 1960s, he was appointed to a Royal Commission on Security (the Mackenzie Commission), called into being after a series of security scandals had rocked the federal government. If the RCMP security service felt any apprehension about being investigated by this former "leftist" leader, it was soon dispelled. In keeping with his past record on the Cold War, Coldwell proved to be the most conservative of the three commissioners.

In 1966, one of the authors of this book interviewed Coldwell about his career. When asked what he considered to be the proudest achievement of his years in politics, he answered without hesitation: "Helping get Canada into NATO."

Coldwell speaking in 1953.

Coldwell (third from left) at a CCF convention in 1958.

Watson Kirkconnell and the Anti-Communist Crusaders

In the United States, throughout the Cold War, numerous freelance anti-Communist crusaders and self-styled anti-Communist organizations (such as the John Birch Society and the Christian Anti-Communist Crusade) flourished on the margins, and sometimes closer to the mainstream of American life. In Canada, there was greater deference to authority and less evangelism, but there were some freelance crusaders here as well who kept up a drumbeat of anti-Communist propaganda.

In English Canada from the 1940s through the 1960s, one man stood out as an anti-Communist agitator. No marginal figure, Watson Kirkconnell was an academic and scholar, a man of impeccable respectability. A professor of humanities, a key founder of the Humanities Research Council of Canada, and the president of Acadia University, Kirkconnell was an establishment figure. He campaigned on behalf of universities, encouraged scholarship and learning, and advocated the importance of free inquiry to a liberal society. He was, at the same time, a vociferous propagandist against the evils of Communism, who used popular demagoguery to denigrate and caricature opponents, and often insisted that those with whom he disagreed should be silenced.

Kirkconnell first came to public notice during the war when, as someone gifted with languages, he was employed by the government to encourage ethnic support for the war effort. He not only combatted pro-Nazi sentiments among some groups, but struck out at what he considered a far greater menace to a free society, Communism. In fighting Communism, Kirkconnell discovered a second métier that he would pursue for decades. He published a short, popular book on the Communist threat to civilization, *Seven Pillars of Wisdom*, as well as a number of pamphlets on the same theme. While Canada was allied to the USSR in a war against Fascism, his anti-Communism was not always appreciated by Ottawa.

With the coming of the Cold War, he found a ready audience and sponsors. In 1947, the Canadian Chamber of Commerce began a campaign among its membership to spread the anti-Communist message. A centrepiece of the campaign was a pamphlet, prepared by Kirkconnell, sounding the alarm about an imminent Soviet takeover, spearheaded by a treacherous fifth column of Communists and Communist sympathizers in Canada. In *Saturday Night* magazine, he warned of Communist influence on Canadian campuses, claiming that such organizations as the Student Christian Movement and the National Federation of Canadian University Students had been infiltrated by Reds.

Kirkconnell carried his crusade into all areas of Canadian life. As president of the Humanities Research Council, he tried, with little success, to mobilize academic scholarship in a mission to combat the threat to Western civilization. At the same time, he wrote scripts for radio shows beamed to workers in mining and lumber towns, and made personal appearances at service clubs across the country where his inspirational speeches were accompanied by an anti-Communist slide show.

As time went by, it became more apparent that Kirkconnell's popular message was in conflict with his profession of liberal education and scholarly inquiry. On the anti-Communist circuit, he was demagogic, intolerant, and self-righteous, attitudes at odds with the defence of a free society. He also marginalized himself, even from some anti-Communist conservatives, by taking up an eccentric crusade against the fluoridation of water, which he insisted was "a Communist plot to make Canadian brains susceptible to domination," and by falling in with some crank groups with dubious fundraising schemes.

It is difficult to say what impact Kirkconnell's message may have had on Canadians, but by the 1960s, when he published his memoirs, it was evident that his evangelism had gone out of fashion.

In Quebec in the 1940s and 1950s, Kirkconnell had an equal in Robert Rumilly, a prolific historian and commentator on public affairs. Rumilly was a conservative Roman Catholic, an immigrant from Europe where he had been associated with a pre-war French Fascist group. Rumilly believed that Communism was the mortal enemy of Catholic civilization, and he acted as a kind of respectable propaganda arm for Premier Maurice Duplessis' authoritarian rule over the province. He denounced what he called the Communist infiltration of Quebec institutions, with Radio-Canada (the French-language Canadian Broadcasting Corporation) being a particular obsession. Unlike Kirkconnell, Rumilly often mixed anti-Communism with anti-Semitism, and was more aggressively McCarthyite in attacking individuals as alleged Communists. One of his constant targets was Pierre Elliott Trudeau, later to become one of Canada's most prominent prime ministers. Although his poisonous pen did considerable damage during the 1950s, the influence of Rumilly and other anti-Communist crusaders in Quebec went into eclipse with the Quiet Revolution of the early 1960s.

There were some freelance Canadian anti-Communist organizations in the early Cold War era, most of which disappeared after a decade or so. A former general manager of the CBC, forced out of office by financial irregularities, published an anti-Communist newsletter throughout the 1950s. The Imperial Order Daughters of the Empire and the Catholic Women's League combined to back The Alert Service, which provided anti-Communist items to the press and was run by Marjorie Lamb ("A redhead out to beat the Reds"). Pauline McGibbon, later a lieutenant governor of Ontario, was funded by corporations to provide anti-Communist news to New Canadians. The most persistent — and the most extreme and openly anti-Semitic — of these groups was The Canadian Intelligence Service, run for decades out of Flesherton, Ontario by Ron Gostick. Gostick was sometimes joined by Pat Walsh, who claimed to be a former undercover Communist for the RCMP.

Whether extremist or more moderate, freelance anti-Communism did not have as much of a run in Canada as it did in the U.S., where it found a more enduring audience. Here, anti-Communism was more of a government monopoly, jealously guarded by the RCMP, but the various figures and groups on the fringe show how the Cold War did spill over into Canadian society.

John Grierson and the National Film Board

John Grierson, accused of being a Communist during the Gouzenko spy scandal.

John Grierson was one of the most memorable and important figures in the development of twentieth-century Canadian culture. Already an innovative documentary filmmaker in his native Britain before the war, Grierson came to Canada and built the fledgling National Film Board (NFB) of Canada into an organization with a worldwide reputation. Prior to the arrival of television in the 1950s, film was a crucial element in the construction of national identity, and the NFB was instrumental in this task. Even today, its *Canada At War* series offers an indelible record of this country's contribution to that conflict.

Grierson was also a man described to Lester Pearson by the U.S. ambassador to Canada in 1947 as "one of the most subversive characters now alive." Hauled before secret hearings of the Royal Commission investigating Igor

John Grierson.

Gouzenko's evidence of Soviet espionage, he was rudely interrogated about his political beliefs and bullied to admit his alleged Communist sympathies. Four years after Grierson's departure from Canada in 1945, the NFB fell victim to an anti-Communist purge, with scores of filmmakers driven out of government employment, and Grierson's successor as NFB commissioner forced to resign under a cloud of suspicion. It was the Canadian version of the highly publicized Hollywood witch hunt by the U.S. House Committee on Un-American Activities.

How did John Grierson, the innovative filmmaker and successful cultural bureaucrat, become a subversive blacklisted in North America? And how did his remarkable documentary film board become, in the eyes of the prime minister of Canada, "quite a Communist nest"? This is a story of how artists and idealists whose radical ideas were tolerated, and whose creative energies were welcomed by a government fighting a war against Fascism, suddenly found themselves on the wrong side of history. Victory in the war was quickly followed by the Gouzenko affair and the onset of the Cold War. Almost overnight, Grierson and his film board became "security risks."

There is no doubt that Grierson was "progressive" in his politics. His British documentary films had exhibited a strong social conscience. The early NFB had a self-styled democratic mission to depict "real people in real situations." Grierson himself was not a Communist, but he attracted a talented group of radical young people around him, and among these were a few Communist Party members. All became suspects.

The new Cold War security consciousness was supposed to be about screening out the kind of Soviet spies identified by Gouzenko. The NFB was not a sensitive agency with access to classified information like the Defence Department. Nevertheless, it became a prime target, with its employees falling under intensive RCMP surveillance, the subjects of mushrooming secret police files. Like the Hollywood witch hunt in the U.S., the purge at the NFB was directed not at spies but at subversives, politically incorrect dissidents. It had nothing to do with counter-espionage, but represented an ideological purge to root out anyone who might produce cultural representations that clashed with the new official anti-Communist orthodoxy.

Why was the NFB singled out as a target? Grierson had made many enemies during his years as bureaucratic entrepreneur and impresario in wartime Ottawa, among rival civil servants, and in the private Canadian film industry. Even though Grierson himself was gone after 1945, his organizational creation and his acolytes caught the backlash. The late 1940s was pay-back time for the NFB's enemies.

The groundwork for a large-scale purge was being quietly laid behind the scenes as the RCMP security service carefully prepared massive dossiers on the filmmakers. Finally, in 1949, a story planted in the business press revealed that the Defence Department, concerned about the political unreliability of the NFB, was dropping the agency as producer of its training films. With this, the publicity dam burst, and the NFB became publicly identified as the prime security weak point in the government of Canada.

The cover story of the purge — "security" — cannot be taken at face value. A closer look behind the scenes reveals two primary sources for the anti-NFB activity. The small private Canadian film industry was resentful of a successful competitor that was also a government monopoly. One private filmmaker in particular, "Budge" Crawley, actively worked to further the purge as a source for the RCMP against his public-sector competitor. The other antagonist was the U.S. government, behind which stood the Hollywood movie industry. The industry not only wanted to crush competition from independent national film companies abroad, but particularly disliked "un-American" public-sector filmmakers. And, of course, some conservative sections of Canadian society were scandalized by the NFB's "radical" ideas. Among these were some cabinet ministers.

Grierson's successor as film commissioner, Ross McLean, vainly tried to limit the impact and scope of the purge, but was quickly brushed aside, and indeed driven right out of the country into exile in Paris to work for UNESCO. His successor was Arthur Irwin, a journalist from *Maclean's Magazine* who had no background in film, but was considered politically trustworthy to preside over a purge of left-wingers.

As for the impact of the purge, there are two versions that have circulated for decades. The official version, as announced in Parliament and reiterated by Liberal politicians and bureaucrats over the years since, was that only three employees were dismissed. Irwin later recalled that the RCMP presented him with a list of thirty-six security risks, but that in conjunction with senior civil servant Norman Robertson, he whittled this down to three, and this number, although not the names, was announced in Parliament. The unofficial story, as recounted in interviews with the filmmakers themselves, is that scores of people were systematically driven out.

Recently declassified documents from the RCMP security service files directly undermine the official version. The RCMP later did its own accounting and concluded that roughly the same number as had appeared in its initial list of "risks" presented to Irwin were in fact purged. The Mounties got their men (and women) after all.

The two versions can be reconciled quite simply. The NFB hired few permanent employees, keeping most on contract. The three announced terminations were all permanent employees. The other thirty or more simply did not have their contracts renewed, or bowed out "voluntarily" before they could be fired. However disingenuous the official version, it has served as a cover story extolling the liberalism of Canada in the Cold War era in contrast with the repressive Hollywood witch hunt and the ravages of McCarthyism in the U.S. public service. In fact, the number of thirty-five to thirty-six is proportionately comparable to the numbers purged and blacklisted in Hollywood, considering the ratio of population between the U.S. and Canada is about ten to one.

There is another dimension to this story that does not reflect well on Canada. In the U.S., the "Hollywood Ten" and the many others blacklisted for years eventually received public vindication. Publicly accused as traitors at

the time, eventually the wheel turned. The victims of the purge have become cultural heroes, praised in Hollywood movies featuring the likes of Woody Allen, Robert De Niro, Robert Redford, Barbra Streisand, and Jim Carrey. Their accusers are now depicted as witch hunters and stool pigeons.

The NFB victims were not publicly accused and have never received public vindication. Many in fact found their post-NFB careers blighted, with the shadow of the purge following them everywhere. Unlike their American counterparts, they have never experienced closure on this ugly experience.

Nor did the NFB ever recover the vibrancy and energy that had characterized it in its early, "radical" days. The board became a civil service filmmaker, generally safe and not too daring, although occasionally housing innovative talents, such as the award-winning animator Norman McLaren. But the romance of its early years is gone, a victim of a smug Canadian McCarthyism that was practised primly behind closed doors.

Hal Banks: Anti-Communist Racketeer

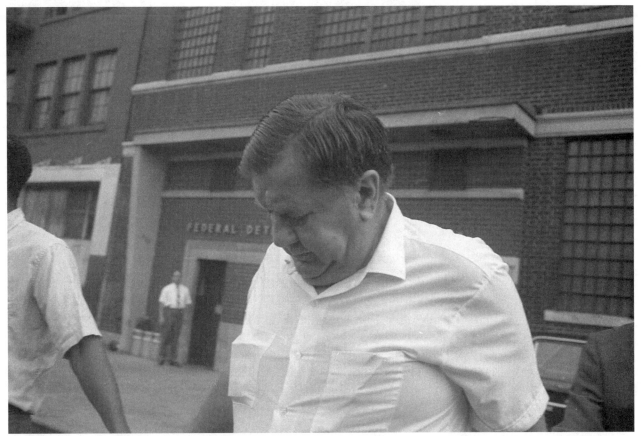

Hal Banks at the federal courthouse during his extradition hearing in the United States in 1967.

The battle against Communism was waged on all fronts, including the waterfront. The Communists lost the battle of the Canadian waterfront, not to the forces of freedom, but to a strong-arm, gangster-filled union, the Seafarers International Union (SIU), led by a notorious American labour racketeer, Hal Banks. As a hired thug, Banks was imported illegally into Canada, with the complicity and active encouragement of the federal government. Long after he had done his job by routing the Reds, the brutality and sleaze in his union led to an official inquiry and criminal charges, but Banks skipped the country to return to the U.S.

How did this gangster become "Canada's sweetheart"? Only in the hysterical context of the early Cold War could such a bizarre story unfold.

In the late 1940s, seamen on Canadian merchant ships were organized under the Canadian Seamen's Union (CSU). Ship owners did not like the CSU, a militant union that had forced minimum working conditions and better pay in the contracts it negotiated during the war. They had had little success in beating back the CSU, which was very popular with its members

CSU members protesting SIU tactics, 1949.

Hal Banks conferring with his lawyer during his extradition hearing.

for standing up on their behalf. As it happened, the CSU was Communist-led. In the gathering Cold War, this was a godsend to the owners, as it gave them a club with which to beat their adversary. The CSU was also a Canadian union at a time when the American Federation of Labor (AFL) was bringing strong pressure to bear on the Canadian Trades and Labour Congress (TLC) to bow to international (i.e. American) unions. AFL unions, including the SIU, were strongly anti-Communist. Here was the solution to the ship owners' problem. The SIU began organizing on the Canadian waterfront in competition with the CSU, and were clearly favoured by the owners.

No one could have been under any illusions about what kind of union the SIU was. It already had a track record in the U.S. for strong-arm tactics and intimidation. Hal Banks had an American criminal record, and was thus inadmissible to Canada under Canadian rules. Not only was he admitted, he was virtually invited into the country. And when he applied for acceptance as a landed immigrant, he was helpfully provided with a special application form that omitted the usual question about criminal convictions. In 1954, a board of inquiry recommended deportation, but the Minister of Citizenship and Immigration stepped in and explained that Banks had come to Canada to "clean up a difficult labour situation," and "had been of real service to Canada." The board was overruled, and "Canada's sweetheart" stayed.

In 1949, the CSU began a strike, which soon spread to foreign ports where dockers were urged by sympathetic local unions not to unload Canadian ships. In the context of the time, with Marshall Plan shipments arriving in European ports, this quickly became an international crisis, viewed by Washington and London, as well as Ottawa, as a dangerous example of

Communist-inspired sabotage of ship-
ping. The Canadian government
outlawed the strike. The AFL successfully pressured the TLC to kick the
CSU out. The SIU violently smashed
CSU picket lines, sometimes even
using firearms. International support
crumbled, and the strike was soon lost.
Having failed disastrously, opposed by
the owners and by the government,
the CSU was on the run, and eventually collapsed and disappeared. The
SIU was triumphant. By the close of
the 1940s, Hal Banks was king of the
Canadian waterfront. Seamen shipped
only through SIU hiring halls.

Adding insult to injury, in 1951,
the Canadian government, under pressure from the U.S., instituted Royal
Canadian Mounted Police security
screening for Great Lakes seamen.

Hal Banks.

This was completely unnecessary, since Bank's SIU hiring halls had its own
blacklist, a "Do Not Ship" list of former CSU supporters, but it gave further
evidence of state backing for the SIU monopoly on the waterfront.

Through the 1950s, SIU brutality and corruption was unchallenged.
Savage beatings were freely used against anyone questioning Banks' iron-
fisted hold. All who crossed Banks were, of course, labelled "Communists."
Finally, in 1962, the mess on the Great Lakes was so out of control that a
judicial inquiry was ordered under Mr. Justice T.G. Norris. One hundred
and eight volumes of testimony were elicited and a devastating report was
published that concluded, among other indictments, that "Banks has been
lawless from the beginning, and it was a mistake to bring him to Canada."
No doubt, but importing Banks had been quite deliberate. The official atti-
tude had been like that of the American president who said of a particularly
malodorous Latin American dictator: "he may be a son of a bitch, but he's
our son of a bitch."

Hal Banks in custody, 1964.

Following Norris' recommendation, the SIU was put under federal
trusteeship in 1963. Banks, facing criminal charges, skipped his adopted country in 1964. Authorities claimed to have no idea of his whereabouts, but a
reporter tracked him down to a yacht off New York. In 1967, he was ordered
extradited to Canada by a U.S. court. No less than the American secretary of
state, Dean Rusk, quashed the order. Banks, it seems, always had friends in
high places, whether in Canada or the U.S. He died in 1985, having never
been brought before a Canadian court.

Cold War Logic: Investigating Lotta Hitschmanova, the Unitarian Church, and the United Church of Canada

Lotta Hitschmanova in the uniform of her Unitarian Services Committee, November 17, 1961.

"Fifty six Sparks Street, Ottawa." For a generation of Canadian television viewers, these words could mean only one thing: Dr. Lotta Hitschmanova, a world-renowned humanitarian, was ending a commercial for her Unitarian Services Committee (USC) Canada. From the perspective of the Cold War and state security, however, these were the words of a potential subversive. Not only would Hitschmanova be targeted for investigation by the counter-subversion branch of the Royal Canadian Mounted Police, but so would religious organizations such as the Unitarian Church and the United Church of Canada.

Born in 1909 in what would become Czechoslovakia after the First World War, the diminutive Hitschmanova found herself on the run when Hitler's Germany occupied her homeland. Settling in Canada in 1942, she began work with other refugees. That dedication led her to form the Canadian branch of the Unitarian Services Committee and brought her name into the ever-burgeoning filing system of the Cold War version of the RCMP.

The attention began in the late 1940s as the police sought to ascertain what both the new organization and the person behind it were all about. The initial investigation may have been inspired by events in the United States where an anti-Communist crusade alleged that USC's Boston branch was under Red control.

The RCMP opened a file on Hitschmanova and obtained information about her, including copies of correspondence from "reliable contacts," otherwise known as police informants within the Ottawa Branch of the Czechoslovak National Alliance, a group to which she also belonged. Despite the investigation, the police failed to discover anything "that would cast an unfavourable reflection on her from a political point of view." Nevertheless, the occasional report on her organization continued into the 1970s.

The RCMP's examination of the fifteen-thousand-member Unitarian Church and some of its affiliated organizations was not so sporadic. To put it simply, the Mounted Police viewed the Unitarian Church as a haven for hidden Communists, or what the Mounties called "closed-club members." It was not that the church itself was a Communist organization or Communist front

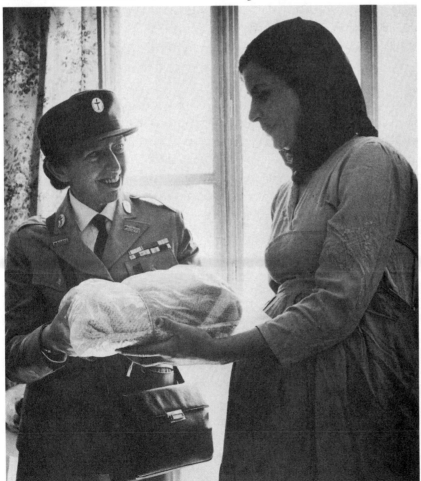

Hitschmanova on Unitarian Services Committee business.

A refugee being assisted by the
Unitarian Services Committee.

(even the RCMP at its worst escaped such crudities), but rather that it seemed to attract Communist members and, as an institution, appeared to defend causes also supported by Canada's Cold War enemies. Even more fundamental from the perspective of the police, Unitarianism as a philosophy viewed the alien Red ideology "objectively, free from the antipathies which have characterized its reception by most other organized religions. It thus provides Communism with a foothold in a society which is chiefly hostile to Communism and all it entails."

One particular Unitarian club, the Ottawa branch of the Unitarian Men's Club, became the focus of additional police attention. Its aim, noted one policeman, involved activities "towards peace ... [and] like any peaceful movements attempts are made for subversive infiltration." In the late 1950s, the Mounted Police employed informants within the club to monitor "suspects" in attendance and to provide detailed accounts of meetings. Of special interest were talks given by guest speakers such as social democrats Tommy Douglas and Eugene Forsey, with the latter deemed as in no way "communistically inclined," and the Soviet ambassador to Canada, of whose address the Mounties somehow obtained a copy. Even the questions asked after a talk and the money contributed in collection plates fascinated the sticklers for detail in their scarlet uniforms. Again, as with the church as a whole, the club escaped the subversive label but its executive was considered "infiltrated ... by persons ... suspected of Communist sympathies" creating a forum wherein "points embarrassing to the Canadian government" could be freely discussed.

It was not just Unitarianism and its various facets that concerned Canada's intelligence agency. The nation's largest Protestant denomination, the United Church of Canada, was also investigated because of its involvement in certain causes. The first police report was written in 1947, and a permanent file on the church was opened in 1948 after its annual meeting passed a resolution in which the word "synthesis" was repeatedly used — a tipoff, the police

decided, to the underlying "Marxist character" of the gathering. Again the justification was similar as to that applied to Unitarianism: "Although it is inconceivable that any devoted theologian would be converted by such a dialogue [between Christians and Marxists]," wrote one officer, "the mere fact that Christian leaders are willing to associate and/or discuss differences with Communists has given the Communist an appearance of respectability." Hence the investigations searched for attempts by subversives to influence or infiltrate the church with the longer aim of influencing the wider society and possibly government policy in a number of areas: youth protest and education, Communist China, poverty, and peace.

In the end it made no difference to the anti-subversive unit of the Mounted Police whether Communists really sought to manipulate religion to their own ends. Merely the suggestion that they did through the espousal of causes by religious groups that ran counter to Cold War orthodoxy sufficed. The old firefighting principle operated. Where there was smoke, there had to be fire; the Mounted Police were determined to discover who had struck the match.

The Marshall Plan and NATO

An RCAF CF-100 flies over Niagara Falls, March 16, 1959.

In the late 1940s, Canada came of age as an international actor in peace-time. Before the war, Canada had been so much in the shadow of Britain as to barely register on the world stage as an independent presence. After the war, she emerged as a middle power with her own distinctive role to play. Her emergence coincided with the emergence of the Cold War. This had important consequences for Canada's new international personality.

In the first post-war decade, Canada became an important champion of a new liberal internationalism, closely associated with the United Nations (UN) and the maintenance of peace through multilateral negotiation. In 1957, the foremost architect of Canadian foreign policy, Lester Pearson, was awarded the Nobel Prize for peace, as a striking recognition of Canada's role in the Suez Crisis. Canadian contributions to international peacekeeping have, over the years, become an essential element in Canadians' perception of their place in the world.

Canadian negotiators at a meeting to plan North American defence.

Along with this, Canada also embarked in the late 1940s on another track in maintaining peace. Collective security through alliances with other Western powers under U.S. leadership was the second pillar of Canadian policy. This squarely situated Canada as a partisan in the Cold War. The two tracks were not necessarily in conflict, and could sometimes work together, as in the case of the UN military intervention in Korea. Sometimes, however, there were tensions between internationalism and partisanship, and there were times when Canada displayed some of the symptoms of a split personality trying simultaneously to be both a good internationalist and a good Cold Warrior.

It was imperative that Canada safeguard its own national interests, including its own economic interests. Internationalism and Cold War solidarity were all very well, but if they failed to contribute to Canadians' well-being, governments pursuing these goals on the world stage would come under heavy fire at home. Finally, for Canada, there was the age-old problem of national unity to consider. In the past, to-eager support for foreign entanglements had led to tensions between English and French Canada, as in the conscription crises in two world wars. If Canada were to play an enhanced international role, it could not be at the expense of national unity.

All of these problems and tensions were evident over the reconstruction of Europe and the building of the Atlantic alliance. The Marshall Plan and the North Atlantic Treaty Organization (NATO) were key developments in shaping the post-war world. The Marshall Plan was primarily an American-designed and financed recovery plan for war-weakened European economies, with Cold War implications, onto which Canada piggybacked. NATO was a Cold War military alliance that Canada had a hand in shaping,

Canadian Defence Minister Brooke
Claxton at a NATO graduation
ceremony in 1957.

and was to become a primary focus of Canadian military and diplomatic efforts for some four decades.

Both initiatives were broadly supported within Canada, but were not without minority critics. Debate quickly degenerated into what could better be described as a Cold War loyalty oath test. Both were international and domestic "successes" in the longer term, but the way they were brought in does little credit to Canada as a tolerant democracy that is open to all views. Being on the "wrong" side in the Cold War cost dissenters a great deal.

The Marshall Plan, proclaimed in 1947, has had very good press over the years. The image of the U.S. selflessly pouring its dollars into Europe to rehabilitate economies devastated by war is so powerful that successive "Marshall Plans" have subsequently been proposed for the post-Communist states of Eastern Europe after 1989-90, and for the Third World. But Marshall aid was not a selfless or disinterested effort on the part of the Americans, however much it did benefit Western European countries. It was a way of financing an American export surplus, and was sold to a skeptical U.S.

Defence Minister Claxton inspecting NATO troops in 1957.

Congress in exactly those terms. Rehabilitated European economies would provide better markets for American goods and investments. Call it a confluence of interests. Certainly it worked better for Western Europe than Soviet rule did for Eastern Europe, where a kind of negative Marshall Plan ground down the economies behind the "Iron Curtain."

For Canada, the Marshall Plan posed a challenge. Canada too needed the recovery of pre-war European markets for its agricultural exports, especially wheat. Canadian officials succeeded in striking a special deal with the Americans: Canada would be allocated a quota of Marshall dollars for Europeans to purchase Canadian exports. This was highly advantageous to Canada, and represented something of a coup for Canadian negotiators. Best of all, Canada could sell the arrangement as being in the interests of peace and in the interests of Canadian commerce. And conservative, anti-Communist Quebec was persuaded that Marshall aid was bolstering the Christian and Catholic West.

Marshall's critics — mainly on the left wing of the trade-union movement and among a few academics and journalists — worried about the division of Europe between capitalist West and Communist East that was being consoli-

President Eisenhower departing from a NATO summit, December 19, 1957.

dated. The Communists saw it as a capitalist trick, a point that few Canadians were likely to accept, but there were more considered arguments about the hidden motives behind the plan. No matter whether such arguments were considered or ill-considered, little if any criticism was tolerated. Trade unionists and Co-operative Commonwealth Federation members who opposed the Marshall Plan were silenced and sometimes expelled. Independent commentators in the media were chastised as pro-Communist if they gave voice to anti-Marshall views. In one case, Glen Shortliffe, a Queen's University professor was intimidated into silence for his independent criticisms on the Canadian Broadcasting Corporation, when alumni threatened to cut off financial support for his university.

The North Atlantic Treaty Organization (NATO), signed in 1949, provided a more significant test of Canada's commitment to collective security, since it involved tangible military contributions. Canadian negotiators fought hard for the inclusion of Article 2 of the Atlantic Charter, which spoke of strengthening the social elements of Atlantic solidarity, thus echoing the liberal internationalism of Canada. However, U.S. Secretary of State Dean Acheson poured scorn on this, insisting that "the plain fact, of course, is that NATO is a military alliance." The first secretary general of NATO, Lord Ismay, once somewhat cynically summed up the purposes of NATO as threefold: "to keep the Russians out, the Americans in, and the Germans down." By the early 1950s, following the Korean War, Canada had a permanent infantry brigade group stationed in West Germany, air bases in France and Germany, and its Atlantic naval fleet largely under NATO command.

NATO was sold in Canada in much the same way as the Marshall Plan, as a loyalty oath test. Dissent was, for the most part, qualified as pro-Communist. As such, there was little informed debate and not much public education. In 1952, a Gallup poll discovered that almost two-thirds of Canadians had either never heard of NATO, or could not correctly identify it, yet three-quarters were sure that it was a good thing, whatever it was.

Over the Cold War years, Canadian diplomats were insistent on the value of the NATO commitment in providing a voice for Canada, and a counterbal-

Claxton sending aid to the Belgian army under the Marshall Plan, 1957.

ance to the overwhelming power of the U.S. in North American defence. In the latter Cold War years, the Canadian military commitment became controversial, as peace campaigners pointed to NATO as an obstacle to détente with the USSR. Although these debates became impassioned, it is ironic that the decision to bring home the boys (and girls) from Europe was ultimately made on purely fiscal grounds by a Conservative government in the late 1980s, just as the Cold War was drawing to a close. Remarkably, this decision drew little public attention or criticism.

With the end of the Cold War, NATO has transformed itself into a very different kind of organization, now encompassing some of the armies of Eastern Europe that were formerly locked into the antagonistic Warsaw Pact, created by the USSR as a counter to NATO in the early 1950s. Even Russia is now considered a partner to the Atlantic Alliance. NATO actually fought its first military campaign well after the end of the Cold War with the successful 1999 military intervention against the Serbs in Kosovo, to which Canada contributed some limited assistance.

PART TWO

The 1950s

The 1950s were the model Cold War decade. The mould had already been cast in the late 1940s, but serious dissent against the Cold War would not get underway until the 1960s.

Internationally, it was far from being a quiet decade. It opened with a major war in Korea in which Canada participated at the cost of hundreds of Canadian lives. There were twin international crises in 1956, when the Red Army crushed the Hungarian Revolt, and Britain and France joined Israel in an ill-advised invasion of Egypt that gave birth to United Nations peace-keeping and a Nobel Prize for Peace for Canada's foreign minister, Lester B. Pearson. Canada joined the U.S. in the defence of the North American continent and signed the North American Air Defence (NORAD) pact that has endured into this century. And on New Year's Day, 1959, Canadians woke to the news that bearded revolutionaries had overthrown the pro-American government in Cuba. Soon Fidel Castro would bring the Caribbean island located ninety miles off the U.S. coast into the Communist orbit, and it would become a Cold War flashpoint early in the next decade.

Domestically, the 1950s were somewhat calm in comparison to the turbulent decades that preceded and followed. Canada became suburban and Canadians seemed content to retreat to private family life and traditional social values, and to enjoy the fruits of abundant consumerism after two decades of depression and war. The political world did not remain settled, however. In 1957, twenty-two years of uninterrupted Liberal rule came to a

Joseph Stalin, 1953.

Russian soldiers lined up for review, May Day, 1953.

An anti-Soviet protest in Winnipeg, 1955.

sudden end. The upset victory of the Progressive Conservatives was led by a charismatic prairie populist, John Diefenbaker. The following year, Diefenbaker returned to the polls and won the largest landslide victory in Canadian history.

Cold War thinking was not entirely uncontested in the 1950s. There were a few critics who spoke out against Canada's anti-Communist alignment with the West, but they did so at their peril. Dr. James Endicott of the Canadian Peace Congress challenged the Cold War orthodoxy. For his pains, he was identified in the press and by the government of Canada as Public Enemy Number One. Although not publicly known at the time, the Cabinet actually considered (but finally rejected) treason charges against Dr Endicott. In Quebec, autocratic Premier Maurice Duplessis led a virtual reign of terror against "Communists," and others who could be smeared with the same brush. Elsewhere in the country, there were cases of what would be called "McCarthyism" in the U.S. — careers were blocked or in some cases wrecked by charges of Communism. These charges were sometimes accurate and were sometimes not. Behind the scenes, the RCMP were carefully building networks of informers and secret sources throughout civil society. They were accumulating extensive "subversive" dossiers on Canadians that two decades later would be condemned as excessive and unjustifiable by a Royal Commission of inquiry. The government's closely guarded security screening process widened its net throughout the decade. In the late 1950s, it rooted out sexual "deviates" in a campaign against homosexuals that a later prime minister would describe as "odious." In this case, social prejudice in the conservative 1950s was reinforced by the government-directed "Red scare," and the lives of scores of individuals were blighted.

The Soviet military commemorates the 32nd anniversary of the 1917 Communist revolution, 1949.

Although the 1950s may seem conservative and anti-Communist in contrast to later, more disputatious, decades, they were not monochromatic. The official picture was frayed around the edges. Even if the "Communist-fronted" ban-the-bomb movement was rejected by most Canadians, the fear of nuclear war lay like a dark cloud over the decade. Anyone who grew up in the 1950s can vividly recall the omnipresent spectre of "The Bomb," and how it haunted a decade otherwise devoted to the ideals of progress and prosperity. However fervent the zeal of those crusading against the godless totalitarian tyranny of Communism, there were always Canadian doubts about the American doctrine of "massive retaliation," and about the ethics of nuclear "brinksmanship" with the Soviets. American Cold Warriors might declaim "better dead than Red," but Canadians were not quite so sure.

There had always been Canadian suspicion of the excessive crusading zeal of Americans. There was considerable Canadian smugness, not always justified, that we had avoided the extremes of McCarthyism that had bedevilled the U.S. in the early 1950s. In 1957, when distinguished scholar, diplomat and Canadian ambassador to Egypt Herbert Norman was driven to suicide by witch-hunting U.S. senators, who had raked up his student past of years earlier, the Canadian reaction was one of unalloyed moral outrage and anger at the U.S. Canadian-American relations recovered, but it was obvious that, as a junior partner to Uncle Sam, Canada was not always "ready, aye ready."

The ambiguities of Canada's role in the Cold War can be summed up in

Red Square, May 18, 1961.

the figure of Lester Pearson. As Minister of External Affairs until 1957, Pearson gained the most prominent international reputation ever attained by a Canadian diplomat. Pearson was a strong advocate of the Cold War and often showed considerable crusading fervor zeal in denouncing the evils of Communism. Yet he was also an able diplomat who sought peace over Cold War "victories," and this often earned him the enmity of the U.S. Cold Warriors. He won the Nobel Prize for peace, and he also won a place in the files of J. Edgar Hoover's Federal Bureau of Investigation as a suspected Soviet agent.

In retrospect, it is clear that beneath the relatively tranquil surface of the 1950s, tensions were building. A new generation of opposition to the Cold War's grip over Canadian society was germinating. And in 1959, the death of Maurice Duplessis signalled the beginning of deep changes in Quebec. These would later shake Canada to its roots, and render the simplistic "freedom versus Communism" categories of the Cold War increasingly irrelevant.

Russian troops parade in Red Square with bayonet rifles, 1952.

The Vietnam Before Vietnam: the Korean War

Chinese prisoners of war in Korea, May 21, 1951.

On June 25, 1950, the armed forces of North Korea advanced across the 38th parallel that divided the Korean peninsula between the Communist People's Republic to the north, and the pro-Western Republic of Korea to the south. The invasion quickly turned into a rout, as Communist forces overran the southern capital of Seoul within days, and continued to advance rapidly down the peninsula. The United Nations Security Council, in the temporary absence of the Soviet delegate, voted for military assistance to the beleaguered South, but American armed forces failed to stem the Communist tide. By September, the Communists held all of Korea save for the small Pusan perimeter in the southeast corner.

In the face of this desperate situation, the Americans pushed hard for military commitments from their Western allies, including Canada. Stretched thin following post-war demobilization, Canada was reluctant to commit troops to a faraway conflict in Asia, but came under relentless U.S. pressure, abetted by the United Nations Secretary General. In August 1950, Canada gave way and

A Canadian soldier fighting with UN forces in Korea.

agreed to send ground troops (including the Princess Patricia's infantry, which would later serve in Afghanistan in 2002). This was met with general approval by press and public.

Then, in the fall, a successful American counterattack was launched with a daring landing at Inchon, on the west coast near Seoul, under General Douglas MacArthur. Following Inchon, the tide turned, and American-led forces under the United Nations flag drove up the peninsula. They pushed back the North Koreans toward the Yalu River that marked the boundary with China, which had just fallen under Communist rule the year before. The Canadian government, especially External Affairs Minister Lester Pearson, harboured private qualms about America's war aims. MacArthur's reckless drive toward the Yalu set off alarm bells with regards to drawing the Chinese into the war and widening the conflict in a dangerously unpredictable fashion. Quiet diplomacy by Pearson and the British was brushed off by the Americans, who wanted their allies' military contribution, but not their advice. With the warnings ignored, the Chinese poured across the Yalu in November, and the UN forces were once again put on the defensive, retreating by early 1951 to below the 38th parallel. Soon, fighting stabilized around the middle of the peninsula, where it was to remain for the next two and a half years.

Canadian alarm about MacArthur's bellicosity and barely concealed intent to extend the war yet further by bombing China and "rolling back" Communism may have had little impact, but in the spring of 1951, the president of the United States, Harry Truman, was sufficiently incensed by MacArthur's insubordination and Caesarist ambitions to take the drastic step of firing his popular commander.

MacArthur's departure did not, however, significantly lessen the tensions with America's allies. In December, 1950, British Prime Minister Clement Attlee flew to Washington over fear that the U.S. might use atomic weapons, a fear shared by Pearson. These fears were never entirely abated. The Americans had little time for their allies or their concerns. In 1952, Pearson, together with India, tried to broker a peace settlement at the UN. The American secretary of state, Dean Acheson, was enraged at this Canadian impertinence.

There was an incident in 1952 that further frayed relations between Canadian officials and the U.S. The situation had turned ugly in a UN prisoner-of-war camp on the island of Koje. The Americans claimed that thousands of North Korean and Chinese prisoners were refusing repatriation at war's end and demanding political asylum in the South. This claim was as much propaganda as fact. At Koje, Communist prisoners were actually carrying out a violent uprising. The Americans, without seeking official Canadian consent, dispatched Canadian troops to help quell the revolt. Lester Pearson made a statement in Parliament based on American information that he later learned was less than truthful. In fact, Pearson was angry at the use of Canadians in this situation, and angry at not being consulted. But the differences were papered over in public, and the Canadians remained in Koje for as long as required.

The Korean War was a very bloody conflict, with horrific civilian casualties numbering in the millions. U.S. air power, including blanket fire bombing of cities, reduced North Korea to rubble. Dams were deliberately targeted, with resulting floods and destruction of the North's food supply. There was extensive misrepresentation of UN military success, and an unremitting propaganda campaign that depicted a "white hats, black hats" image of Communist atrocities and Western rectitude. North Korea was clearly a brutal dictatorship, but the regime in the South was corrupt and reactionary. Yet, almost no criticism of "our Koreans" ever reached the mainstream Western media.

All these features would later become known as the "Vietnam syndrome," with reference to that later controversial conflict. But in Vietnam, the official version of events was challenged repeatedly and often to good effect. Korea was a Vietnam before Vietnam. The press was docile, and rarely questioning. Dissent on Korea came from the left, which in the early days of the Cold War was generally dismissed as Communist-inspired or in sympathy with the enemy. The Canadian Peace Congress raised claims that the Americans were using "germ warfare." There was no attempt to investigate these charges, since they could be rejected as Communist propaganda. Indeed, the Cabinet discussed laying treason charges against James Endicott for spreading this claim. In the later Vietnam conflict, dissent became so widespread that it could not finally be dismissed as Communist. Korea was simpler, and cruder.

Publicly throughout the war, Canada tended to stand with the U.S. and the UN command. Privately, Pearson and other Canadian officials harboured growing doubts about how recklessly the Americans risked a wider conflagration. These doubts rarely reached the public. Canada did, however, resolve in the future not to get involved in American military interventions abroad. When war was threatened over a crisis in the straits of Taiwan in 1955, Pearson made it clear that the Americans were on their own so far as Canada was concerned. Canada did not contribute militarily to the Vietnam War in the 1960s and 1970s. Instead, Canada turned in the latter part of the 1950s to a mission of UN peacekeeping that it has continued ever since. Only after the end of the Cold War, in the Gulf War in 1991 and the war against terrorism in Afghanistan, has Canada returned to making small military contributions to interventions abroad.

A Korean armistice was concluded in 1953 by the incoming American president, Dwight Eisenhower. It more or less recreated the status quo along the 38th parallel, after three and a half years of blood and destruction. Over three-hundred Canadian servicemen died in action.

Lester B. Pearson: Cold Warrior or Liberal Subversive?

Lester Pearson as leader of the opposition in 1959.

By any measure, he was one of the most distinguished Canadians of the twentieth century. Born in 1897, Lester B. ("Mike") Pearson served in the First World War, graduated from Oxford, and became a leading diplomat with important postings to London and Washington. Rising to under-secretary of state of External Affairs, Pearson then moved into politics, becoming Minister when his old boss, Louis St. Laurent, succeeded Mackenzie King as prime minister in 1948. He had been considered seriously for the post of secretary general of the United Nations in 1946, but was vetoed by the Soviets. During the Suez Crisis of 1956, it was Pearson who pioneered the United Nations peacekeeping force for which he was awarded the Nobel Prize for peace in 1957. After the defeat of the Liberals in the 1957 federal election, Pearson became the leader of the Liberals in opposition. For five eventful years, from 1963 to 1968, he was prime minister of Canada, presiding over the birth of the national Medicare system, the Canada Pension Plan, and the new Canadian flag, among other initiatives.

Pearson in 1952.

A protestor demonstrating against Pearson's support for nuclear weapons in Canada in 1963.

His death in 1972 was the occasion for a great state funeral.

Mike Pearson was the most prominent architect of Canadian foreign policy in the Cold War era. He was the senior diplomat during the Marshall Plan and the formation of North Atlantic Treaty Organization (NATO) in the late 1940s, and steered Canada into an internationalist stance in the world quite unlike the isolationism of the interwar years. But what sort of internationalism was Pearson championing for Canada? Here, the image is somewhat ambiguous.

Sometimes Pearson seemed to be guiding Canada firmly toward an active acceptance of the burdens of collective security, whether via the United Nations when Canadian forces were sent under the UN flag to battle the Communist North Koreans and Chinese in the Korean War, or when Canada took a strong role in the foundation of the NATO alliance against the Soviet threat to Western Europe. In 1963, Pearson, as leader of the opposition, attacked the Diefenbaker Conservative government at the time of the Bomarc missile crisis for failing to fulfill Canada's obligations under the North American Air Defence (NORAD) alliance for the defence of North America. Pearson pledged his Liberal Party would accept nuclear warheads for the Bomarcs stationed on Canadian soil, and won the 1963 election on an apparently pro-American platform.

As advocate of Canada as America's loyal Cold War partner, Pearson could often sound a strident anti-Communist note, especially in the late 1940s when his countrymen had to be first persuaded to join in the global struggle. "The crusading and subversive power of communism," he declared, "has been harnessed by a cold-blooded, calculating, victoriously powerful Slav empire for its own political purposes…. Our frontier is not now even on the Rhine or rivers further east. It is wherever free men are struggling against totalitarian tyranny…. It may run through the middle of our own cities, or it may be on the crest of the remotest mountain."

He reacted with hostility to those on the left of the political spectrum who criticized Canada's support for the Cold War. He regularly denounced the Reverend James Endicott and the Canadian Peace Congress [see chapter on Endicott] as subversive tools of the Soviet Union, sometimes sounding not so very different than J. Edgar Hoover when he did so.

Pearson the tough-minded Cold Warrior was not the only Pearson. There was also the internationalist and supporter of the UN, the promoter of the international peacekeeping force, and a "dove" on the issues of peace and war. Canada sent troops to Korea, but Pearson did his best at the UN to try to broker a peace accord to end that bloody conflict — and earned the enmity of the U.S. secretary of state, Dean Acheson, for his efforts. In his memoirs, Pearson wrote ironically of a "very difficult negotiation between Corporal Pearson and General Acheson." For his part, Acheson later referred contemptuously to Pearson as an "empty glass." Following Korea, which Canadian policy makers privately found a trying experience, Pearson tended to counsel Canadian prudence when it came to supporting American brinkmanship in Asia, as in the crisis over the Straits of Taiwan in 1955.

These tensions came further to the fore during the Vietnam War in the 1960s. Although Canadian companies made money out of the U.S. involvement in that agonizing conflict, the Canadian government officially stayed out of any military commitment. This was an American show, and when it started to go badly, Pearson offered public advice to President Lyndon B. Johnson that was not appreciated. In 1965, just two years after coming to office in Canada as a pro-American hawk on the nuclear weapons issue, Pearson accepted an invitation to give an address at Temple University in Philadelphia. Johnson had just escalated the war by ordering intensive bombing of North Vietnam, and the domestic divisions over American involvement were beginning to build toward the traumatic intensities of the late 1960s. Into this burgeoning maelstrom, Pearson stepped in with a cautious but clear suggestion that the administration consider a pause in its bombing campaign in order to explore peace negotiations. Lyndon B. Johnson exploded in indignation. Summoned to a grim meeting at the presidential retreat at Camp David, Maryland, Pearson was bullied and ranted at by a raging president who towered menacingly over the smaller prime minister. According to one report, Johnson went so far as to snatch Pearson up by his lapels and shake

Pearson holding his Nobel Peace Prize, 1957.

Lester Pearson with John Diefenbaker in Ottawa, photographed March 29, 1968.

Pearson meets with Indian Prime Minister Jawaharlal Nehru, November 9, 1955.

him. The presidential language was straight out of the locker room, including an accusation that the Canadian leader had "pissed on my rug." Pearson came away pale and unnerved.

Most of these signs of American displeasure with Pearson were kept away from the public eye, although the criticism of American policy in the Temple speech was widely noted. What was not known at all to the Canadian public, but certainly to Pearson himself at the time, was that this Canadian Cold Warrior was a target for American anti-Communist witch hunters. J. Edgar Hoover's Federal Bureau of Investigation (FBI) kept a file on Pearson, begun during the Second World War and continuing through the period when he was prime minister, that was labelled "Espionage – R." "R" stood for "Russian." The declassified version of this file is approximately two inches thick. It is filled with entries by FBI agents about Pearson's subversive political views, his alleged Communist associations and, rife with malicious gossip, hearsay accusations that sometimes betray serious ignorance and misinformation about Canada, and base innuendo. It is now apparent that when the Washington witch hunters went after Herbert Norman with fatal results, Norman was a mere stalking horse. Their real quarry was Lester Pearson.

Pearson felt very badly about Norman's suicide, perhaps accepting some personal responsibility for failing to come more publicly to his colleague's side. Like most Canadians of whatever political stripe at the time, he was also very angry at the Americans who had driven this distinguished Canadian diplomat and scholar to his death. For a time, he even threatened to cut off the exchange of intelligence information on Canadian citizens with the U.S. Eventually the flap died down, and business as usual returned between the U.S. and Canada, and between the Royal Canadian Mounted Police and the FBI. But Pearson knew full well that the U.S. Senate internal security sub-committee that had publicly hounded Norman to his death, really had Pearson himself in their sights.

Ten years earlier, just as he was crusading among his countrymen for Canadian commitment to the American-led Cold War, Pearson had warned

Pearson meeting with Lyndon Johnson, January 22, 1964.

Canadians against succumbing to the "black madness of the witch hunt" that was already engulfing American life. Now, directly threatened himself by that same witch hunt, Pearson refused to run and hide. Instead, he stared down the bullies. Secure in his own mind that he had nothing in his past and nothing in his actions of which he should be ashamed, he in effect dared the committee to go ahead and reveal their allegations. Under pressure from the U.S. State Department and White House, the witch hunters backed down, perhaps recognizing that they could only discredit themselves, and not the Nobel Prize for peace winner, in Ottawa.

Pearson in the late 1950s.

This did not, however, put an end to the whispering campaign against Pearson in American right-wing circles. Nor did it close the FBI file on him, which continued to accumulate bits and pieces of rumour and innuendo gathered from the various ideological garbage bins in which FBI investigators poked. In the mid-1960s, during a particularly rancorous period of parliamentary partisanship under a Liberal minority government, the former prime minister, John Diefenbaker, embittered by the loss of his government and apparently willing to use any means to discredit and undermine his successor, threatened to open the "loyalty" question in Canada. Diefenbaker had mysteriously come into possession of the anti-Pearson material accumulated by the Senate committee. He privately tried to blackmail the prime minister into suppressing an old Tory security scandal involving one of Diefenbaker's former Ministers [see chapter on Munsinger affair] by threatening to make

Pearson with Pierre Trudeau in Ottawa, June 25, 1968.

Pearson's "security" case public. Pearson in effect told Diefenbaker to go ahead and hang himself if he wished. Diefenbaker, like the FBI and the senators, backed down.

Yet traces of the mud lingered on, to be stirred from time to time. The memoirs of the special counsel to the Senate committee, published in 1968 when Pearson retired as prime minister, made thinly veiled allegations against him. And then long after his death, an American teaching in Canada, James Barros, published a book on Herbert Norman in 1986, in which he asserted, on derisory evidence, that Pearson was likely the Soviets' "ultimate mole." This posthumous mudslinging appears mercifully to have died with the end of the Cold War, and Lester Pearson's reputation as a national and international statesman remains undiminished.

What are we to make of Pearson

Lester Pearson meeting with President John F. Kennedy, May 10, 1963.

and the Cold War? How could such radically different images have been associated with the same man, and the same record? Perhaps the ambiguities surrounding Pearson's role simply reflect the ambiguities surrounding Canada's role in the Cold War, and especially Canada's relation to its senior partner, the United States. In the post-war era, a new internationalism for Canada necessarily involved a commitment to the collective security of the West, as well as a commitment to the United Nations, and to peace in the world. Sometimes these commitments came into conflict, particularly when the U.S. had a different interpretation of strategy. The Americans tended to stress military power and "brinksmanship," while the Canadians were more inclined to emphasize multilateral diplomacy and peace making. Pearson was occasionally in the uncomfortable position of having to challenge the Americans. As a master of "quiet diplomacy," Pearson tried to make sure that disagreements were kept behind closed doors. The Americans frequently paid little regard to private advice that conflicted with their own agenda, and sometimes Pearson felt it necessary to gently establish a public stance for Canada that differed in degree from that of the U.S. When this happened, as it did over negotiating peace in Korea and Vietnam, the Americans reacted with irritation at such impertinence from a junior partner. Extreme right-wing Cold Warriors in the U.S., such as Hoover's FBI and the witch hunters in Congress, mistook cues from the White House and State Department, and concluded that Lester Pearson was a subversive and a security risk.

Pearson was in fact a principled supporter of Western collective security against Soviet totalitarianism. He genuinely believed that Soviet Communism represented a threat to liberal and democratic values, and to international peace and stability if Soviet aggression were not contained. But he also believed deeply in a world of liberal internationalism, and was passionately committed to peace and to negotiating differences and avoiding the awful spectre of nuclear war. In these various commitments, Pearson faithfully reflected the values of his own country. That some, although certainly not all, Americans chose to interpret differences of opinion over means as evidence of disloyalty and treason was a sad reflection of the occasional American insensitivity and arrogance toward Canada that stained the partnership of the two North American nations during the Cold War era. In the end, the reputation of Lester Pearson, like the friendship of the two countries, survived.

E. Herbert Norman: The Man Who Might Have Been

April 1957 marked a low point in Canadian-American relations. On April 4, the Canadian ambassador to Egypt, E. Herbert Norman, deliberately took his own life by jumping from a rooftop in Cairo. This was no private tragedy: his suicide had been preceded by public allegations from a U.S. Senate committee that Norman was a Communist spy for the Soviet Union. Canadians, from Norman's colleagues in the External Affairs department, to editorial writers in every Canadian newspaper, to ordinary Canadians hearing the news, were shocked and outraged, and their anger was directed squarely at their close friend and Cold War ally, the United States.

Norman, by virtually unanimous Canadian estimate, had been a victim of the American anti-Communist witch hunt. Canadians had long believed that their country had escaped the lunacies of McCarthy-era America, that Canadians were more responsible, sober, and tolerant than their excitable and evangelistic neighbours to the south. Canadians had watched the sinister finger pointing of Senator Joe McCarthy on television, and shuddered. Perhaps somewhat smugly, they had congratulated themselves on being too mature to

Herbert Norman in Nagano.

allow such destructive antics. And now, just as the McCarthy era seemed to be fading into the past, it had reached beyond the American border to claim a Canadian public servant as a last human sacrifice.

Nor was Norman any ordinary diplomat. He was a noted scholar, a pioneer Western Japanologist whose 1940 book *Japan's Emergence as a Modern State* was a classic work on political economy. He had served as an invaluable and trusted advisor to U.S. General Douglas MacArthur in the latter's role as proconsul during the post-war occupation and reconstruction of Japan as a democratic capitalist state. He had most recently been a player in the post-Suez Crisis negotiations for a United Nations emergency force that would shortly bring Lester Pearson the Nobel Prize for peace.

Now this distinguished Canadian scholar and diplomat had been driven to his death by witch-hunting Americans. In his private diary, the Canadian ambassador to Washington, Arnold Heeney, described the state of Canadian-American relations in the wake of Norman's death as "thoroughly bad." In Ottawa, Lester Pearson saw the reaction in the country as a wave of anti-Americanism that "exceeded anything in his experience."

The crisis was soon papered over, and Canadian-American relations returned to their earlier, less volatile state. But the Norman affair remained a sore point. In 1986, three decades after Norman's death, two books appeared on the Norman affair. Both were written by Americans, but could not have been more different from one another. Roger Bowen's *Innocence is Not Enough* is a sympathetic biography, written by a fellow Japanologist with a great respect for Norman's scholarly achievement and a strong sense of the injustice that had been done to him by the accusations of disloyalty. The late James Barros' *No Sense of Evil*, on the other hand, had no doubt that Norman (not to speak of Lester Pearson [see chapter on Pearson]) was indeed a Soviet mole, or "agent of influence." Barros drew on the same sources as the Senate committee, with the same right-wing Cold War frame of reference. With these two books and the commentaries and reviews that followed, the Norman affair was reborn. With questions asked in the House of Commons, the Department of External Affairs commissioned a respected retired diplomat and academic, Peyton Lyon, to write a report in 1990 on the loyalties of Herbert Norman. Lyon, who was given unrestricted access to the classified documentation on Norman, concluded that Norman had always been a loyal servant of his country, and scathingly criticized the Barros interpretation.

In the 1990s, the National Film Board produced a sympathetic documentary film on Norman's life and death, and in 2000, the sixtieth anniversary of

Norman's book on Japan was commemorated with a new edition. It is interesting that both these projects were given support and encouragement by the Japanese, for whom Norman remains a highly respected, even revered, figure — a Westerner who first explained Japan to the West, and who also helped explain Japan to the Japanese themselves. The final verdict of Canadians on Norman is similarly respectful: a distinguished scholar, diplomat, and public servant who was shamefully and tragically driven to his death by Americans who pushed the Cold War too far.

Herbert Norman presents his ambassadorial staff to Egyptian President Nasser, September, 1956.

Why had Norman become a "witch" to be hunted? The story of his persecution is in a sense the story of the Cold War itself. Norman was in the wrong place at the wrong time. He attended Cambridge University in the 1930s at the same time as infamous Cambridge traitors such as Burgess and Maclean [see chapter on The Great Molehunt]. He had kept company with known Communists and Communist sympathizers, and was hence guilty by association. Worse, he had the annoying knack of always being ahead of his time: an anti-Fascist in the late 1930s before the war against Fascism; a sympathizer with the anti-colonial struggles of the Indians before the decolonization of India; a supporter of democratic and progressive forces in Japan at a time when the American occupation was making its peace with the Emperor and the conservatives. These premature opinions made him suspect. Worse still, he had drawn open intellectual inspiration from Marxism, as was quite evident from his published works on Japan. On all these counts, he was guilty of the offence ironically described in Orwell's 1984 as "thoughtcrime." Worst of all, unlike others who had dabbled in left-wing politics in the 1930s but then laundered themselves in the anti-Communist post-war atmosphere, Norman would neither renounce his own past nor turn in the names of friends to the witch hunters. If he refused to be a born-again anti-Communist, the witch hunters reasoned, he must himself be a Communist.

There was a first brush with the Federal Bureau of Investigation (FBI) over a library of books on Japan that an old Japanese friend of Norman's who had been studying in the U.S. had to abandon when he was repatriated to Japan at the outset of the Pacific war. Norman tried to recover this library but clashed with two Boston FBI agents who were suspicious about his motives. Thus began Norman's FBI file. Later, when he was serving under General MacArthur in Japan in the late 1940s, Norman roused the hostility of MacArthur's extreme right-wing intelligence chief, General Willoughby, who opened a military intelligence file on Norman. It was filled with circumstantial evidence and politically biased characterizations. The latter was

Norman with Douglas MacArthur.

hardly surprising since General Willoughby was an open admirer of Franco's Fascist Spain.

Norman was named in Senate committee hearings at the beginning of the 1950s. Since the FBI was behind the naming, Canada had to respond. Norman was brought in for two rounds of questioning by the RCMP in 1950 and 1951, in which he was grilled on his past associations and opinions. Freely admitting that he had been close to the Communists at Cambridge in the 1930s, but denying that he had ever been a party member, as such, Norman struggled to explain the context of the time (global depression, the rise of Fascism, the threat of war) that had led to his political opinions . The Mounties were not sympathetic, even though Norman's diplomatic colleagues were.

Deeply upset, Norman offered to resign in the interests of Canada, but this was refused. Cleared by the Canadian government of any wrong doing, Norman's career went into brief hiatus as he was sent to the relatively unimportant post of high commissioner to New Zealand to allow the Americans to cool off. Within a few years, he was back in the thick of things in the international hot spot of Cairo. Then, in 1957, the old accusations were raised once again, and a despairing Norman finally ended the persecution by taking his own life.

Publicly, Canadian anger over this senseless tragedy was directed at the United States. Behind the closed doors of Ottawa, however, matters were not quite so simple. Some of the misinformation on which the FBI had acted, and which had fallen into the hands of the congressional witch hunters, was based on a faulty RCMP security report that had been sent to the FBI in 1950. As Minister of External Affairs, Lester Pearson had vainly tried to block the transmission of this report. The misinformation that it contained continued to work its mischief in the U.S. until the tragic denouement of the affair in 1957. If this were not bad enough, Pearson knew that it was he who was in fact the real target of the American witch hunters. Norman had been likely no more than an unfortunate stalking horse for bigger game [see chapter on Pearson].

In short, the whole Norman affair, thoroughly unpleasant as it was, was like a rock which, once turned over, revealed even more unpleasant things crawling underneath. Here was the dark underside of the Cold War for Canadians. The "case" of Herbert Norman was that of a man who might have been, an ideological construction of Cold War paranoia and suspicion. Herbert Norman the man — distinguished scholar, diplomat, and humanist — perished, a Canadian martyr to the Cold War.

Now that the Cold War is truly over, the final verdict of history should be to honour Norman's memory, and to condemn the mean-spirited mudslingers who drove him to his death.

Maurice Duplessis' War on Communism

Protestors outside the Soviet embassy in Ottawa in 1959.

Nowhere in Canada in the first post-war decades was the Cold War more popular than in Quebec, and nowhere did Communism rouse greater antipathy. Before the Quiet Revolution in the early 1960s, Quebec was the most socially and culturally conservative province in Canada. The Roman Catholic Church still dominated life in Quebec, controlling educational and health services for the Francophone majority, and defining the everyday philosophy of Quebecers. Of course, there were dissenters, but the church by and large held undisputed sway.

The Catholic Church had every reason to oppose Communism, an atheistic creed that contested the church for people's loyalties. In some of the countries within the Soviet bloc, such as Hungary and Poland, Catholic clergy had been subject to persecution. In some Catholic countries, such as Italy and France, mass Communist Parties in politics and the trade-union movement were serious rivals to Catholicism. Quebec was a protected Catholic backwater, apparently insulated from the winds of

A wounded protestor at the asbestos strike of 1949.

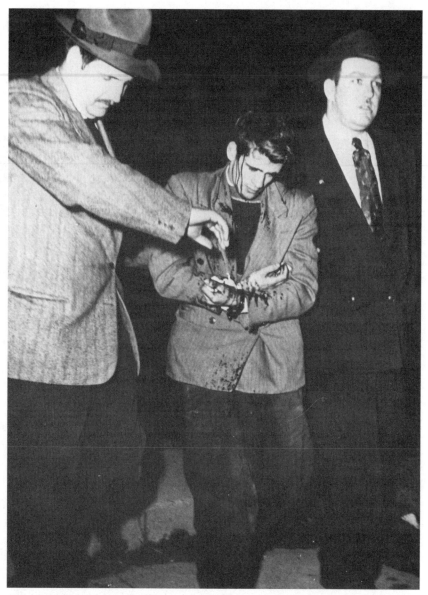

change (that is, before the floodgates opened in the 1960s). The church, and the dominant political force in Quebec from the 1930s through the 1950s, Maurice Duplessis' and his Union Nationale party, were determined to keep it that way.

Duplessis was a Quebec nationalist long before the emergence of a sovereignty movement. He was also a social and cultural conservative. Duplessis was an effective demagogue and authoritarian with little regard for the niceties of liberalism, which he considered an alien creed, almost as bad for Quebec as Communism. In the late 1930s, he passed the notorious Padlock Law, which permitted the Quebec authorities to close any premises deemed to be used for the propagation of "communism or bolshevism by any means whatever"; to prohibit the publication of any ideas propagating Communism or Bolshevism; and to destroy any such material seized. No definition of "Communism" or "Bolshevism" was offered; it was up to the Quebec attorney general to determine what fell under this rubric. The law was used

Protestors at a church during the asbestos strike of 1949.

aggressively by Duplessis in the 1930s, and then trotted out again in the Cold War era. Twenty years after its passage, the Padlock Law was declared unconstitutional by the Supreme Court of Canada in 1957. In the meantime, Quebec had earned the dubious distinction of being regarded as one of the jurisdictions most inimical to civil liberties in the Western world.

Duplessis routinely intervened with the full force of the law — and sometimes beyond — to crush strikes and labour organizers, with the latter usually described as "Communists." The vicious battle over the asbestos strike of 1949 was an epochal moment in modern Quebec history, and made the reputation of Pierre Elliott Trudeau, who vocally supported the strikers and would later become prime minister of Canada. Duplessis also passed labour legislation in 1949 that made it illegal for unions to hire Communists, Marxists, or anyone guilty of trying to subvert, sabotage, or overthrow the established order, with wide discretion to the attorney general with regard to who might fall within these broad parameters. Any union containing among its officials or representatives such individuals, or who were associated with or affiliated to any organization containing such persons or under the influence of Marxist doctrine, could be decertified by the province. Labour protests stopped the Bill in 1949, but in 1954, Duplessis passed much the same legislation — and made it retroactive to 1944. With this law, Quebec could claim credit for the toughest anti-Communist labour law in North America, even outstripping the U.S. Taft-Hartley Law that the federal Liberal government pointedly declined to emulate.

Police assigned to crowd control during the asbestos strike of 1949.

Maurice Duplessis.

Notorious for patronage, corruption, and intimidation, Duplessis' Union Nationale machine never shrank from demagogic use of the fear of Communism to smear its hapless Liberal opposition in Quebec — whose leaders were charged with being secret Communists or Communist sympathizers — or even the more successful Liberal government in Ottawa. In 1956, an election advertisement for the Union Nationale pointed to a trade agreement between Canada and Poland permitting the importation of Polish eggs. The ad screamed "Les Québécois forcés de manger des oeufs Communistes!" (Quebecers forced to eat Communist eggs!).

Duplessis' biggest and longest-standing anti-Communist publicity stunt was the interminable battle over the Polish art treasures. These were crown jewels and other rich objects spirited out of the royal castle of Cracow when Hitler swept over Poland in 1939, ending up in Ottawa for safekeeping. When Canada established diplomatic relations with the post-war Communist government of Poland and arranged for the return of the treasures, a diplomatic representative of the anti-Communist wartime government-in-exile managed to transfer the treasures to a convent in Quebec. A Royal Canadian Mounted Police inspector visited the convent to inquire about the treasures' whereabouts. Duplessis seized on this incident to denounce federal violation of a cloister of Quebec nuns, on behalf of the dreaded Communists. Invoking provincial jurisdiction over property and civil rights, Duplessis pledged to protect these treasures in perpetuity from the atheist hands of the Communists. This became an all-weather, all-purpose, no-cost Cold War issue that Duplessis trotted out again and again. The treasures were finally returned to their rightful owners but only, as it were, over Duplessis' dead body. Upon his death in 1959, arrangements were set in motion and completed in 1960, in time for Poland's millennial celebrations.

The most spectacular, and absurd, example of Duplessis' anti-Communist stance was the scandal of the Duplessis Bridge. In 1949, a year-and-a-half old bridge named after the premier, spanning the St. Maurice River at Trois-Rivières (Duplessis' hometown) collapsed, killing eight people. Duplessis and

A Hungarian national who travelled from the Yukon to demonstrate.

his flunkies immediately took to the airwaves, denouncing the collapse as Communist sabotage. A government commission of enquiry tried to keep this inane theory alive, but to little avail. Structural faults in the design and patronage in the contracts could not be traced to Communism, even among the more credulous of Duplessis' followers.

In the atmosphere of what historians would later refer to as Quebec's "dark ages," Duplessis was generally very effective in his anti-Communist demagoguery. However, this did not mean he was sincere. In fact, his use of the Red issue was often cynical to an extreme. He campaigned tirelessly against the National Film Board (NFB), at a time when that institution was subjected to Red-baiting and loyalty purges [see chapter on John Grierson and the NFB]. Denouncing the imposition of an "alien ideology" on Quebec, he went so far as to ban NFB films from use in Quebec schools, confiscating those already in use. This campaign suddenly halted in 1950, when the federal government announced that a new NFB headquarters was to be built — in Montreal. To make matters even more ironic, the NFB's architect was some-one publicly named as a Communist in U.S. testimony. Duplessis breathed not a word about this.

By the 1960s, Quebec awoke from its dark ages, and Maurice Duplessis' anti-Communist crusades were forgotten. For cynical demagoguery, they had in their heyday no match in the rest of Canada. Only Senator Joe McCarthy was in the same league.

Redcoats Versus Reds: the RCMP Security Service

A mountie on horseback, photographed October 8, 1948.

The RCMP was, and is, a unique institution in the Western world. Nowhere else is a police force a national icon. The Mounties, with their red serge jackets, distinctive hats and horses, are an instantly recognizable symbol of Canada. Throughout Canadian history, the Mounties have, since their inception, represented a potent myth of the Crown preserving peace, order, and good government on the frontier. Celebrated in countless dime-store novels, Hollywood movies, and song (who can forget Nelson Eddy and Jeanette MacDonald in *Rose-Marie*, even if neither had ever been to Canada?), the Mounties "always got their man."

For the first three decades of the Cold War, the Mounties maintained the myth, and even enhanced it, as the front line of defence against the Communist menace to Canadian society. A national police force, the Mounties were also the nation's security arm. It was the RCMP that chased down Soviet spies, the RCMP that watched for Communist sabotage, the RCMP that quelled situations such as violent strikes that could lead to public disorder and undermine faith in our free institutions. It was the RCMP that

ran security screening and kept the files on who the bad guys were who
threatened Canadian society.

Within the RCMP, there was a special section that was variously designated
over the years, generally known as the security service. It was dedicated to
tracking and blocking threats to the security of Canada. It had extraordinary
powers at its disposal, but no specific legal mandate, and was accountable to no
one except the RCMP Commissioner with regards to how it used these powers. It could, and did, spy on Canadians through human sources, undercover
agents, and later telephone taps and electronic bugs. It maintained close relations and shared intelligence with J. Edgar Hoover's Federal Bureau of
Investigation (FBI) in the U.S. and MI5 in the United Kingdom.

From its inception, the security service was never in any doubt as to who
the main enemy was. It was the Bolshevism of the Russian Revolution of
1917, and the Communist Party of Canada and its fronts and dupes who followed the Soviet line. Sometimes, as during the war against Fascism, it was
compelled to monitor other targets, but it never forgot Communism, which
was always considered the main enemy.

Canadian police bugging devices.

With the Gouzenko affair and the coming of the Cold War, the security
service could devote itself full time to chasing Reds. This mission led them to
spy on political parties, trade unions, universities, social and cultural groups,
ethnic associations, even church groups. In the 1950s, when the threat of war
with the USSR loomed large, the Mounties were charged with the task of
preparing lists of people to be interned in the event of hostilities, an operation
known as Profunc. This gave them the green light to identify anyone, anywhere, who might be suspected of pro-Soviet beliefs. Although they would have
known few details, it seemed for many years that most Canadians applauded
this role, asked few (if any) questions about Mountie methods, and assumed that
if anyone were a target of RCMP surveillance, they must deserve it.

J. Edgar Hoover's FBI in the U.S. used its prestige as Communist fighters
to stoke the fires of McCarthyism in American society. Hoover fed the congressional witch hunters with a steady stream of information under the table,
and then turned the climate of fear to the political advantage of the FBI. To
their credit, the Mounties never really tried to capitalize politically on their
Cold War prestige. In the Canadian tradition, they thought of themselves
above all as servants of the Crown, and were in agreement with the government that anti-Communism should be kept safely within the hands of the
constituted authorities. But behind closed doors in Ottawa, they tirelessly lobbied decision makers about the need for eternal vigilance, and they often,
although not always, got their way on tough security measures against anything that smacked of Communism.

Before the advent of electronic data processing in the 1960s, the paper
blizzard in the security service's subversive files quickly became unmanage-
able, and they had to cut back voluntarily. Nor could they keep up with the
backlog of government and immigration security checks they were asked to
perform. Oddly enough, during the darkest days of the Cold War in the
1950s and early 1960s, governments never did fund the RCMP security oper-

ations to the same degree that they provided rhetorical support.

Many of the problems that plagued the Mounties were a result of lodging security intelligence with a paramilitary police force. The methods appropriate to a criminal investigation force were not always appropriate to the delicate task of the "political policing" of Canadian society. The training of Mounties, which was a rigorous and demanding regimen designed to produce tough cops, did not foster the qualities required for subtle intelligence analysis. Sporadic efforts to upgrade the intellectual level of the officers and develop a more sophisticated understanding of the nature of the Communist enemy produced spotty results. Civilian analysts were hired, but found it difficult to prosper in an organization pervaded by the hierarchical esprit de corps of the "Horsemen." In the early 1960s, the practice of sending officers to university to beef up their academic qualifications (and sometimes to spy on university professors and students) was begun. However, once they had broadened their horizons, many of the Mountie graduates found security service work tedious and unfulfilling, and left the force for greener and more challenging pastures.

Things started to unravel for the RCMP security service in the 1960s and 1970s, when they had to refocus, not on the traditional Soviet Communist threat, but on domestic threats to security not directly connected to Moscow. Violent Quebec separatists emerged in the 1960s. In combating this new threat, the RCMP became embroiled in divisive domestic politics. Similarly, the emergence of a "new left" in English Canada brought the Mounties and their methods under more critical scrutiny.

Eventually, in the 1980s, the security service would be taken away from the RCMP and reconstituted as a new civilian agency. Before that, the Mounties had a fairly free ride through the early years of the Cold War, and were widely viewed as the true champions of Canada against its enemies. Their shortcomings as a security force would slowly build, until finally the dam broke and major reform would become necessary.

The Mounties and the Ladies Auxiliary

The Royal Canadian Mounted Police (RCMP) were a great national symbol, but the Cold War hunt for subversives involved them in secret activities that might have given even their most ardent supporters pause for thought — if they had known about them. There is, for example, the strange case of the Mounties' decades-long intensive surveillance of a Sudbury Ladies Auxiliary.

The object of the RCMP's attention was the Ladies Auxiliary, Sudbury Local, International Union of Mine, Mill and Smelter Workers (Mine-Mill). For years, conscientious Mounties in the Sudbury detachment of the security service earnestly and meticulously compiled files on every meeting and every development in the Ladies Auxiliary. If $50 or $100 were donated to charities, the Mounties recorded the exact allocation of every dollar (and ominously noted from time to time that $10 or so was "unaccounted" for). If the ladies held a bake sale, there was an entry into the RCMP file recording how many cookies were sold, and the net profit. If members discussed and passed a resolution regarding some matter of public interest (say, smokestack emissions),

Mountie watchers duly entered into the files a summary of the discussion and a breakdown of the vote. All of this would then be transmitted to headquarters in Ottawa for inclusion in the voluminous files of the Counter-Subversion branch (or the Anti-Communist branch, as it was known in the 1950s).

There was an apparently simple explanation for all this attention: Mine-Mill had long been targeted as Communist-led. Indeed, in the late 1950s, the union was the object of a vicious decertification attempt from the more conservative Steelworkers union, the Co-operative Commonwealth Federation, the Catholic Church and the RCMP. To the Mounties, there was no question that any organization associated with Mine-Mill was, obviously, a Communist front. Ergo its intensive surveillance of its Ladies Auxiliary.

We can now peruse censored versions of these files via Access to Information requests. There appears to be nothing whatsoever to justify the slightest suspicion about the union women. No doubt the Mine-Mill women were a bit more radical in their opinions than, say, an Anglican ladies auxiliary. But no member of the Mine-Mill Ladies Auxiliary was ever charged with espionage, sabotage, or sedition, or anything else in the Criminal Code. So why did the national police pay such close attention to them?

There was the Cold War to consider. To the Mounties, Communist subversion meant that that the moral fibre of the state and society was being undermined by the covert activities of Moscow's fifth columnists. They might not be able to define a subversive to the satisfaction of legal scholars, but they knew a subversive when they saw one. And Ottawa had charged the force with responsibility for fighting Communism.

Armed with these marching orders, the Mounties would inevitably want to keep a close eye on the Ladies Auxiliary of the Mine-Mill union local. An organization affiliated with a Red-led union was, by definition, a front for the Communists. In an internally circulated memo, Mounties were instructed in the Communist tactics of infiltration and subversion: "Whether it is an international movement or a small town women's sewing circle, the reds try to get in and if they are successful, they exert every effort to get to the top. And their tactics are extraordinarily successful." The Mountie watchword was that one rotten apple can taint an entire barrel. Their job was to search out the bad apples.

The Mounties never seemed to ask themselves just what the Communists were going to do with the Sudbury Local of the Ladies Auxiliary. When the members raised money for the Canadian National Institute of the Blind (CNIB), was this laundered Moscow gold that would somehow taint the CNIB?

There is another, more sinister, aspect to this surveillance. The McDonald inquiry into the RCMP reported in 1981 that the security service held files on no less than 800,000 individuals and organizations. The detail in the files that have been declassified reveals that such a wealth of information could not have been gathered without the active collaboration with the police of thousands of ordinary people, rank-and-file supporters of unions and other organizations, office holders, organizers, envelope lickers, fundraisers. The intimate details of decisions made by the Ladies Auxiliary in the 1960s in tiny meetings held in a variety of locales, including school basements, kitchens, and living rooms, could not possibly have been derived from bugs and wire-taps. The force had neither the technology nor the resources to wire the entire country in those days. For these reported meetings, there was someone there, someone whom to all outward appearances was a member, a friend, and colleague of the others, someone who was going home at night and reporting to her RCMP contact everything that had transpired.

Multiply this by thousands for organizations across the land, and we have a picture of a country honeycombed with secret police informers. Ironically, the RCMP darkly warned of the numbers of dupes, sympathizers and fellow travellers who could be manipulated by a hard core of Communist party operatives. The security service too constituted a hard core of operatives and spread out their own army of secret informers and collaborators.

What motivated people to lead double lives as members of organizations and as after-hours informants to the police? We will never know for certain, but we can guess. In some cases, the motive may have been mercenary: the service would pay for good information. In fact, it liked to pay, since this established a hold over informants. The Mounties were not above using a bit of blackmail: security screening was an effective device for enlisting involuntary informants, if the alternative was to lose one's job or be deported from Canada as a security risk. In other cases, there were people with idealistic motives, who were genuinely concerned about Communist influence in their unions or associations — people whose idea of public-spiritedness extended to secretly informing on their fellows. The Mounties, after all, carried very high prestige in the eyes of the Canadian public, which is one good reason why the government in this era liked to use the Mounties as its security service. Informing to the Redcoats might be seen as doing one's patriotic duty.

Eventually, as the Cold War wore down in the 1980s, the Canadian public and its government finally began to wake up to the negative impact that the activities of the secret police were having on Canadian life, and in 1987, the Counter-Subversion branch (now housed in the Canadian Security Intelligence Service) was closed down, and its files destroyed or sent to the National Archives. The Ladies Auxiliary was not that much of a threat after all.

The Mounties Watch the CBC

Adrienne Clarkson, pictured in 1965.

When television arrived in Canada in the early 1950s, it quickly became the most important vehicle for Canadians to see themselves and their society. Much of the television watched by Canadians was American, but the public broadcaster, the Canadian Broadcasting Corporation (CBC), helped define Canada through its Canadian programming. One of the most avid audiences attracted by the CBC for its Canadian shows was the security service of the RCMP. Standing on guard as always, the Mounties were concerned about left-wing types gathered around the creative side of the CBC, and about the pro-Communist messages that they might be trying to transmit. Canadians might be watching Father Knows Best, Leave It To Beaver, and Hockey Night in Canada, but the ever-vigilant Mounties were watching for evidence of subliminal subversion that might have slipped through.

Beset by anti-Communist émigré groups, CBC Radio's international service was, like the National Film Board, purged of "pro-Communist" elements and rededicated to promoting the message of the Western way of life abroad. Personalities working for the domestic radio and television service were also threatened with being screened as security risks from time to time. The careers of some people suffered, although never on the scale of those employed by the National Film Board.

There were some "left-wingers" at the CBC and a few who were, or at least had been, Communists. Looking into the declassified files of the security service, it seems that the Mounties were not just after individual security risks, they also fancied themselves cultural critics who reviewed the offerings of the CBC for hidden subversive messages. For instance, in 1953, a Mountie investigator devoted a report to an ideological deconstruction of various CBC broadcasts. A radio play called *Who Killed Cock Robin?* was "quite consistent with Communist propaganda" because it suggested "opposition to war and support of peace." A television play by Ted Allan (who was indeed a Communist) was "reviewed by members of our Toronto Office" and judged by these critics to be "Communist propaganda." In 1955, the RCMP commissioner ordered an investigation to gather five or six examples of an "organized effort to disseminate Communist propaganda" through CBC-TV, and to see what could be done to counteract this, and even if "ways or means could be adopted to do away with such programs."

Operating behind closed doors, the RCMP television critics did not exercise the kind of power wielded in this era by U.S.-free enterprise witch hunters such as the authors of the notorious publication Red Channels, who could destroy an artist or entertainer's career with a single public listing. But the Mounties were not without quiet influence. In 1955, for example, the CBC cancelled a scheduled production of an opera to be conducted by Ivan Romanoff when the president of the CBC, Davidson Dunton, "received a complaint" that this production was being produced by "subversive elements." Apparently, the opera was based on the work of the Russian writer Gogol, the anniversary of whose death was being celebrated by the Communists. Dunton bowed to the pressure, which came, not from the public, but from the RCMP itself. In short, the Mounties were not merely cultural critics, but cultural critics with clout. This was a typically Canadian variant of censorship. Unlike the Americans, who did these things noisily and in public, the RCMP-inspired censorship was behind the scenes and discreet.

CBC Radio did offer a more favourable environment to a Canadian refugee from McCarthyism in the U.S., Reuben Ship. Deported from the U.S. as a subversive, Ship wrote a hilarious parody of McCarthyism, *The Investigator*, that was produced on the CBC. This was a satire about a McCarthy-like figure investigating, in a committee with Titus Oates, Torquemada, and Cotton Mather, the presence in heaven of subversives such Socrates, Milton, and Voltaire, who are to be deported to "Down There." McCarthy finally turns his suspicions of treason on those in high places, finally leading to the "Chief." Denounced by Ed Sullivan as Communist propaganda and banned from the U.S. networks, it circulated widely in bootleg version in the States. It was allegedly even heard appreciatively by President Eisenhower who, as in the satire, became the eventual target of Senator McCarthy. Ship eventually fled North America for Britain, but he took with him the leading female CBC-TV personality of the 1950s, Elaine Grand, who went on to a long and distinguished career in British TV.

The RCMP critics continued to watch television programs into the 1960s and did not like the more liberal and open atmosphere. In 1961, a television show about anti-Americanism featuring a journalist and future senator, Philip Deane, and the famous writer Farley Mowat (who was banned from entering the U.S.), elicited the following grumpy Mountie review: "It appeared that the script was written by an unknown person who endeavoured to promote Communist propaganda." The same year, an interview show, *Close-Up*, featuring African-American singer Harry Belafonte, was the subject of an indignant review: "A brazen, non-subdued, uninterrupted half hour display of Communist propaganda at its best," the Horseman critic fulminated somewhat incoherently. The CBC interviewer, he wrote, "led her subject down the alley of communism and from all appearances he was quite willing to follow her." In 1964, a performance of the Ibsen play *The Master Builder*, brought forth the critique that "it followed the materialistic communistic propaganda all through." A future Governor General of Canada, Adrienne Clarkson, seemed to attract thumbs-down attention as a television personality, although the specific reasons for this have been excised by the censors from the declassified documents.

The CBC survived the Cold War. It would have been interesting to see how its Mountie critics might have fared if their reviews had been made public.

The Fruit Machine

J. Edgar Hoover associated gays and lesbians with Communism and convinced civilian officials that they were a security threat in the late 1950s.

The Cold War was a time of high anxiety. Some of this anxiety was well grounded. There was very good reason to fear war and nuclear holocaust when both blocs practised the dangerous art of "brinksmanship" while building up arsenals of death that could destroy all life on the planet many times over.

Some of the anxiety had substance, but was greatly exaggerated. The fear of Communism had some basis in the Soviets' iron rule over Eastern Europe and in the record of Soviet espionage. But in the early years of the Cold War especially, these fears grew into paranoia about "subversion" and Reds under the bed, resulting in McCarthyism and witch hunts.

And then there was anxiety that had no basis whatever, prejudices and bigotries that assumed the respectable cover of the Cold War. Nowhere was this more apparent than in the extension of the Red Scare to a "Lavender" Scare, from a hunt for Communist subversives to a hunt for homosexual subversives. The story of how homosexuality became classified as a Cold War security risk

on par with Communism is one of the strangest aspects of the era. In its ludi-
crous excesses, it might even be considered humourous — until one considers
the broken lives, shattered careers, and the hate that the official campaign
against homosexuality engendered. It was a discreditable chapter in Canadian
history, so much so that a later prime minister, Brian Mulroney, would refer to
it as "odious."

Like so much during the Cold War, the idea that an anti-Communist purge
should be accompanied by an anti-homosexual purge did not originate in
Canada but was imported from the U.S. The Royal Canadian Mounted Police
(RCMP) did adopt the crusade against homosexuality with alacrity, however, so
much so that the Mounties became the activists on this file.

During the early years of the security screening program in Ottawa, there
was no mention of homosexuality as a security risk. In the U.S. at this time,
there was a social panic about homosexuality that quickly spilled over into the
Cold War security system. In 1950, at the same time that Senator McCarthy
was launching his career as a witch hunter, the U.S. government started systematically removing gays and lesbians from the public service as security risks on
grounds of "moral turpitude." Ostensibly, homosexuality was a security risk
because of its supposed vulnerability to blackmail by foreign espionage agents.
In reality, it was rank prejudice run amuck. In any event, blackmail was only
possible because homosexuality was criminalized during this era. With the
blackmail argument, homosexuals were in effect subjected to double jeopardy.

Inevitably, pressures to conform to American practice were soon felt in
Canada. The RCMP, at the time an all-male paramilitary police force with a
strong macho strain in its self-image, took up the challenge with enthusiasm.
They had developed very close links to the Federal Bureau of Investigations
(FBI), and tended to take direction from their American colleagues. In retrospect, there is a certain irony in an anti-gay crusade by an FBI that was directed
by J. Edgar Hoover, a lifelong bachelor with a close and enduring friendship
with his assistant director, Clyde Tolson. If the RCMP detected any such irony,
they never let on. In the late 1950s, they persuaded the civilian officials that
were overseeing the security screening system that homosexuality constituted a
serious risk, and that homosexuals should be identified and removed from sensitive positions. The civilian officials were persuaded only reluctantly. They
retained some liberal scruples about this kind of investigation and feared, correctly as it turned out, that some talent would be lost to the Canadian public
service if gifted and valuable people were pushed out on these grounds.

Once underway, the anti-gay and lesbian purge quickly spun out of proportion. Special "anti-queer" squads were set up, and all sorts of questionable
methods were employed to track down every last offender they could find. The
most effective method proved to be the crudest: intimidation to force names of
other suspects — intimidation made easier by homosexuality's criminalization
and the Mounties' dual role as security service and a national police force
enforcing criminal law. Since the alleged basis of the problem was Soviet blackmail, it is highly ironic that the RCMP itself in effect employed blackmail to
extort names. By 1967, when the hunt peaked, the Mounties had amassed eight-

thousand files on known or suspected homosexuals, of which well less than half were actually employed in the public service.

In their crusading enthusiasm, the Mounties strayed further afield than traditional police methods. They tried to enlist science in the cause, giving contracts to a Carleton University psychologist to sketch out the psychology of sexual "deviance." And then, in what must rank as the single looniest endeavour of the entire Canadian Cold War, they set up an internal project to design technology to detect homosexuality. This was to be a chair with various sensing devices in which subjects were strapped to measure responses to carefully selected stimuli. This quickly became known in the Mountie locker rooms as the "Fruit Machine." It never got past the experimental stage and was never actually used, but it remains as a monument to a mania that consumed resources and fixed the attention of otherwise sane and rational adult human beings.

It was a mania with grave consequences. It is unclear just how many people were driven out of the public service as a result of the purge, but there is evidence of hundreds of dismissals or forced resignations. Beyond this, there were many who ducked out of the firing line first. There is certainly no question that many more public servants suffered in the gay purge than in the Red purge. And many more were in high positions. The story of John Watkins, the former ambassador who died while undergoing interrogation, is recounted elsewhere in this book. Watkins, it should be noted, was the object of attempted Soviet blackmail, but resisted. In fact, the government knew of very few such cases, and none for certain that had actually succeeded.

As some had feared, many talented persons were lost to government as a result of this purge. One case is that of the late John Holmes, an exceptionally talented young diplomat with a promising career ahead of him in External Affairs. Holmes was forced out in 1960. Thankfully, he was permitted an honourable exit to head the Canadian Institute of International Affairs. He became one of the most distinguished Canadian scholars of international affairs and historian of Canadian foreign policy, ending his career at the University of Toronto.

As for the purge, by the late 1960s the wind was no longer in the Mounties' sails. Pierre Trudeau, before becoming prime minister, had brought about a change in the law to remove the criminal stigma from homosexual acts between consenting adults, making the famous statement that the state had no place in the bedrooms of the nation. The Charter of Rights in the 1980s finally made it clear that discrimination on the basis of sexual orientation was a violation of fundamental freedoms. Now, there are no legitimate grounds for assessing sexuality as a security risk. The change has happened elsewhere as well. In Britain in recent years, the first gay spy couple were posted abroad by British intelligence. And in Washington, the Central Intelligence Agency and the National Security Agency now hold a joint annual "Gay Pride day," when gay and lesbian spies celebrate their sexuality.

While it lasted, the gay purge was an ugly and destructive episode, one of many that lurked under the umbrella of the Cold War.

Long Knife, Gideon, and the Spy Who Came Back from the Cold

The KGB board game demonstrates the public's interest in spy stories during the 1950s.

It is a spy story that might have come from the pages of a John Le Carré novel. It has double agents, deception, betrayal, and finally a spy who came back from the dead. It even has a happy ending, of sorts. And it happened in Canada.

It began in 1952, when the Cold War was at its very coldest. The Korean War was raging, Josef Stalin was still ruling the Kremlin, and the Rosenbergs were on death row. A young man in his late twenties stepped off a ship at Halifax, slipped past Canadian Customs by flashing false American citizenship, and boarded a train for Montreal. There he entered a washroom in the train station, found a cubicle marked with chalk, and retrieved from under the toilet tank lid a birth certificate and other identity documents for David Soboloff, a Canadian who had left Canada as a child with his parents without leaving any record of his departure. David Soboloff was now reborn.

The new "Soboloff" was a Soviet spy, trained in the KGB's Moscow spy school to speak unaccented English, and to be so familiar with daily life in

Canada that he could pass as a Canadian. His job was to create a "legend," a false identity so convincing that he could eventually be activated as a spy working undercover on Moscow's orders, sent on assignment into the United States, where he would appear as simply another Canadian migrant.

Things did not go as planned for Soboloff. He proved difficult for his Soviet handlers, not fulfilling his assignments. He was young and attractive, and drew the attention of women. While passing through Kingston, Ontario, he met a woman with whom he fell passionately in love. She returned the passion, but unfortunately was married — to a Canadian Army corporal. This was definitely not in the KGB playbook, but Soboloff was smitten and would not break off the dangerous affair. Finally, he confessed his true identity to his lover, who persuaded him to go to the RCMP. He travelled to Ottawa, stepped into a phone booth, and called the Mounties to tell them that he was a Soviet spy and wanted to come clean. Soboloff became "Gideon," the code name assigned him by the RCMP, who had suddenly had a counter-espionage bonanza in their laps.

Gideon was assigned to Terry Guernsey, the ace anti-Communist investigator in the force at the time. Guernsey decided that Gideon should be run as a double agent, playing his Soviet handlers along while feeding them disinformation provided by the RCMP and passing back valuable intelligence on the KGB. It was called Operation Keystone. Keystone was a coup for the Mounties, suddenly elevating them in the eyes of their counterparts in the U.S. and United Kingdom. During the Second World War, a double agent operation with a captured German agent had been badly bungled by the RCMP, embarrassing them in the eyes of British intelligence. This was a chance to redeem the force's reputation abroad and score some serious points in the Cold War spy game. Gideon began playing a double game, not always pleasing either his KGB or his RCMP handlers, but still producing some good value for his new masters.

Then Gideon was recalled by the KGB to Moscow for a "temporary" visit. This sent tremors through both Gideon and his Mountie handlers. It might be a trap, in which case Gideon would never return. On the other hand, if genuine, it offered a golden opportunity for the RCMP and Western intelligence to learn more about the dreaded Moscow Centre. Gideon was given a choice: pack it in, and be given a new Canadian identity — or play on further in anticipation of greater gains. Gideon chose to play on. It was a very unwise choice. He departed for Moscow and did not return. Nothing more was heard of him.

What the RCMP brass did not know was that one of their own number, who had had a brief involvement in handling Gideon, had shopped him to the KGB. An RCMP officer, given the appropriate code name "Long Knife," was living well beyond his means, and accumulating a lot of debt. He contacted the Soviets and was offered the sum of $3,500 (about a year's salary for a Mountie of Long Knife's rank at the time). In exchange, Long Knife gave them, among other things, Gideon's name. The recall to Moscow was a ruse. Gideon was lured back to whatever fate lay in wait for a traitor to the Soviet state. The RCMP assumed that this meant death. Long Knife had delivered the Mounties' prized double agent into the jaws of the enemy.

When this became known, Long Knife's fate was less drastic than that believed to have befallen Gideon. Although Long Knife was criminally culpable, the Mounties did not want a public trial that would reveal the ugly truth. Long Knife was quietly sacked from the force. At the time, no one outside a small circle in the RCMP and the KGB knew anything of the nasty drama that had been played out.

It took another two and a half decades for the Long Knife and/or Gideon story to come to public notice. Investigative journalist John Sawatsky broke the story in a book published in 1982, but chose not to reveal Long Knife's identity. Four years later, he was finally identified as James Morrison, still alive and still unpunished for his act of treachery. Embarrassed by this, the RCMP finally brought charges, and Morrison was sent to prison for eighteen months.

Another decade passed, the Cold War came to an end, and the Soviet Union collapsed. In 1997, a stunning surprise ending to this long drama was revealed: Gideon was not dead after all, but was back in Canada.

It turned out that he had not been executed in the 1950s, as everyone had assumed. He had instead spent twenty-five years in Soviet gulags, eventually emerging as a "nonperson" left to struggle on the margins of Soviet society. But he carried a secret with him all those years. When he had been sent into the USSR on his last mission as a double agent in the 1950s, the Mounties had prepared an escape plan for him if things went awry. He had been given a secret password, and instructions on how to contact British intelligence (the RCMP had no foreign intelligence capacity). In the late 1980s, with the Soviet Union in chaos, Gideon finally activated the now ancient plan. He travelled to Latvia, and made contact with British intelligence. Word was relayed to Canadian Security Intelligence Service, which had by now succeeded the RCMP as Canada's security service. The prime minister of the day, Brian Mulroney, decided that Canada owed a debt to this man who had suffered so much on behalf of his adopted country. Under British auspices, he was spirited out of the USSR under a false identity and brought back to Canada.

Canada decided that it owed Gideon a pension payable from the time he had first left for Moscow, with interest accumulated for all the years he had been unable to collect it. Gideon, who had entered the country illegally as a spy, was now at last a bona fide Canadian, honoured by his adopted country, in comfortable retirement. He lives in Ottawa, spending his time happily browsing through second-hand book shops, and is surprisingly lacking in bitterness over the turns that fate has dealt him.

This is one Cold War spy story with a happy ending.

The Reverend James Endicott and the Peace Movement

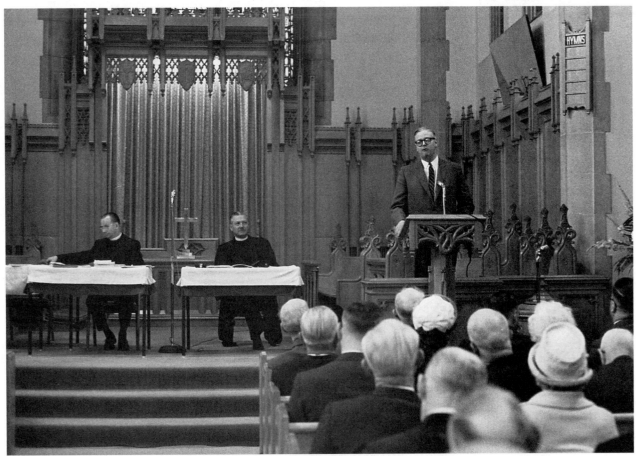

The Cold War era was dominated by the threat of nuclear war. By 1949, both sides had possession of weapons with the potential to destroy all life on earth, and an apparent willingness to resort to such weapons, if necessary. In the face of this menace, there was continual debate in the West between "hawks" and "doves," between those who advised deterrence through strength and those who wanted the antagonists to negotiate away the power of life and death over the planet. Both sides were represented within government, but it was generally the hawks who held the upper hand as the superpowers' mutual suspicion prevented serious compromise. Not surprisingly, this division also spilled over into society, with peace movements emerging to challenge popular Cold War sentiments.

In the early years of the Cold War, there was only one serious peace movement in Canada, the Canadian Peace Congress. The leading figure was the Reverend James Endicott, an extraordinary charismatic figure, who quickly assumed in the eyes of the Canadian government, the media, and con-

Reverend James Endicott addressing the United Church Conference in 1966.

servative Canadians for the most part, the status of Public Enemy Number One — or, in the words of a Winnipeg newspaper, "the Prince of Darkness."

Dr. Endicott was a United Church clergyman, the son of a prominent churchman who had been a missionary in China and Moderator of the United Church. Born in China, Dr. Endicott himself spent many years in that country as a missionary. During the Chinese civil war that led to the victory of Communism in 1949, he became an outspoken critic of the Chiang Kai-Shek regime and friendly toward the Communists, who represented, he believed, the forces of progress in an impoverished land. These views made him unpopular with Cold Warriors, who saw the Communist victory as a major defeat for the West.

Following his return to Canada in 1947, Dr. Endicott threw himself into an activity that made him even more controversial. He founded the Canadian Peace Congress, which began campaigning for nuclear disarmament. An impressive speaker, he drew crowds everywhere. He also drew the unfavourable attention of the U.S. as well as the Canadian governments, both of which regularly sent spies to report on Congress activities.

The Canadian peace movement was affiliated with the World Peace Council, identified by Western intelligence as a Communist front organization run by Moscow. Everywhere in the Western world, Communist party members hastened to join the national peace councils. Canada was no exception. To the RCMP, there was no question that Dr. Endicott and the Congress were tools of the Soviet Union. This was also the frequently expressed opinion of Canadian newspapers at the time.

Although some members of his immediate family were Communists, and despite his own evident sympathies for the Chinese Communists, Dr. Endicott was never a Communist Party member himself. There is not much question, however, that he and the peace activists in his organization did tend to act as apologists for the Communist regimes. In the early Cold War, there was a kind of mirror logic at work. If you were critical of the West, you were an apologist for the East, and vice versa. The Western camp stood for "freedom," and the Eastern camp stood for "peace." Those in the West who spoke of "peace" were labelled Communist sympathizers, which made peace campaigning uncomfortable and sometimes even dangerous. Nevertheless, the Canadian Peace Congress went into the streets and managed to collect some 300,000 signatures on the so-called "Stockholm Declaration," calling for great power negotiations to eliminate nuclear weapons.

Things turned ugly with the outbreak of the Korean War in 1950, and the commitment of Western troops, including Canadians, to battle the Communists. China and North Korea made charges that the U.S. was engaging in "germ-warfare." Dr. Endicott travelled to China and North Korea and publicly endorsed the germ warfare charges. He returned to angry accusations of treason. In Toronto's Massey Hall, he addressed a crowd of 10,000 people who filed in past the taunts and jeers of anti-Communist demonstrators. Publicly denounced by the highest officials in the land, including the Minister of External Affairs, Lester Pearson, the Canadian Peace Congress was now widely attacked in the press, denied meeting halls, banned from the CBC, and subjected from time to time to intimidation and physical violence — from fisticuffs to firebombs.

What was not known publicly at the time was that the government of Canada seriously considered laying charges of treason against Dr. Endicott. Documents were prepared and the matter went to the Cabinet for consideration. In the end they backed off. Since the only penalty then for those convicted of treason was death, wiser heads prevailed on the argument that proceeding would only make Dr. Endicott a martyr and increase sympathy for his cause. Moreover, the Americans proved to be unenthusiastic about a public trial that Dr. Endicott could use as a platform to further publicize his germ-warfare charges.

In 1953, Dr. Endicott was awarded the Stalin Peace Prize, an act that outraged many Canadians. A few years later, de-Stalinization in the USSR prompted a general recall of the medals, and their replacement by new Lenin Prizes. Dr. Endicott refused, preferring to retain his — Stalin's head and all.

In 1956, the Soviet invasion of Hungary at the same time as the Suez invasion of Egypt by Britain and France produced a crisis throughout the Western peace movements. The Canadian delegates to the World Peace Council argued for a forthright denunciation of all foreign invasions, including Hungary, which did not please the Soviet-line delegates.

Despite this display of independence, Canadian opinion had effectively marginalized the Canadian Peace Congress by this time. In the late 1950s, the Peace Congress fell into a prolonged decline from which it never recovered. Despite this failure as an organization, the cause toward which the movement had worked had actually advanced by the end of the 1950s. Peace and nuclear disarmament had been placed on the agenda of the superpowers for serious negotiation, and the issues had begun to move into the mainstream of Canadian life, especially with the campaign to ban nuclear testing and the evidence of serious health risk from radioactive fallout. By the early 1960s, the peace torch had been passed to a new generation of Canadian activists, such as the Voice of Women and the Student Union for Peace Action, working alongside a new worldwide campaign to "ban the bomb." These groups were less imprisoned by the Cold War mirror logic that had entrapped the Canadian Peace Congress. In 1963, the U.S. and the USSR signed the Test Ban Treaty, signalling a major victory for the peace movement.

As the passions of the early Cold War cooled, Dr. Endicott began to receive recognition from his country for his services to peace and disarmament. In the 1980s, he was presented with a special award of merit by the city of Toronto. And his own United Church, which had repudiated him in the early 1950s, issued an official apology for the "much personal hurt and anxiety" it had caused him, and affirmed the "faithful and courageous contribution he has made to the cause of peace and social justice." He died in 1993 at the age of ninety-four, one of the more memorable Canadian personalities of his time.

Paul Robeson and the Concert at the Border

Paul Robeson.

On May 18, 1952, upwards of 40,000 people gathered at the imaginary line dividing British Columbia from Washington state to listen to one man sing. His name was Paul Robeson, and he was close to being Public Enemy Number One in Cold War America. His government had prevented him from travelling to Canada to sing, so instead his audience came to him in a show of solidarity and admiration for a man who stood tall in the face of the Cold War power of the American state.

Paul Robeson was an African-American who, through ability and determination, overcame the hostility and harassment of a racist America to become world famous. Initially, his fame was based on his skill as a singer and actor. Robeson, however, also displayed repeated determination to fight for a more egalitarian society. Such words were not popular in the early years of the Cold War. Testifying before the U.S. House Committee on Un-American Activities in 1946, the singer made no effort to hide his admiration for Communism. Now he had become a threat and the considerable powers of the American government were brought to bear against him. Television and radio barred him. Concert halls refused to book him. Robeson's albums vanished from stores. To complete his status as an invisible man the U.S. State Department seized his passport in 1950 to prevent him from travelling abroad. Because of his political beliefs, the man from Princeton, New Jersey, had become a prisoner in his own country.

In January 1952, escape arrived in the form of an invitation to sing for the annual meeting of the International Mine, Mill and Smelter Workers Union in Vancouver. Travelling to Canada did not require a passport and Robeson accepted the offer. At the border a month later, he quickly discovered that the U.S. government had no intention of allowing him to leave. Instead, a telephone line transmitted his distinctive voice in song across the 49th parallel to

Paul Robeson, barred by television and radio in the early 1950s, speaks to the media.

A pamphlet describing Paul Robeson's struggle.

Robeson in 1958.

the ears of those in attendance at the labour conference.

The events of February led to a return visit to the border in May. Here, Robeson came to straddle the 49th parallel near the peace arch. And here, thousands of people gathered on both sides to hear him sing in person. On that spring day, after being introduced by a Canadian union leader, he did not disappoint his audience and for a brief period the chains of the Cold War were broken. Three more annual concerts followed this first effort until Robeson finally had his passport returned. Nevertheless, the symbolism of the event lived on and fifty years to the day, a concert was organized to commemorate the courage and sacrifice of a remarkable man and to support his fight to make the world a better place.

On the day that the U.S.-Canadian border served as the battleground of his fight, Robeson ended the unforgettable concert with a song and lyrics that he had made his own: "I keeps laffin' instead of cryin' / I must keep fightin' until I'm dyin' / And Ol' man river, he just keeps rollin' along."

The Symphony Six

A member of the Toronto Symphony Orchestra, photographed in 1960.

It appeared innocuous enough except that in the logic of the Cold War, the adjective innocuous no longer applied. The Toronto Symphony Orchestra had been invited to perform in Michigan, a task that required a visa. What seemed a mere formality was anything but for six members of the orchestra. Dirk Keetbaas, a flautist, bassists Ruth Budd, Abe Manheim, and Bill Kuinka, and violinists Johnny Moskalyk and Steve Staryk found that their journey could not extend beyond Canadian territory. The "Symphony Six," as they would be dubbed, had their requests for visas denied by American authorities without any reason being offered. Even worse, their employers quickly fired them over the visa mess and rumours abounded about their secret Red proclivities having been discovered.

At the time, the incident provoked an outcry in some quarters. A rally, condemned by the notoriously right-wing *Toronto Telegram* as a "Communist meeting," was held on behalf of the six. As two uniformed Mounties sat in the front row, a variety of speakers lambasted the authorities over the affair. One of the speakers, Langford Dixon, the music critic at the *Globe and Mail*, was fired

Farley Mowat, November 22, 1958.

soon after his speech to the gathering. The Toronto Symphony continued its tour and none of the other musicians — perhaps out of fear of suffering a similar fate as the now unemployed six — spoke out on behalf of their banned ex-colleagues.

Long before September 11, 2001, the issue of border security between Canada and the United States affected relations between the two nations. During the Cold War, instead of barring the entrance of terrorists, the United States sought to ban the entrance of perceived ideological threats. In the case of the "Symphony Six," those targeted had been linked to real or imagined left-wing causes, either in the present or in their past.

They were not alone in having their lives affected by American immigration decisions. Another prominent case involved Glen Shortliffe, a Queen's University professor prevented in 1949 from entering the United States to take up a new job because of his allegedly subversive views. Periodically, other cases — some receiving more attention than others, as in the case of author Farley Mowat who was denied entrance into the United States in the 1980s — would materialize over the subsequent decades.

How the Immigration and Naturalization Service (INS) selected individuals to whom to deny entry is an interesting story in itself. With the Cold War the INS had established the Service Lookout Book, more accurately described by one Canadian official as a "black list." Simply put, if your name appeared in the book, you did not get into the United States. To discover the identity of these supposed subversives, the INS subscribed to numerous left-wing Canadian periodicals and received information from the Royal Canadian Mounted Police, other Canadian police forces and governmental agencies, as well as individual Canadians. Once the American agency had a name in mind, the RCMP would often be approached for any additional information. The force was often reluctant to supply it since the INS would frequently use the information to bar entry into the United States, making little secret of the original source of some of the details. Confusion frequently occurred over names, and Canadians, including two University of Toronto students barred in 1954 in apparent cases of mistaken identities, often complained openly to the federal government about their treatment.

Because of these high-profile cases and ensuing negative publicity, the Canadian government made several attempts between 1949 and 1956 to have the United States change the use of the Service Lookout Book. The government wanted the INS to receive all of its information on individuals in Canada from the RCMP alone, and for the list of names contained in its black list to be cross-referenced against Canada's national police force's "subversive indices." Names not on the Mountie list were to be excised.

After talks in June and August, 1956, between the INS and the RCMP, agreement was reached. The INS agreed not to conduct its own security investigations in Canada and that all enquiries would be directed to the Mounted Police. Exclusions of individuals arriving from Canada would not be done until consultation occurred with the RCMP. Finally, the Service Lookout Book, containing the names of 2,150 Canadian residents and citizens, would be turned

Enjoying dinner at the Toronto Symphony Orchestra, 1960.

over to the force so that the persons could be verified as genuine subversives.

The Department of External Affairs had a role to play in the new system as well. Should a complaint over an exclusion be lodged, officials from the department would immediately, in the words of External Affairs Undersecretary Jules Léger, "check with the RCMP: if we learn that he [subversion had a masculine voice in the Cold War] has an established subversive record, we reply to him that 'the case is entirely within the jurisdiction of the United States Government, and that it would not be appropriate for the Canadian government to intervene.'" In his memorandum, which was read by Prime Minister John Diefenbaker, Léger also addressed the most controversial aspect of the agreement — precisely why the RCMP should supply sensitive information about Canadians to American agencies in the first place. Besides mentioning that the system prevented "innocent Canadians" from being labelled subversives, the senior civil servant pointed out the Cold War "You scratch my back, I'll scratch yours" reality of the intelligence relationship between the two countries:

> The RCMP receive in return from the United States security agencies a great deal of information affecting Canadian security, mostly of course about residents of the United States but also to some extent about persons living in other parts of the world, including voluntary statements made by Canadians to INS; it has always been considered that the balance of advantage in the exchange of security information with the United States has been in favour of Canada.

McCarthyism on the West Coast

John Marshall.

In the early years of the Cold War, there were many examples of anti-Communist hysteria spilling out into Canadian society. Canada was never as subject to McCarthyism on a large scale as was the U.S. in this period. Still, the efforts of the Ottawa establishment to contain and manage Cold War fever did not always succeed.

The trade-union movement was one place where accusations of disloyalty and subversion were rife, and a number of trade unionists were purged for being too close to the Communists, or for holding suddenly unpopular political opinions. But trade unions were a Cold War battlefield, where Communist organizers had been active since the 1930s. Other areas of Canadian society, apparently less engaged in political controversy, were also subject to bouts of McCarthyite intolerance, and there were those who lost their jobs or had careers destroyed when self-appointed watchdogs of political orthodoxy decided to punish dissenters.

Two particularly blatant examples occurred in British Columbia. B.C. was a bit of a hotbed of conflict between capital and labour, and Communism had more followers on the West Coast than anywhere else in Canada, save Ontario. But the two worst examples did not occur on the trade-union front, but in the B.C. legal profession, and in the Victoria public library.

Gordon Martin was a young native British Columbian who had served his country during the war with the Royal Canadian Air Force. Married with two children, he opted to take advantage of the educational opportunities offered to war veterans by taking a law degree at the University of British Columbia. Following graduation in 1948, he applied for admission to the B.C. bar. Normally, this would follow almost automatically, but Martin was rejected.

The benchers stated that the reason Martin had not been admitted was that he was a member of the Communist Party, and thus failed a test of the bar that members' character be of "good repute." Moreover, anyone called to the bar was required to swear an oath that they would defend the sovereign against "traitorous conspiracies." Martin had been willing to swear such an oath, but in the benchers' opinion, the word of a Communist could not be trusted. The Communist Party was a legal political party in B.C., but the benchers were of the view that the Communist Party was an "association of those adhering to subversive Communist doctrines." Martin was of course free to hold his political opinions, but those opinions made him "not a fit person" to practise law in B.C.

To make matters worse for Martin, there was no appeal to the courts, which declined to intervene in the administrative jurisdiction of the bar. His years of study, the expenditure of his veterans' credits, and his successful completion of all the requirements to enter the profession had been swept away. He had been deprived of fundamental rights, with no recourse.

There was considerable unfavourable publicity about Martin's plight. The B.C. government wished to clear the air. An amendment was passed to the Legal Professions Act that permitted Martin to appeal to the B.C. Court of Appeal, and the attorney general agreed to pay his costs.

In a unanimous 1950 judgment, the Court of Appeal rejected Martin's plea, and fully backed the benchers' original decision, taking the opportunity to denounce the "alien philosophy" of Communism. No further appeal was undertaken (this was long before the Charter of Rights), and so Martin's career as a lawyer was aborted. He set up shop as a television and radio repairman on Vancouver Island.

Other law graduates at this time were subjected to an inquisition by the B.C. benchers on their political opinions, including Harry Rankin, later a leading radical lawyer and Vancouver alderman. Rankin and others were told to sign an American-style loyalty oath that they were not Communists, did not belong to any Communist association, and had "no intention of following any communist association in the future."

A few years later, in Victoria, another McCarthyite controversy over freedom of expression blew up, this time in the local public library. John Marshall, a young graduate of the University of Toronto library school, was

Senator Joseph McCarthy (right), in the early 1950s.

offered a post heading the new bookmobile program in late 1953. Married with two young children, he bought a house in Victoria and settled down for what looked like an interesting challenge. The Library Board had other ideas. An in-camera meeting in early 1954 resulted in an announcement that the appointment had been rescinded. No reasons were officially given, but anonymous sources had indicated to the board that Marshall had a "left-wing" past. He had been associated with the Manitoba branch of the Canadian Peace Congress, and had for a few months edited a paper with ties to the Communist Party.

There was a wider context for the Marshall decision at the time. Various local anti-Communists, some on the Victoria city council, had been insisting that "subversive" books be banned from the library. The mayor had even put forward a plan whereby the RCMP would work with the chief librarian to weed out any offending titles. Defenders of free speech gathered both inside and outside Victoria. Marshall himself appeared before the Library Board on his own behalf, but put his plight in wider context:

> It might be held that because of what I am or what I believe, I may in some way abuse my position in the future. This assumption comes dangerously close to justifying, on the part of employers, an attempt to

enquire into the political, social or economic beliefs, and into the religious principles, of an employee. No employer has such right in a democratic country.

Except for one member who vainly tried to defend Marshall's rights, the Board was unmoved. The chief librarian and others resigned in protest, but it was to no avail. Marshall and his young family left Victoria, which acquired an unenviable reputation as the book-burning capital of Canada in the 1950s.

As it turned out, John Marshall's career was not destroyed. He had offers from other libraries across Canada. Eventually, he settled in Toronto, and in the mid-1960s was offered a position in the University of Toronto, where he eventually retired as a professor of library science. In 1998, then in his seventies, he was invited back to Victoria by the Greater Victoria Public Library, where he was honoured and given an apology for what had been done to him four decades earlier.

At the time, the Victoria Library was once again in the midst of a political controversy over unpopular ideas. Times had changed, and now the controversy was over the library's decision to allow meetings of racist groups to take place in library space. Some of the left-wing people who had been active in supporting Marshall in 1954 were now on the side of censorship. John Marshall was not, and neither was the Victoria Library, which had learned some lessons from the unhappy experiences of the Cold War.

McCarthy speaking at the Republican convention, 1952.

Imperial Order Daughters of the Empire

An IODE meeting at the Royal York Hotel in Toronto, 1960.

An old, imperialist women's organization found a new calling in the tumultuous post-war era. The Imperial Order Daughters of the Empire (IODE), which began in an era when British imperialism was connected to the prevailing form of nationalism in English-speaking Canada, required new relevance in the Cold War as Canada moved further into the American orbit and farther away from its British roots. One path to relevancy was to fully embrace the dominant discourses of the Cold War period, particularly anti-Communism. Thus, the IODE set out to do its part on the home front as it had done in the century's two world wars.

One form of contribution concerned immigrants to Canada. The IODE created a Citizenship Department, which launched itself into a program of Canadianization, "involving the true meaning of Citizenship in all its aspects." The prime target for the IODE's affections were those tainted souls who had escaped Eastern European communism, chiefly from Hungary with its failed revolution in 1956, and the close to ten thousand who had arrived in Canada

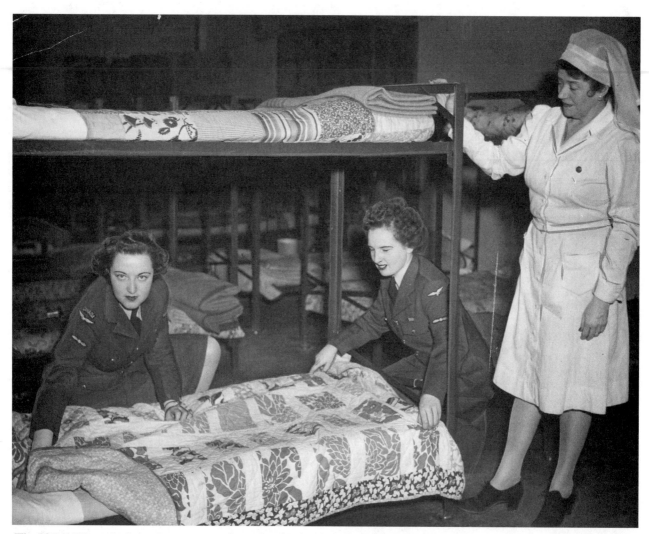

The IODE Women's Active Service Club prepares beds to help with civil defence, 1946.

from Czechoslovakia after the Soviet military intervention in 1968. There to greet the refugees were IODE members, who set up operations in Canada's main port cities, the chief points of entry in the 1950s. They offered the newcomers aid in a variety of ways, including providing them with "unbiased" news in their native languages.

The other route to Cold War relevancy involved preparations for the next war. While the IODE was not ready to take up arms or build bombs, it did offer to help with civil defence preparations. At the height of the tensions of the early 1950s, more than one thousand IODE members attended the Canadian Civil Defence College at Arnprior, Ontario. Here, a wide range of Canadians, including police officers, received civil defence training. Although the IODE never had an opportunity to use its skills in the aftermath of the attack by a godless enemy, the new skills came in handy for dealing with an act of God when Hurricane Hazel blitzed southern Ontario in 1954.

Preparing for the Third World War: The Radar Lines, the Diefenbunker, and Internment Plans

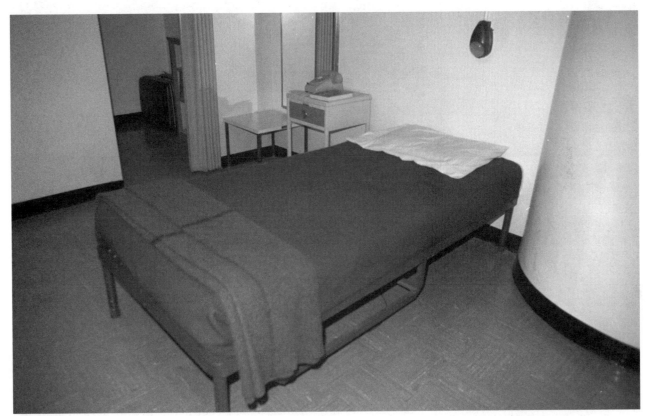

A cot inside the Diefenbunker.

Hovering in the background throughout the Cold War was the fear that the war would become an open one involving direct conflict between the United States and the Soviet Union. Through its geographical proximity to the United States, and its economic and military relationships, Canada would inevitably be involved in a conflict that would amount to a Third World War. To prepare for any attack involved planning for numerous contingencies.

First, there was a need to be able to detect an opening attack by the Soviet Union against the United States. This would most likely involve Soviet bombers flying over Canadian soil on their way to drop their nuclear payload on American targets. In the 1950s, three separate radar systems were built in Canada, all at the behest of the United States and with controversy surrounding their financing and who would control them. In the case of the latter, the Canadian government held that any defence establishments on its soil had to be under Canadian control. Any American military presence should be mini-

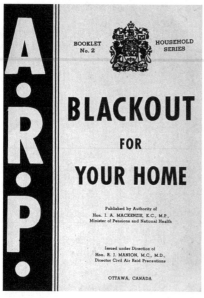

(above left): An emergency preparedness pamphlet prepared by the Canadian government.

(above right): Civil defence students learning rescue tactics, May 17, 1951.

An American military policeman guarding an atomic test site in Nevada, April 14, 1955.

mized or, if that failed (as essentially it did when as many as fifteen-thousand U.S. soldiers were in Canada by the middle of 1950s), Canada had to command this presence. This proved idealistic. At the American base in Newfoundland, U.S. governmental institutions such as the post office and the Internal Revenue Service operated, and even Canadian civilian employees were subject to the legal system of their southern neighbour.

The first radar system to be built, the Pinetree Network, was in service by 1954 to the north beyond major Canadian cities; it stretched from Vancouver Island to Newfoundland. When the Americans demanded another line further north, the Canadian government opted to employ already existing technology, and created the Mid-Canada Line in 1957. It featured ninety-eight radar stations, both manned and unmanned, stretched across Canada along the 55th parallel, and was in operation until 1965. That still did not satisfy American military planners, who then requested a radar system in the Arctic. That project, the most famous of the three, became known as the Distant Early Warning (DEW) line and was operational by 1959. Built along the 70th parallel, it featured forty-two radar stations across the Canadian north. Because of changing technology, close to half of the DEW line stations had already been mothballed by 1962.

Should the bombers be detected and not deterred by controversial defence systems such as the Bomarc missiles, which were designed to defend the United States anyway, then the possibility of a nuclear attack had to be addressed. To ensure its continuance, between 1959 and 1961 the Canadian government constructed a large underground complex, quickly nicknamed "the Diefenbunker," after the prime minister at the time, to protect over five-hundred politicians and bureaucrats for at least one month after a nuclear strike. Located outside the small eastern Ontario town of Carp, a short drive

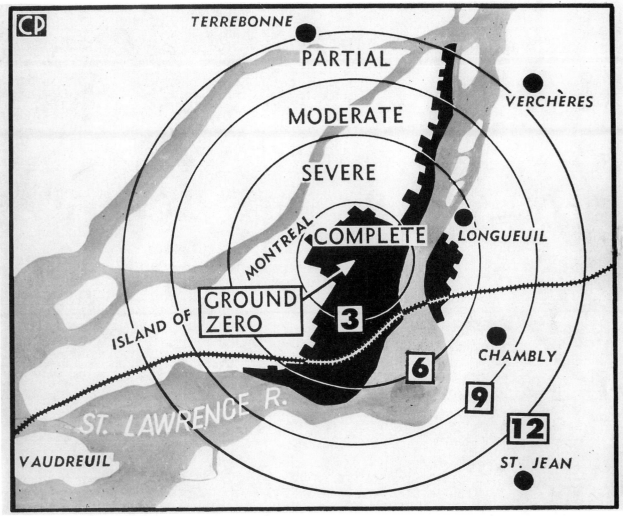

An illustration of the nuclear blast range if an atomic bomb were to fall on Montreal, May 2, 1963.

An atomic blast at a Nevada test site, 1961.

from Ottawa, the 100,000-square-foot structure was designed to withstand the detonation of a five-megaton nuclear weapon as close as one mile away. It contained a CBC Radio studio, a hospital, and a vault for the Bank of Canada. Only once, however, did a prime minister set foot inside the complex — Pierre Trudeau stopped in for a quick tour in 1976.

Finally, in the event of the Third World War, preparations had to be made to deal with those considered in the logic of the Cold War to represent a "fifth column" on the home front: Communists and other subversives. Internment was their destiny. The Royal Canadian Mounted Police (RCMP), under the heading of PROFUNC (Prominent Communist Functionaries), established and spent considerable resources meticulously maintaining lists of individuals, including their current addresses, whom they deemed to be subversive. Not only that, but the Mounted Police also established lengthy and detailed lists of "potential Communist hideouts" — safe locations across Canada where those targeted for internment might try to evade capture. For most of the Cold War, the primary characteristic of police targets was membership in the Communist Party of Canada. In 1970, the list of names totalled 762, mainly at locations in southern Ontario, with 174 women and 36 age six-

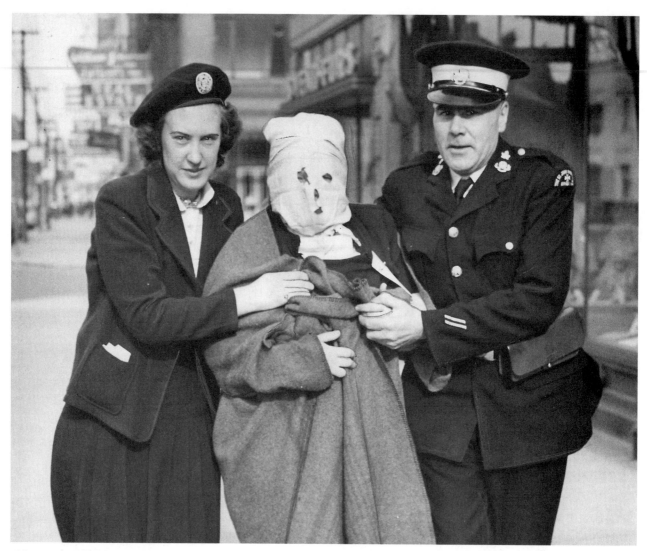

(above): A mock burn victim, April 9, 1951.

(below): Schoolchildren in an air-raid drill, November 28, 1951.

teen and under. Another 300 individuals, the police added, might need to be interned once hostilities began.

After war ensued, the subversives were to be arrested and put in short-term holding facilities until room could be made in federal prisons, specifically in Drumheller, Alberta and Warkworth, Ontario. The final destination for female subversives was Joyceville, a penitentiary outside of Kingston. Even elaborate rules for handling those to be interned were designed. Disobedience might be met with "Punishment Diet Number One," literally consisting of nothing but bread and water.

With détente in the 1970s and Gorbachev in the 1980s, all of the elaborate planning for another world war came to naught. Stations along the various radar lines were mothballed even before the Cold War ended, and then almost completely eliminated in its aftermath. They continued to have an impact on the environment though, as PCBs and other chemicals remained present at many of the decrepit stations, and new fights began over who would pay for the clean-up instead of the construction costs. The Diefenbunker became another Cold War artifact in 1994 when it was decom-

(above left): The CBC radio studio inside the Diefenbunker.

(above right): A poster promoting emergency preparedness.

(below): Emergency rations and supplies.

missioned and eventually re-emerged as a Cold War museum. By that time, the Third World War internment plans had also joined the relic pile on the orders of the Liberal government in 1983. Only the internment files remained behind as evidence of the antagonism of the age.

Radioactive Nation: Canada's Contribution to the Age of Weapons of Mass Destruction

With a blinding flash of light and an enormous explosion in the desert of New Mexico, the world officially entered the age of weapons of mass destruction on July 16, 1945. Less than a month later, Japan would twice experience the atomic wrath of its enemy. Although the United States held a monopoly on nuclear weapons until 1949 when the Soviet Union exploded its own device, it was not the only nation to have experimented with nuclear energy by the end of 1945. With American and British support, Canada gave high priority in the summer of 1944 to the development of a research facility at Chalk River on the upper Ottawa River under the administration of the National Research Council. The world's first nuclear reactor outside of the United States, ZEEP (Zero Energy Experimental Pile), was activated in September, 1945. By the middle of the

DANGER KEEP OUT RADIOACTIVITY

ATOM

1950s, Canada had accumulated enough plutonium to construct its own atomic weapon, and it still had an air force capable of delivering it. The decision had already been made, however, not to follow that path. Instead, Canada would develop nuclear technology for peaceful use while simultaneously helping make its ally's war machine possible by playing the role of uranium dealer to the American atomic junkie.

That uranium came from the pitchblende in the soil of Canada's rocky north. The initial source was Port Radium, located on Great Slave Lake in the Northwest Territories. Established in 1932 by a private company, Eldorado Gold Mines, Limited, the site was destined to produce ore that the company's refinery in Port Hope, Ontario, would turn into radium for use in medical treatments. By the start of the Second World War, demand for radium had fallen and the mine closed.

Resurrection soon arrived with the atomic age. In 1942, the mine reopened to fill an order from the United States government for sixty tonnes of uranium destined for the Manhattan Project, the program that would lead to the creation of the world's first atomic bomb. Although in the aftermath of Hiroshima and Nagasaki, the Canadian media would trumpet the participation of the nation's uranium in the enterprise, the harvest of Port Radium remained secondary to that being produced by mines in the Belgian Congo.

The Canadian government could not have cared less about chest thumping. It was more interested in security, paramount during the war. In particular, it worried about a private corporation controlling the national supply of uranium, so it secretly began to buy up shares in the company. Then in 1944, it went all the way, and made a brief announcement that Eldorado had

An atom smasher at the University of Wisconsin, October 17, 1945.

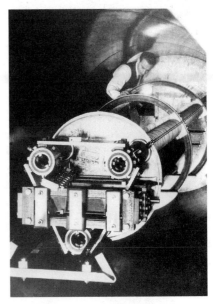

(above): A radioactive fallout suit, April 12, 1955.

(right): A kindergarten air-raid drill, June 14, 1954.

become a Crown corporation under the complete control of Ottawa's mandarins and politicians. By this time, American interest in Canadian uranium had declined considerably, and despite the takeover, the future of uranium mining was far from certain.

Again fate resuscitated the uranium industry. No sooner had the Second World War ended than the Cold War commenced. With a large Soviet military presence in a now ideologically divided Europe, nuclear weapons as a deterrence to conventional attack figured highly in American military planning. Then, with the development of the Soviet bomb in 1949, the American monopoly ended and the atomic arms race began. Nuclear weapons required nuclear fuel and although Canada's uranium deposits were not as plentiful as those in Africa, their closer proximity to the U.S. and Canada's position as a close American ally rendered them particularly strategically significant. Until the end of the 1950s, almost all of the uranium mined in Canada went south of the border where the American military stockpiled a huge nuclear arsenal that eventually surpassed 10,000 bombs. In 1959, the total value of Canadian uranium production was $331 million, and of that amount, $311 million was exported. Economically, uranium mining proved lucrative for Canada. It was the country's top mineral export and third only behind timber and lumber as the leading overall export.

Supplies of any natural product are finite, however. In 1960, the ore at

Port Radium reached its conclusion, and with it, so did the mine. New supplies had already been developed. Barely thirty miles south of the Northwest Territories southern boundary, Eldorado had established the Beaverlodge mine at the north end of Lake Athabasca in the early 1950s. It was not only a mine that materialized out of the Canadian Shield. An entire community, Canada's first and only Cold War city — fittingly named Uranium City — was built by the company, almost completely at its own expense, in northern Saskatchewan. At the conclusion of the 1950s, it was a bustling town of over 5,000 people with all of the amenities of any similarly sized entity across Canada.

The 1950s, however, were to be a golden age for uranium mining in Canada. Already before the end of the decade, demand from the American military, finally satiated by its enormous collection of nuclear weapons and by a growing domestic supply, had dropped; it ended in 1960. Declining demand and excess supply soon depressed the price. Uranium City saw its population decline as the projections of growth evident in its name proved illusory. Ottawa began to purchase uranium in order to protect the industry and to ensure its future. Indeed, some uranium mining continued in Canada as the country entered the twenty-first century.

Even in locations where uranium mining had ended, its impact lingered on — Canada's part in the American war machine came at a human cost to its own people. In mining the uranium around Great Slave Lake, Eldorado employed labourers from the Dené community of Deline. Without any health protection, Dené men hauled ore for $3 a day between 1942 and 1960. Local

Synchronizing watches during a civil defence exercise, May 29, 1956.

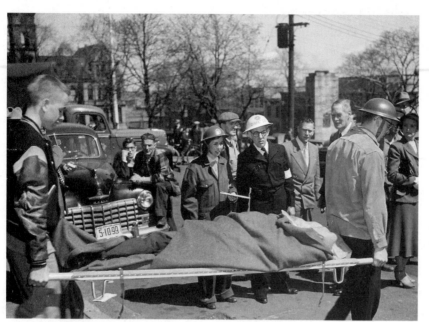

Montreal's Civil Defence Organization, April 3, 1954.

children came into contact with mineral dust. The community consumed fish from contaminated ponds. All the while, U.S. and Canadian officials had an awareness of the health risks. Safety precautions, however, threatened the supply of cheap labour and cheap uranium. In 1959, Gordon Churchill, the Minister of Energy in the Diefenbaker government, publicly denied that there were any "special hazards" connected to uranium mining.

The Dené of Deline discovered otherwise. In the small community, at least fourteen men involved in uranium work between 1942 and 1960 have died of a variety of cancers. A federal government examination in the 1990s reported that Deline suffered twice the medical problems of any other Aboriginal community in Canada. The Dené alone did not experience the health risks. One study of Port Radium miners found ten incidents of lung cancer out of seventy-six men who spent more than five years mining uranium.

The mining that poisoned the lives of the Dené and others clearly had military purposes. Nevertheless, even Canadian efforts at fostering the peaceful use of nuclear energy had unintended and negative consequences. In 1974, India exploded its own atomic bomb, and it soon became apparent that Canadian technology had played a role in its weapons program. It was not through the CANDU (Canadian Deuterium Uranium) reactor, a 1960s development designed by a public and private consortium under the control of Atomic Energy of Canada Limited, but through plutonium derived from an earlier reactor that Canada had sent to India as part of nuclear cooperation in the 1950s and early 1960s and with the promise that the reactor would be used for peaceful purposes.

With the explosion, the Trudeau government immediately ended assistance to India's nuclear program. It was too late, however. India's weapons program continued, and in 1998, it conducted several nuclear tests to the chagrin of much of the world, including its neighbour Pakistan, which detonated its own bomb in response. Speculation as to the continuing role of Canadian technology in India's program centred on whether the pre-CANDU reactor used in the 1974 test, along with tritium, a by-product from the heavy water involved in the operation of CANDU clone reactors, might have been involved. Secrecy surrounding the India program meant such queries would remain speculative but troubling ones for the Canadian government nonetheless. Like radioactivity that lingers on where uranium and its relatives have made an appearance, Canada's Cold War participation in the arms race promises to have implications well into a post-Cold War future.

North American Air Defence (NORAD) Command

CF-100 interceptors, March 16, 1959.

The style of announcement was that of an afterthought. On August 1, 1957, the government of Prime Minister John Diefenbaker announced through a press release that, for the first time, Canada and the United States had formed a new "integrated operational control of ... air defence ... forces" under the joint control of military officers of both nations. On an anonymous Canadian summer day, private discussions going back years had turned into the North American Air Defence (NORAD) command.

The beginning of this new joint defence plan was on another August day seventeen years earlier. In 1940, with Canada's ally and historical benefactor the United Kingdom teetering on the edge of defeat to Nazi Germany, leaving Canada virtually defenceless, William Lyon Mackenzie King and his government sought out a new big brother, the United States. King met President Franklin Roosevelt in Ogdensburg, New York, to create the Permanent Joint Board on Defence to synchronize the defence of the northern half of North America. Although never publicly debated and marking the

NORAD's coat of arms.

The main entrance of NORAD's underground Cheyenne Mountain complex.

beginning of a much closer relationship with its southern neighbour, the arrangement was popularly received in the desperate Canada of 1940.

There was a deeper subtext, however, to the new relationship. It had been initiated at the request of the United States, and in their meeting, Roosevelt had pressed King to allow American bases in Canada. As such, the summit represented the shape of things to come in the new Cold War. The United States, now viewing Canada as a potential battleground or at least a transit route for Soviet bombers on their way to drop their payload on American cities, began to clamour for an even tighter defence arrangement.

The clamouring led to the erection of radar defence lines such as the Pinetree Network and the Mid-Canada Line, and mounting coordination and contact between the Canadian and American militaries. In 1951, the first Royal Canadian Air Force officers began liaison assignments at the U.S. Air Force's headquarters in Colorado Springs. Under the Permanent Joint Board on Defence, Prime Minister Louis St. Laurent's government gave permission to the U.S. military to attack incoming Soviet aircraft in Canadian airspace. Diefenbaker's new government added permission for the U.S. to utilize nuclear-equipped missiles to shoot down Soviet planes over Canada.

For the U.S. Air Force, nonetheless, joint planning was not enough since it still provided Canada, at least in theory, with the freedom to say "no." The objective became a completely integrated command structure, although the American military remained reluctant until the mid-1950s to directly broach the subject because Canadian officials had expressed concern about infringements on sovereignty. American military planners also feared that Canada might attach any new relationship to the already existing North Atlantic Treaty Organization (NATO) and, in the process, bind their southern neighbour's hands when it came to continental defence. In the end, a more circuitous route was pursued.

That path led through the Canadian armed forces. Although the Canadian military's leadership had articulated momentary reluctance to move toward a more integrated command, in December, 1956, a committee of the two nations' military recommended just that step, in particular the appointment of a single commander. Only the details remained to be articulated, and the two militaries did that quickly in early 1957. By February, both militaries had approved the new command, and the U.S. government added its support in March.

NORAD headquarters.

Now it was up to Canada's politicians to offer their blessings to the agreement. One problem prevented the Liberal government from quickly addressing the subject. An election was scheduled for June 1957, and the government had no desire to touch a topic that might provide nationalist ammunition for its political opponents. The decision now awaited the winner of the election.

To the victors went both the spoils and the spoilage. For the Conservatives and John Diefenbaker, electoral triumph necessitated addressing the further integration of the defence systems of Canada and the United States. The Canadian military attempted to convince the defeated Liberal government to approve the measure "subject to confirmation" by their successors, but the Liberals refused. Diefenbaker and his Defence Minister, George Pearkes, now received their inheritance.

Not until the end of July did the two men finally deal with the issue. They did so in an entirely brief fashion, an approach encouraged by General Charles Foulkes, the chief of the Canadian defence staff. Foulkes misled his political masters by telling them that avoiding delay was crucial and that the outgoing government had already approved the agreement. After examining it for a day, Pearkes passed the document on to his boss. The prime minister

Early-warning DEW line site in the Arctic, March 20, 1959.

NORAD surface-to-air missile.

opted not to consult the rest of his Cabinet and, on August 1, the press announcement was made, one in which the new agreement was erroneously portrayed as part of NATO. A Canadian was appointed as second in command, and NORAD command posts (built into a mountain in Colorado Springs, Colorado, and down a mineshaft in North Bay, Ontario) were established in both nations.

The lack of reflection and debate about the new agreement would quickly come to haunt the Diefenbaker government. By the fall of 1957, the media and opposition commenced demanding what the new defence arrangement entailed. The prime minister wrongly claimed that the Liberals had approved the agreement while in government, and he inaccurately coupled NORAD to NATO; he continued to repeat that line in the coming months, namely, that it was nothing different from previous Canadian alliances, perhaps in the belief that if he said it enough it would come true. Out of public view, Diefenbaker's inherent streak of paranoia emerged as he became convinced that disloyal civil servants within External Affairs, where considerable opposition to the agreement existed, had leaked material to the Liberals.

Under ongoing pressure, the government finally agreed to a parliamentary debate about NORAD in June, 1958. In what one newspaper described as an "ambiguously worded excursion," Diefenbaker again portrayed NORAD as intricately attached to NATO, and he denied any loss of Canadian sovereignty. The Liberals, while not condemning the effort to further integrate the defence systems of the two nations, attacked the handling of the entire affair, especially the lack of consideration and consultation. In the end, when the time for the vote on a resolution supporting NORAD arrived, the Liberals joined with the Conservatives to support it. On the other hand, in a sign that Cold War political consensus was not complete, the Co-operative Commonwealth Federation voted against the new relationship.

For Diefenbaker, it was an immediate victory and the issue appeared to be finally settled. Presumption, however, did not equal reality. Additional aspects of continental defence, in particular the stationing of nuclear weapons in Canada, would render the political life of the man from Prince Albert and his government decidedly miserable.

The Birth of a Peacekeeping Nation

Egyptian President Nasser in Gaza, May 17, 1956.

An event of the Cold War inspired a new pillar of the post-war identity of Canadians. It also demonstrated the nation's new foreign policy reality in the post-Second World War era. In July 1956, Egypt, to the shock of the French and British governments, nationalized the Suez Canal, the 160-kilometre path between the Red Sea and the Mediterranean Sea. The outraged British government compared the move to Nazi Germany's acquisition of territory in the 1930s. Despite residing on Egyptian territory, the politics of imperialism had long denied Egyptians control of the canal. President Gamel Abdul Nasser, a strong nationalist, was no longer willing to suffer his nation's humiliation.

This created a new grievance and in October, 1956, Israel, working in co-operation with naval and air support from Britain and France, and later ground troops from those nations, seized the canal. The move exacerbated international tensions already elevated over the Soviet Union's assault on Hungary. Egypt was a Soviet ally, while France and Britain resided in the American camp. In this crisis, nevertheless, the United States turned its back

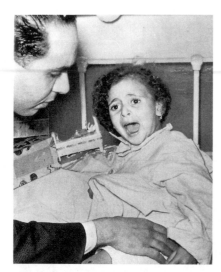

(above): A wounded child during the Suez Crisis.

(above right): Egyptians at Suez Canal ruins, 1956.

The body of an Egyptian air-raid victim, 1956.

on its allies, criticizing their involvement in the crisis and demanding the invaders' withdrawal from the canal zone. Washington, however, drew the line at accepting a Soviet proposal for a joint force of the two nations to repel the invaders of Egypt.

North of the U.S.-Canadian border, the government of Louis St. Laurent found itself in a difficult position, since the Canadian public was split almost exactly down the middle over the emergency. Then there was Canada's historical position of siding with Britain when it came to such international emergencies. The Suez Crisis marked an end to that approach. Lester Pearson, Minister of External Affairs, privately made it clear to a London apparently shocked by the temerity of the Canadian colonial, that it could no longer depend on his nation's automatic support. He then flew to New York to take part in a United Nations debate about the crisis. During the debate, Pearson, who would win the 1957 Nobel Prize for peace for his efforts, argued that a return to the status quo was not good enough. A better approach, he suggested, was the creation of a United Nations military force to keep the peace while a permanent settlement was being negotiated.

Pearson honed the idea and slowly brought the major parties onside. With an American presidential election just around the corner, Washington wanted the matter dealt with as expediently as possible. Britain and France offered support as well, out of the mistaken belief that they would contribute troops and maintain de facto control over the canal. Indeed, the two countries went ahead and landed soldiers in the Sinai. Egypt, withstanding the worst of the attack, also approved the plan. In the early morning of Sunday, November 4, 1956, fifty-seven members of the United Nations supported Pearson's plan with not a single vote against it.

Now the emphasis was on implementing the plan. A Canadian general took charge and Canadian soldiers made hurried preparations for transport to the region. A major obstacle to Canadian involvement quickly arose. The Egyptian government opposed Canadian involvement because of the nation's strong ties to its British enemy, evident in the British-style uniforms replete with a Union Jack patch that Canada's soldiers sported. After the standoff, which proved discomfiting to Ottawa, a compromise was reached, and three-hundred support troops instead of front-line soldiers left for the Sinai. There, a Canadian presence would remain until the Six-Day War of 1967 when Nasser ordered them out.

A blockade of sunken ships at the Suez Canal, 1956.

While Canada performed a leading and historic role in a bout of international diplomacy, at home the government found itself under attack because of its stance. The opposition Conservatives derided the Liberals for having turned the nation's back on the United Kingdom and France. Many newspapers across the land echoed that approach, including the *Calgary Herald*, which accused the government of having "run out on Britain." During a heated debate in the House of Commons, both St. Laurent and Pearson made it clear that the rules of the past no longer applied in the era of the Cold War. Canada, Pearson chastised the official opposition party, would no longer be a "colonial chore boy" who chimed in with a "Ready, Aye, Ready," as a Conservative leader had once advised Mackenzie King to do at a moment's notice.

Egyptian prisoners during the Suez Crisis.

PART THREE

The 1960s

The contrast between the two men who met on May 16, 1961, could not have been greater. On that day, wrinkled John Diefenbaker, Conservative prime minister of Canada from 1957 to 1963, greeted the new Democratic president of the United States, the suave and young John Kennedy, on his first presidential visit to Ottawa. That Kennedy could not properly pronounce Diefenbaker's name seemed symbolic of the relationship between the two men. After all, Diefenbaker was a man of the First World War, and Kennedy, its sequel. The grey Diefenbaker seemed better suited to the 1950s and the administration of Republican Dwight Eisenhower, a man more comfortable on the golf course than in the company of the likes of Sinatra and Monroe. Kennedy, on the other hand, appeared handsome and dynamic. With his beautiful wife Jackie on his arm as they toured Ottawa, the president seemed to serve as the ultimate symbol of the new decade. Looming above both men, however, was the Cold War, which would fundamentally affect both of their governments and their respective nations.

For much of the decade to follow, the Canadian economy, at least in the industrial belts, roared with the equally blossoming economy to the south. Unemployment remained low as the first wave of the "baby boom" entered the workforce. A smaller number followed the academic route, attending Canada's rapidly expanding system of post-secondary educational institutions.

By the middle of the 1960s, Canada, although hardly unique in this respect,

Buying food for the bomb shelter, 1961.

(opposite): Russian premier Khruschev and his wife.

Moscow Circus, September 20, 1967.

Hungarian anti-Soviet rally, 1956.

would be the site of rising levels of protest, some aimed directly and indirectly at the Cold War — for example, the nuclear arms race and the social and political conformity encouraged in the 1950s. The peace movement blossomed, attracting young adherents, and soon found an additional cause in the American involvement in Vietnam. Others turned to more radical politics, collectively known as the "new left," that offered critiques of both capitalism and Stalinism. "Rock 'n' Roll," illicit drugs, and sexual liberation soon dominated an increasingly rebellious youth culture. Other movements arose to challenge racism and sexism, and the position of Quebec in Canada. Emblematic of the degree to which Canada had changed in the 1960s, Pierre Trudeau swept to power in 1968 with promises to liberalize Canadian society through legislation.

Although a new decade of the Cold War started quietly enough on the domestic front, it was a different tale internationally. A major issue in the 1960 presidential election in the United States was which candidate would be tougher on the Soviet Union. Bandied about was a phantom "missile gap," specifically in the form of an American shortfall in the nuclear arms race. For a variety of reasons, it was John Kennedy who won, and it was John Kennedy and his administration that sought to uphold their end of the superpower rivalry.

Cuba, under the leadership of the bearded Communist Fidel Castro, represented one tempting target. The Bay of Pigs debacle followed, strengthening Castro's hold in Havana and furthering a growing divide between Ottawa and Washington over Cold War policy. This divide would widen in 1962 over the continuing debate about equipping Canada's military with nuclear weapons, and then with the Cuban Missile Crisis. By the federal election of 1963, Canada's relationship with the Kennedy administration had become an important issue, one exploited to its full potential by John Diefenbaker.

The other significant foreign policy decision taken by the Kennedy administration in the early 1960s was to increase American commitment to the government of South Vietnam in its struggle with the Communist North. The policy taken by Kennedy would live on after his death as Lyndon Johnson significantly expanded his nation's military participation in stemming the expansion of Communism in Southeast Asia. In turn, this involvement sparked criticism from around the world. Even the Canadian government, initially a cheerleader for Washington when the bombs began to drop, urged caution and a negotiated settlement.

By the second half of the decade, domestic and foreign issues began to converge and spiral out of control. Although privately admitting his nation could not win, Johnson continued the escalation of U.S. involvement in Vietnam. Violence erupted in American city after city, and in 1968, two prominent public figures, Robert Kennedy and Martin Luther King Jr., were assassinated. Out of this apparent chaos, a majority of those Americans who bothered to vote turned to Richard Nixon to make things right once again. Nixon's solution to the Vietnam quagmire fell from the hold of B-52 bombers.

U.S. President Nixon.

While the Soviet government may have enjoyed the American predicament, it had headaches of its own. To stem the flow of its citizens westward, Moscow's ally of East Germany had constructed a wall in 1961. In 1968 the problem was in Czechoslovakia, where liberalizing leadership had come to power. Fearing a domino effect much as the U.S. did, although from the opposite perspective, Soviet and other Eastern European militaries brought the movement to an end and confirmed the repressive nature of the Soviet system for much of the world.

By the end of the 1960s, the world was very different. Yet, in terms of the Cold War, it remained in a virtual state of suspended animation. The Soviet Union and the United States continued to be bitter adversaries. Only the location of their proxy conflicts had changed from ten years before. Moreover, the Canadian government, while occasionally pulling the tail of the American elephant next door, continued to be content to follow whichever path the pachyderm trod.

A model basement fallout shelter, April 19, 1961.

John Diefenbaker

Diefenbaker during the flag debate, 1964.

One of the stranger figures in the Canadian Cold War was John Diefenbaker. Member of Parliament (MP) and prime minister, he was both a strong anti-Communist and someone who defended civil liberties and repeatedly annoyed Washington, D.C.

Born in Ontario in 1895, Diefenbaker and his family moved in 1903 to a homestead near Prince Albert, his future federal riding, in what two years later would be the province of Saskatchewan. After serving overseas in the First World War, the transplanted Ontarion turned to law as his vocation of choice. Soon, however, the political bug infected him. What followed was a losing streak worthy of the worst sporting team imaginable. The lawyer and politician lost five consecutive elections at three different political levels before finally winning a seat in the House of Commons in 1940. Even then, the defeats continued as he twice failed to capture the leadership of the Conservative Party before finally emerging victorious in 1956, three decades after his political life began and at the age of sixty-one. Diefenbaker's lengthy struggle to reach the pinnacle of Canadian politics reinforced many of his negative characteristics, especially paranoia about the media and potential rivals, all of which ultimately emanated from a deep sense of insecurity.

Not surprisingly with such a complicated individual, Diefenbaker was a man of contradictions when it came to the Cold War. Desirous of the leadership of his party in the latter half of the 1940s, he could Commie bash with the best of them. In 1948, the year of the Berlin blockade and airlift, as a leadership candidate he positioned himself as an impeccable anti-Communist, calling for greater public education as to the dangers of the Red menace and a halt to the "pampering of those who indulge in Communist subversive activities." Yet other forces prevented him from becoming a Cold War caricature of the likes of his colleague George Drew [see chapter on Drew]. When the Gouzenko spy scandal became public, Diefenbaker took great delight in pointing to the support that the Labour Progressive Party, as the Communist Party of Canada was then called, had provided the Liberals in the 1945 federal election. He had no apologies to make, Dief told the House of Commons, for never having received Communist support. His ultimate point, however, did not follow the course that his initial comments suggested. Instead, the Conservative MP, drawing upon his legal background, criticized the Liberals for the violation of civil liberties through the secret arrests and interrogations of those incriminated by the documents supplied by Igor Gouzenko.

Diefenbaker at a Zionist convention.

A similar paradoxical Diefenbaker emerged in the aftermath of Herbert Norman's suicide. In the House of Commons, the now leader of the opposition explicitly blamed the death of Canada's ambassador to Egypt on American witch hunting. His speech moved his arch-enemy, Lester Pearson, so much that he sent a personal note of gratitude. Within days, Pearson's ally of the moment was back on the attack after the government offered conflicting accounts on security investigations of Norman and his Communist associations.

Diefenbaker's Cold War inconsistencies were even more evident once he became prime minister in 1957. First, there was the matter of the security screening of prospective federal government employees, a policy that represented a clash between the prime minister's anti-communism and his support for civil liberties. Diefenbaker chose the former when he accepted the policy that his government inherited from its Liberal predecessor. This policy, passed in 1955, allowed Canadians to be denied employment with the government, even prevented from appealing or being notified of the reason for the rejection of their security clearance, because of real or imagined ties not only to the Communist Party but to a belief in the principles of Communism in general.

More troubling for Diefenbaker was the inclusion of homosexuality, under euphemisms such as "weakness of character," among the justifications for rejecting an employee along security lines. The prime minister ordered a review but instead of ending the use of this criterion, it was expanded, and in the process hundreds of lives and careers were negatively affected, if not destroyed because of state-sanctioned homophobia [see chapter on the "Fruit Machine"].

Diefenbaker addressing the United Nations.

It was in the area of foreign policy, however, specifically with respect to Canada's relationship with the United States, that Dief the Chief's Cold War schizophrenia achieved its widest display. Part of his complex stance was clearly based on the personal animosity between him and the younger President John F. Kennedy, who considered "Diefenbawker" to be a "boring son of a bitch." Another factor was Anglophile Diefenbaker's suspicion of the United States, something reinforced by Howard Green, his Minister of External Affairs, and by repeated efforts of the U.S. government to influence and pressure its northern neighbour. Finally, there was Diefenbaker's governing style that often avoided making difficult decisions. All of these factors would come into play over the Progressive Conservative government's policy toward stationing nuclear weapons on Canadian soil and its response during the Cuban Missile Crisis.

Initially, Diefenbaker had been among the hawks circling about Fidel Castro's Cuba and its Soviet partner, a stance that ran against the more conciliatory approach of his government's Department of External Affairs. He expressed concern about the Castro government's pro-Soviet leanings, and in a speech before the United Nation's General Assembly in 1960, the prime minister lambasted the Soviet Union. These comments came during the Eisenhower administration. With John Kennedy, personality played a role, as did the growing tensions as the new president expressed a determination to vigorously resist Communism. In the case of Cuba, that involved signing off on the Bay of Pigs debacle [see chapter on the Cuban Missile Crisis]. Still, Diefenbaker continued to support the tough American line on Cuba, labelling the island a "bridgehead of international Communism." In the process, he occupied a position contrary to that of Howard Green, who offered to moderate between the two antagonists, and External Affairs, which the prime minister forced into producing a statement after the Bay of Pigs that was viewed as supportive by Washington.

Diefenbaker at the UN.

With Cuba, however, animosity toward Kennedy and distrust of his administration would trump Diefenbaker's revulsion toward Communism. On October 16, 1962, a U-2 spy plane over the island nation captured on film the construction of a ballistic missile site. Six days later, as Kennedy prepared to make the information public on television, the United States' partner in NORAD, Canada, was finally informed via a letter from the president and shown the photographic evidence by the American ambassador. Diefenbaker's hackles quickly rose over what he saw as a snub by Kennedy, who had taken the time to telephone the prime minister of the United Kingdom with the news. After the president spoke on television, Diefenbaker appeared before the House of Commons and called for a calm and a non-partisan commission to investigate the situation in Cuba. His appeal represented a challenge to the veracity of American claims and was interpreted as such. Behind the scenes, the prime minister ruminated over an American request to increase the level of alert of Canadian forces; two days later, he gave the order, but by that time the Minister of Defence, Douglas Harkness, had already done so on his own initiative. In the end, his government officially supported the American posi-

The Avro Arrow.

tion and the crisis ended peacefully, although there was a political price to be paid for delaying a superpower. Eighty percent of Canadians expressed opposition to the delay when news of it was made public.

Even more damaging in the context of the Cold War was that Diefenbaker had provoked the Kennedy administration, which had the potential to make his political life troublesome over the issue of nuclear weapons that had been in limbo for years. In avoiding a position, Diefenbaker was attempting to juggle completely contrary factions. Howard Green and his undersecretary, Norman Robertson, were completely opposed to the stationing of such weapons in Canada. Beginning with

the Eisenhower administration, the U.S. began to increase pressure on the Canadian government to accept the weapons, arguing correctly that defence systems such as the Bomarc missile were useless without them. In 1959, Diefenbaker announced that Canada would have to accept and that negotiations would follow, and then went into a stalling mode.

In January 1963, the issue of nuclear weapons finally exploded on the political front. After more dithering by the prime minister, the Kennedy administration openly criticized Diefenbaker's nuclear weapons stance, accusing his government of weakening North American defence plans and, in effect, calling Canada's leader a liar. Pressure on Diefenbaker to accept weapons only grew. Canadian newspapers savaged his nuclear shell game while opinion polls showed support for the American argument. Even members of his Cabinet turned against him over his continuing recalcitrance. Both Douglas Harkness and Pierre Sévigny, Minister and Associate Minister of Defence respectively, quit the government, the former in particularly spectacular fashion. The more the opposition mounted, however, the more Diefenbaker stiffened his resolve. With the passing of a non-confidence motion on the issue, the government fell and an election ensued. On the campaign trail, the prime minister, his jowls quivering as he spoke, revelled in his position, proclaiming it as heroic as he reminded audiences that "Canada was in both wars a long time before some other nations were." The election demonstrated some truth in another of his regular campaign lines (which also reflected his paranoia and insecurity): "Everybody's against me but the people." While his government went down to defeat, it was far from decisive as his critics had predicted and hoped for, since his stance against the United States proved popular with many Canadians. The Liberals won a minority government on April 8, 1963, with an increase of only twenty seats over their total going into the campaign, while the Conservatives dropped twenty-one seats from their pre-election standing. Politically, Diefenbaker lived to fight another day.

Diefenbaker meeting with President Kennedy in 1961.

One Minute to Midnight: the Cuban Missile Crisis

A presentation displaying missile launchers in Cuba, 1963.

It was the worst moment in the entire four and half decades of the Cold War. It was the moment when the world came closest to nuclear war. It was one minute to midnight, and the whole world knew it. Apocalypse was averted at the last moment, but the world was changed irrevocably by its close brush with disaster.

How the world came to the brink of nuclear war in October 1962 is a complicated story. The Cuban Revolution that brought Fidel Castro to power on January 1, 1959, also brought an unwelcome radical presence ninety miles off the coast of the United States. In the context of the Cold War, it was strictly a case of siding with the West, or siding with the Communists. The

American UN representatives during the Cuban Missile Crisis.

Castro government was soon seen by Americans as a Communist instrument of Soviet power, and in 1961, the incoming Democratic administration of John F. Kennedy was determined to reverse this threat to American security.

The first attempt at unseating Castro was a fiasco. In 1961, President Kennedy approved a Central Intelligence Agency mission to invade Cuba with a force of anti-Communist Cuban exiles. The attempted landing at the Bay of Pigs, without air cover, was quickly repelled. With the Cubans and the Soviets triumphant, and the Americans humiliated, Cuba had been identified as the flashpoint for the Cold War. The Americans set about planning for various schemes to reverse their defeat, from full-scale invasion plans, to the destabilization and subversion of the regime, and including some outlandish plots to assassinate Fidel Castro. The Soviets were gravely concerned for the survival of a friendly regime in the Western hemisphere. Cuba had become a prize piece on the Cold War chessboard.

The Cold War stakes were even higher than Castro's survival. Despite false charges raised by Kennedy in his 1960 election campaign that the Eisenhower administration had allowed a "missile gap" to appear to America's disadvantage, the Soviets knew only too well that the global strategic position gave a preponderance of power to the West. U.S. nuclear missiles were being stationed on Turkish soil just off the Soviet border. Soviet premier Nikita Khrushchev saw an opportunity to right the strategic imbalance and, at the same time, to guarantee the survival of the fledgling Communist regime off American shores. Secretly, medium and intermediate range missiles were sited in Cuba, directed at the continental U.S. It was a huge gamble by Khrushchev, a high-risk roll of the dice. It very nearly led to a catastrophic global conflagration.

On October 14, 1962, U-2 reconnaissance flights over Cuba detected the first evidence of missile sites. Two days later, President Kennedy was informed, and immediately a crisis management committee, called the ExComm, was formed to develop the appropriate American response to this challenge. Pre-emptive air strikes and full-scale invasion were discussed. On October 22, the Soviets were warned of the imposition of a naval blockade around Cuba. The Warsaw Pact and the North Atlantic Treaty Organization were on high alert. A poll of the American public showed 84 per cent support — and two in five Americans who believed that this would lead to the Third World War.

On October 24 and 25, the world watched in high anxiety as Soviet ships approached the U.S. blockade, and one Soviet tanker was intercepted. The U.S. went to Defence Condition (DEF CON) 2, the highest state of nuclear alert, for the first time. Behind the scenes, there was a direct exchange between Kennedy and Khrushchev on a way out of the crisis. The elements were principally an American pledge of non-aggression against Cuba, and a Soviet promise to dismantle their missiles. Implicit, but not referred to in public, was an American commitment to withdraw their missiles from Turkey. Saturday, October 27, was the worst day of the entire crisis. A U.S. reconnaissance plane flying over Cuba was shot down by a Soviet anti-aircraft battery.

By the end of the weekend, however, the blockade held and the elements of the agreement had finally been struck. Catastrophe had been averted — just.

Three weeks later, the quarantine on Cuba was lifted with firm evidence of the dismantling of all Soviet missiles on the island. Quietly, American missiles in Turkey were phased out. The Americans never did stop their efforts to clandestinely subvert the Cuban regime, and to undermine it by economic sanctions, but after the missile crisis, they eschewed the option of outright invasion.

For Canada, the Cuban missile crisis was a wake-up call. At the official level, Canada had been largely ignored by the U.S. (even though Kennedy was in constant communication with Sir Harold Macmillan, the British prime minister). As the junior partner of the North American Air Defence Treaty, Canada was expected simply to do what was directed by its senior partner. Moreover, the Canadian military acted more in the context of the continental command structure than in response to Canadian civilian authority. The pressures exerted on the Canadian Cabinet of Prime Minister John Diefenbaker exacerbated deep divisions already building up between the hawks and doves [see chapters on Diefenbaker and Harkness and Green]. These divisions would shortly engulf and consume the Diefenbaker government, which was defeated in Parliament and then in a general election in 1963.

For the public, the crisis was a deeply traumatic experience. No one who lived through those days can forget the sense of grim foreboding, of a world drifting ever closer to an apocalypse, and of the sheer sense of powerlessness

The Khruschevs, the Kennedys, and the president of Austria.

LAUNCH POSITION

MISSILE-READY TENTS

MISSILE ERECTORS

A Cuban missile launch site, 1962.

that pervaded all discussion and thought. The fateful decisions on which the very future of the planet depended were in the hands of the leaders of two great superpowers also were apparently accountable to no one but themselves. The overwhelming sense of powerlessness was true of course for ordinary Americans as well, but for Canadians, whose own government was rendered equally powerless, it was even more terrifying.

It is no exaggeration to suggest that the missile crisis marked the breaking of a Cold War spell cast over the Canadian population. Before the crisis, Canadian support for American Cold War leadership had been firm, and dissenters had largely been cast as a pro-Communist minority. After the crisis, opposition to the Cold War mentality grew out of the margins and into the mainstream. It was not that Canadians became anti-American or suddenly discovered some affection for the Soviet system. Rather, it became more acceptable to look for a third way to avoid the nuclear brinksmanship that had neared disaster. Coming face to face with the immensity of the stakes, as people did during that frightening week, was a very sobering experience. After 1962, the peace movement grew, and there was more of a genuine debate in Canadian society about alternatives to the Cold War. In 1965, George Grant published his influential polemic *Lament for a Nation*, and Canadian nationalist movements began to stir.

Howard Green and Douglas Harkness: Cold War Antagonists

(above left): Howard Green in Hamilton, May, 1962.

(above right): Douglas Harkness at a press conference on March 21, 1963.

Starker contrasts in Canadian Cold War policy, especially Canada's relationship to the United States, could not be found than those that existed between two prominent members of the Cabinet of Progressive Conservative Prime Minister John Diefenbaker in the early 1960s. On one side was Dief the Chief's Minister of External Affairs, Howard Green, who strongly opposed the stationing of nuclear weapons in Canada and expressed concern about American military and foreign policy. Occupying the opposite position was Douglas Harkness, the Minister of Defence, who pushed Canada into following the American defence lead during the Cuban Missile Crisis, and then quit the Cabinet over his government's failure to follow what he believed to be its obligations about nuclear weapons on Canadian soil. Cumulatively, the clashes between Harkness and Green, aided by the inaction and paranoia of Diefenbaker, tore apart the Conservative government.

Howard Charles Green was a British Columbian by birth and career. Born in Kaslo, B.C., in 1896, he travelled east to study at the University of Toronto

Howard Green speaking at the University of Toronto, November 26, 1962.

from which he graduated in 1915. Like many young men of his generation, the First World War interrupted his life plans. Green served with the 54th Kootenay Battalion and then, after the war ended, spent time with the Canadian section at British headquarters. Upon his return to Canada, he studied at Osgoode Hall and returned home to begin practising law with a Vancouver firm in 1922.

Eventually, his attention turned to politics. In 1935, generally a bad year for Conservatives since their party was defeated federally by the Liberals, he was elected as a Member of Parliament for Vancouver South, a riding he would represent until 1949 when he successfully switched to Vancouver Quadra. In 1942, he sought the leadership of his party but finished a disappointing fourth on the ballot, just behind John Diefenbaker, with whom he generally enjoyed a good relationship. When the Conservatives, after twenty-two years in opposition, captured a minority government in 1957, Green was among the favourites to be added to the Cabinet, initially as Minister of Public Works, a position he held until 1959. He also served as acting prime minister when Diefenbaker was absent on trips abroad, a sign that the perpetually insecure Diefenbaker believed that Green had no desire for the top spot in the government.

On March 19, 1959, the Minister of External Affairs, Sidney Smith, dropped dead from a heart attack. Media speculation about potential successors ensued. Diefenbaker, wishing to avoid placing a potential rival in such a senior position, selected the unthreatening Green. When it came to his new portfolio, he was far from an inspired choice. Green had not been abroad since his First World War service in Europe. Nevertheless, his belief in strengthening Canada's British ties and a strong aversion to the United States reflected the views of the prime minister.

While a foreign affairs soulmate of Diefenbaker, Green's approach would put him in conflict with the Minister of National Defence, Douglas Harkness. Born in Toronto, Harkness actually grew up in Alberta, attending high school in Calgary and the University of Alberta in Edmonton. He began a teaching career, working at a high school in Calgary, at which his principal was the future premier of Alberta, William Aberhart. Soon, war changed his plans. Even as a high school student, he had been drawn to the military, having joined the Canadian Officer Training Corps. At the age of thirty-six, he was called up for duty once war began in 1939, and the following year he proceeded overseas. As an officer, he saw action, winning a medal for bravery while serving in Sicily.

The war hero immediately entered politics upon his return to Canada. In 1945, the voters of Calgary East sent him as a Conservative to the House of Commons and did so subsequently for nine straight times. Like Green, he became a member of Diefenbaker's first Cabinet in 1957, first serving as the Minister of Northern Affairs and Natural Resources, then as Minister of Agriculture, and finally, from October 1960, as Minister of National Defence.

Within a few months of assuming his position, Harkness found himself in conflict with Green over Canada's defence policy as the first visit to Ottawa of

President John F. Kennedy neared. At issue was whether or not nuclear weapons should be stationed in Canada. Green, an advocate of disarmament and suspicious of the United States, was vehemently opposed to any agreement with the U.S. that involved nuclear weapons in Canada. Harkness and his department supported a speedy decision to deploy such weapons, believing they were necessary for Canada's defence and for it to fulfill its commitments to the North American Air Defence Command (NORAD). Indeed, Canada had agreed to purchase the Bomarc missile, designed to carry a nuclear warhead in defence against oncoming Soviet bombers.

American officials were well aware of the Cabinet squabbling. Green demonstrated his independent streak to the point of offering to mediate differences between the U.S. and Castro's Cuba. This tendency increasingly dismayed the U.S. State Department, and it was suggested that Kennedy address American concerns with Green in a future meeting with Diefenbaker. When it came to the deployment of nuclear weapons in Canada, the Kennedy administration tried to do an end run around Green by sending their ambassador to Canada directly to Diefenbaker in an attempt to cut a deal. Livingston Merchant believed Diefenbaker to be onside, but the prime minister had no desire to alienate Green, and failed to raise the proposed American deal in Cabinet.

The more direct battle between Harkness and Green, indeed between differing philosophies of Canada's relationship to the United States, would occur after the Diefenbaker government had been reduced to minority status in the federal election of June 18, 1962. First, there was the October 1962 Cuban Missile Crisis, in which the Kennedy administration revealed that the Soviet Union was in the process of building sites on Cuba from which nuclear missiles could be launched against the continental United States, and that American forces would launch a "quarantine" of the island to prevent further development of the sites. The date was October 22 and Livingston Merchant and other U.S. officials came to Parliament Hill to meet with Diefenbaker, Green, and Harkness about the situation in Cuba, the reality of which Kennedy was to make public on American television that evening. Canada was naturally approached for its support.

Support was forthcoming but not of the unqualified variety that the Americans anticipated. Green recommended to Diefenbaker that a United Nations' inspection of the sites be conducted and the Chief repeated it before the House of Commons. To many, this suggestion appeared to challenge the accuracy of the American declaration.

More significantly was Canada's military position in the crisis. After Kennedy's address to his citizens, the American military had been put on Defence Condition (DEF CON) 3, a higher state of alert. The Canadian military sought Harkness's approval for similarly increasing the alertness of its forces, a logical step with Canada's close connection to the United States under NORAD. Harkness gave his permission pending what he assumed would be the approval of the higher stage of alert in a Cabinet meeting the next day.

His assumption was wrong. At the next day's gathering, first Diefenbaker

Douglas Harkness at a press conference, May 21, 1963.

opposed the shift, arguing that it would alarm the Canadian public. Even more entrenched in his opposition was Howard Green. "If we go along with the Americans now," he contended, "we'll be their vassals forever." The counter-arguments of Harkness were to no avail. The Cabinet voted against a higher state of alert. This decision prompted Harkness to engage in a major act of political disobedience as he ordered the Canadian military to go ahead and raise its level of alertness to match the status of U.S. forces. When the U.S. forces moved to DEF CON 2, Diefenbaker, without the support of his Cabinet, supplied personal approval to another shift, unaware that his own Minister had approved the previous change.

The Cuban Missile Crisis ended peacefully but the division between Harkness and Green within the Cabinet remained. The final act in their dispute would be played out again over nuclear weapons and Canada's relationship with the United States. At the end of the missile crisis, Harkness proposed the issue of nuclear weapons and Canada be clarified with the U.S. The Cabinet agreed and Diefenbaker selected the Defence Minister and Green, along with one other Cabinet Minister (to act as a referee between the two antagonists), to do the negotiating. The Canadian position, which Diefenbaker and Green wholeheartedly endorsed and Harkness went along with as a form of compromise, was that nuclear weapons would not be stationed in Canada. In a time of crisis, however, they could be transported into Canada to be added to weapons designed to intercept a Soviet attack.

Canada's position was unacceptable to the Kennedy administration, which, along with others, pointed out that Canada had ordered weapon systems designed to carry nuclear weapons. The issue continued to haunt Diefenbaker's increasingly beleaguered government. Harkness pressed Diefenbaker in January 1963 to resume negotiations, but the prime minister refused. Finally, at the end of January, Diefenbaker again appointed a Cabinet committee, which again included both Harkness and Green, to develop a coherent defence policy. Faced with documentary evidence, Green conceded that Canada had made a commitment to accept nuclear weapons, while Harkness also moderated his tone. The committee recommended a swift conclusion to talks with the Americans in order to make clear Canada's policy with regard to nuclear weapons.

Without hesitation, Diefenbaker, who preferred ambiguity until after the next election, rejected his Cabinet's report. He then made a speech to the House of Commons, which was so obscure that those on both sides of the debate interpreted Diefenbaker as accepting their position. Harkness went so far as to issue a press release declaring Diefenbaker's support for acquiring nuclear weapons, a tactic that caused the prime minister's jowls to shake in outrage. His foul mood only worsened when the U.S. state department issued a press release pointing out Canada's commitment to stationing nuclear weapons on its soil. The Defence Minister, who had repeatedly threatened to resign over the issue, now felt that he had no choice.

One final Cabinet showdown remained. It would occur on a tranquil Sunday in the dining room at 24 Sussex Drive. Diefenbaker, with Green sitting close by, opened the meeting by announcing that he intended to call an election over the American intervention on the nuclear issue. Some in his Cabinet demurred, but it was left to Harkness to bluntly state what was on the minds of many in the room: "You might as well know that the people of Canada have lost confidence in you, the party has lost confidence in you, and the Cabinet has lost confidence in you. It is time you went." Diefenbaker erupted in rage. After determining that Harkness' feelings were indeed shared by several in the room, he stormed out, followed by his loyalists, Green among them, labelling his colleagues as "traitors" as he went. Cooler heads eventually prevailed, but Harkness remained resolved in his resignation.

This he made public on the next day, February 4:

> For over two years you have been aware that I believed nuclear warheads should be supplied to the four weapons systems we have acquired which are adapted to their use. ...It has become quite obvious during the last few days that your views and mine as to the course we should pursue for the acquisition of nuclear weapons for our armed forces are incapable of reconciliation. Thus ... I now find I must tender my resignation as Minister of Defence.

His Cabinet career had ended but his political career continued as Harkness won re-election to the new Conservative opposition in the April 1963 federal election.

As for Green, he maintained his loyalty to Dief the Chief as he plotted to save the rapidly collapsing minority government by staving off a vote of nonconfidence over the nuclear issue in the House of Commons. That vote, held the day after the resignation of Harkness, finally put the Diefenbaker government out of its misery and on the electoral trail, a path that led to its defeat by the Liberals under Lester Pearson, and to the end of Howard Green's political life at the hands of the voters in his riding of Vancouver Quadra.

The Munsinger Affair

Gerda Munsinger.

W ho was "Monseignor"? That was the question that hacks in the Ottawa press gallery excitedly asked each other after Question Period on March 4, 1966. The focus of the question-and-answer session had been on a spy scandal involving George Victor Spencer, a Vancouver postal clerk accused of being a Soviet spy. The Conservative opposition under John Diefenbaker launched attack after attack against the handling of the entire matter by Lester Pearson's Liberal government. Most of the fire was on the Minister of Justice, Lucien Cardin, who had ministerial responsibility for the Royal Canadian Mounted Police and its spy service. To fend off the onslaught, Cardin popped tranquilizers and went for Diefenbaker's political jugular: "Of all the members he, I repeat he, is the very last person who can afford to give advice on the handling of security cases in Canada.... I want the right honourable gentleman to tell the House about the participation in the Monseignor case when he was prime minister of this country."

The media soon discovered that there was no "Monseignor." In revealing an older spy scandal to deflect attention from a current one, Cardin had misspoken. Munsinger was the name. Gerda Munsinger. And the most titillating of topics were involved: sex and politics combined with espionage. Some of the interest derived from the familiarity of the scandal, the likes of which had recently been experienced in the United Kingdom, where Defence Secretary John Profumo had resigned over his affair with a prostitute named Christine Keeler who had also enjoyed a relationship with a Soviet intelligence officer. In the Canadian case it consisted of Munsinger, also involved in prostitution and rumoured to have had ties to Soviet intelligence, having had an illicit relationship with one and possibly two cabinet ministers, the Associate Minister of National Defence Pierre Sévigny and Minister of Transport George Hees. What was more, the RCMP had warned Diefenbaker about the relationships in December 1960, and he had done nothing except confront Sévigny about it while leaving him in the Cabinet. In 1964, the Liberals discovered the incident after Pearson instructed the RCMP to allow his government access to its files on all Members of Parliament since 1956. He went so far as to send a letter to Diefenbaker expressing concern about the matter and threatening to call an inquiry, but the matter was put aside for another two years.

In 1966, everyone wanted to know more about the new scandal and details slowly emerged. Cardin announced that "Olga" Munsinger, whom he said had enjoyed improper relationships with Conservative Cabinet Ministers, had died from leukemia in East Germany. In fact, she was very much alive as a *Toronto Star* reporter discovered when he knocked on her door in West Germany. "I suppose you want to ask about Sévigny," was her greeting to her guest, salutations that made public the name of the previously anonymous Conservative Cabinet Minister. Sévigny, in what would become a standard response by politicians involved in sex scandals, took to national television, accompanied by his wife and daughter as backdrops, to deny his involvement with the mystery woman beyond having met her "socially" a few times.

Details about Munsinger, who appeared in living rooms across Canada through an interview on CBC television, also emerged. At birth in her native Germany, she had been Gerda Heseler. Her name change came after a marriage to an American soldier whom she divorced in 1954. By the following year, she was living in Canada and working as a prostitute in Montreal. In 1958, she met Sévigny at a Montreal golf course and soon after became his mistress. Already, however, she was of interest to intelligence services. In 1949, she had been arrested by the West German police on minor espionage charges that involved stealing border passes and currency apparently for the use of Soviet intelligence. It was this record, plus the fact that in 1960 she had applied for Canadian citizenship listing Sévigny and Hees as references, that led the RCMP to her, and then to details about her relationship with the Ministers.

To discover the "truth" about the matter, the Liberal government established a commission of inquiry under Mr. Justice W.F. Spence of the Supreme

The Munsinger Report on sale, 1966.

Gerda Munsinger (right), April 26, 1966.

Court of Canada. After examining relevant documents and interviewing witnesses, who often gave impressions of Munsinger that reflected prevailing gender stereotypes of the age, Spence issued his final report in September 1966. It was highly critical of the handling of the matter by Diefenbaker and his government, arguing that the contact between Sévigny and his German friend had the potential of being a grave security breach. In the end, however, the justice stated that there was not enough evidence to demonstrate a security leak had actually occurred, and the entire matter soon disappeared from the public and political discourse.

Gerda Munsinger in her later years.

John Watkins

John Watkins was a secret casualty of Canada's Cold War. A career diplomat, he served as Canadian ambassador to the Soviet Union from 1954 to 1956. In an era of Cold War secrecy, Watkins possessed the deepest secret possible. He was a gay man in a homophobic world, and his career depended on keeping his personal life to himself. This would have been a difficult task at the best of times. The Cold War made it doubly so. Personal secrets could be exploited by an enemy. Intelligence services employed as a regular tactic a practice nicknamed the "honey trap," in which foreign citizens were sexually entrapped, creating the potential for blackmail. For a married man, the threat would be a package containing revealing photographs sent through the post to his wife. For a gay man, the threat was far greater — public shame and the destruction of his career.

Watkins was a reluctant employee of External Affairs and his life appeared destined for a career in academe. Born near Brampton, Ontario, in 1902, he developed an early interest in music and Scandinavian culture. He attended

John Watkins (left), the Soviet ambassador to Canada, and Lester Pearson on the Black Sea shore.

the University of Toronto, graduating in 1927 with a master's degree. Later, he studied in the United States, including at Cornell University where he earned a doctorate. Returning to Canada, he accepted a position teaching English literature at the University of Manitoba in 1944. Already his abilities, particularly his skill at learning languages, had caught the attention of senior bureaucrats, who had to convince him to write the foreign service exam. In September 1946, he accepted a position as a foreign service officer. Within two years, he had been posted to Moscow as the Canadian Embassy's chargé d'affaires, where he remained until 1951 when health problems necessitated his return to Canada for recuperation. He returned to Moscow as Canada's ambassador for three years in the middle of decade. After that stint, he was promoted to assistant undersecretary of External Affairs, a position he held until his quiet retirement in 1964 to his favourite city of Paris. A distinguished career had ended.

Watkins' retirement, however, would be neither peaceful nor lengthy. With the heightening of tensions in the 1950s, tolerance for difference in Western nations had all but disappeared. The emphasis was on the "normal" in all aspects of society, including personal relationships. Being married with children represented a bulwark against Communism. In turn, homosexuality was on par with those who became a "fellow traveller," and thus a Red. J. Edgar Hoover, the director of the Federal Bureau of Investigation for much of the Cold War, and widely rumoured to have been gay himself, labelled the path to Communism as "perverted" and compared Communists to drug addicts. State discourse regularly equated conversion to Communism with sexual weakness or degeneracy.

For state security services, such as the Royal Canadian Mounted Police, being a homosexual opened up those in positions of authority and power to blackmail [see the chapter on the "Fruit Machine"].

Homophobia eventually ensnared John Watkins. Why he became a suspect has fuelled multiple explanations. One involves a drunken Soviet premier and Lester Pearson. In this version (rejected by one of those actually in attendance), Nikita Khrushchev, well refreshed after several shots of vodka, made a veiled reference to the ambassador's sexual preference in front of Pearson and a visiting Canadian delegation that included Watkins. What directly raised police suspicion about Watkins was a report from a defector from Soviet intelligence. Anatoli Golitsin reported that an effort had been made to sexually entrap a Canadian diplomat in the 1950s. Two subsequent defectors added additional information. An investigation under the homophobic title of "Operation Rock Bottom" was launched. At first, investigators zeroed in on David Johnson, Watkins' successor in Moscow and also a homosexual, who lost his job with External Affairs when this was discovered. Johnson's career, however, did not fit with the details supplied by the defectors. Watkins became the new candidate. The RCMP began studying the paper trail, looking at everything the suspect had written while ambassador and then as an undersecretary at External Affairs. No smoking gun was found to suggest that Watkins had served as an "agent of influence" for the Soviet Union.

What remained was to interrogate Watkins. Two members of the
Mounted Police, one of whom, James Bennett, would ironically later face a
similar style of interrogation because of suspicions that he was a Soviet agent,
flew to Paris to confront the former ambassador directly. There, they convinced him to travel first to London and then to Montreal for detailed
questioning.

On the Thanksgiving weekend of 1964, the three men sat in a Holiday
Inn hotel room in the suburbs to begin the discussion. Watkins, in an era
when society demanded that homosexuality be hidden, was apparently embarrassed to admit his secret. Eventually he confessed to having had sexual
intercourse twice with Soviet nationals while serving as ambassador, and that
Soviet intelligence attempted to use this information as advantage against
him, pressure which he resisted. Those doing the questioning, without any
evidence to the contrary, believed that Watkins had not betrayed his nation.
Near the end of the questioning, the retired ambassador, who had long suffered from heart problems, complained of chest pains. After resting, he
sought a cigarette, but before reaching it, he died from a massive heart attack.
The RCMP quickly covered up the situation surrounding the ambassador's
death, finding a coroner who signed the proper documents without an awareness of the real facts.

Sixteen years later, the story of Watkins' demise began to leak out, first in
the British media and then in Canada when novelist Ian Adams discovered the
misleading death certificate. An enquiry ensued, one that cleared the RCMP
of improper behaviour. In 1982, a Quebec coroner issued a new death certificate that cited natural causes as the cause of death of one of Canada's Cold
War ambassadors to the Soviet Union.

Baby Boomers

The automobile became a facet of suburban life in the 1960s.

The Cold War was not just about events, it was also about demographics. Encouraged by reunions at the end of the Second World War, by the end of the Great Depression, and by Cold War rhetoric that emphasized the family and traditional gender roles as a means for combating Communism, Canadian women and men began to make babies in large numbers, as a previous generation had done at the end of the Great War.

Birth rates soared in Canada, the United States, Australia, and New Zealand, and continued at a high level into the early 1960s. In 1945, slightly more than 300,000 Canadian children were born. Two years later, the number reached 372,000, and by 1952, it broke the 400,000 barrier, a level it would remain above until 1966. In that year, almost half of Canada's population was under the age of twenty-four.

These birth numbers did not extend evenly across the country. Saskatchewan, which had begun an era of depopulation with the crash of the agricultural economy in the Great Depression, experienced a much slower rate of population growth than booming Ontario.

A suburban home, May 28, 1969.

An entire cohort of children born in this period would forever be labelled as the "baby boom generation," a tag that, in suggesting a unified generation, oversimplified and exaggerated that very point. While the baby boomers — through the force of their sheer numbers — altered the society around them at every stage of their lives, whether they were aware of it or not, their suggested cohesiveness was an illusion. Ethnicity, class, gender, region, and even age, among other dynamics, divided the perspective of baby boomers as they had every previous generation of Canadian citizens.

Another unique factor of the boomer experience was where an increasing number of them grew up. The suburbs, or suburbia, as in the United States, became a post-war phenomenon in parts of Canada and reflected the continuing urbanization of the nation as a whole. Although still not affordable for everyone, and reviled by many because of the homogeneity of the houses, owning a home became a possibility for many for the first time, through the help of the Canadian Mortgage and Housing Corporation, increasing access to credit, and aid to decommissioned soldiers. In the insecurity of the Cold War, the suburbs were portrayed as an inexpensive, clean, and safe place to raise the growing number of children of the era.

And as a Cold War phenomenon, these children were undeniably influential across a wide range of areas. Popular culture geared itself toward the young and, in many cases, affluent consumers. The drive-in theatre, by definition made possible by the automobile, became a location where entire families could be entertained without the difficulty of obtaining a babysitter. In 1957, there were 229 drive-ins across the country, as opposed to only seven in existence ten years earlier. The popularity of drive-ins as a location for entertainment outside of the home continued as boomers reached the teenage years, specifically the magical age of sixteen when a driver's license could be obtained, and began to seek entertainment away from their parents.

The impact of boomers extended to other areas of popular culture. Whereas televisions in their large wooden cabinets remained relatively expen-

sive and a shared family experience, radio and record players, once employed by families in the same way as television, had undergone a significant transformation. Cheap transistor radios appeared, well within the price range of teenagers, allowing youngsters to listen to their own music and, in the process, shattering the cultural conformity of just a few years earlier. The same was true of record players, which became smaller and more affordable. In 1957, more than 270,000 record players were sold in Canada, many destined for teenagers' bedrooms. This music revolution culminated in the September 1964 arrival of The Beatles in Canada to play a concert at Maple Leaf Gardens, much to the delight of Harold Ballard, one of the owners of the arena, who happily donned a Beatles' wig for the cameras. Thousands of screaming boomers greeted the mop-topped quartet, signalling again the arrival of a new era of youth culture.

Because of its family nature, television was slower to react to the growing youth culture and efforts were generally aimed at programs that would interest a multi-generational audience. Perry Como still occupied a prominent place on the Canadian television schedule well into the 1960s, whereas other television mainstays on both sides of the border, particularly Ed Sullivan, made efforts to reach out to youth by televising appearances by the Beatles and, later in the 1960s, the Rolling Stones and the Doors.

The youth revolution struck the Canadian state as well. It was forced to adjust to the onslaught of this era of youth in the educational field. British Columbia saw its educational budget rise from $15 million in 1945 to $133 million by 1960-61. New schools were built and extensions added to pre-existing ones. Fresh teachers were hired as well. Even then, problems of overcrowding and large class sizes arose because of the sheer numbers at each level that the boomers reached. In 1961, there were over a million more children in Canadian schools than there had been a decade earlier. Compounding the difficulties for the educational system was the growing tendency of Canadian youth to stay in high school longer.

By the middle of the 1960s, the first of the boomer wave began entering university. As had happened at every stop along the way, higher education attempted to adjust to the influx of students. New universities were constructed, such as Simon Fraser University, a concrete symbol of the modern and affluent post-war era perched on the top of a mountain in Burnaby, British Columbia, while pre-existing universities expanded to welcome the new students.

Despite the growing post-secondary field, only a minority of the boomer cohort attended university. Economically, the 1960s was a boom period, driven in part by the American war economy, which absorbed into the workforce across North America many of those who did not undertake post-secondary studies. This growing workforce also included more and more women.

For those who did enter university, a historically significant portion would be drawn to a variety of protest movements. One target was the university itself. Students fought to democratize institutions that by tradition had ignored

(above): A Ford Mustang, 1964.

(left): An A&W drive-in restaurant, 1969.

the input of those who attended them. Events of the Cold War, including the American Civil Rights movement, radicalized others. Many students, for example, led campus movements against the Vietnam War and Canada's complicity in it. In turn, this convinced some in positions of authority that students were being manipulated by Communists to further their Cold War aims. For other boomers, including the so-called second wave of feminism that emerged as a reaction to the 1950s "father knows best" society, the crusade was about reforming and destroying the patriarchal social structures around them that they believed oppressed women, ethnic and racial minorities, and workers.

A distinctive youth culture emerged that flouted many of the gender, moral, and legal standards of Canadian society. Young men grew their hair long, in the process challenging notions of masculinity. Young women eschewed feminine styles of clothing and other trappings and orthodoxy of traditional gender roles. A revolution in sexual attitudes and sexuality further flayed gender stereotypes of how proper young men and women were to behave. Driven by a decline in the influence of organized religion, by a youth culture that emphasized sexuality, and by a sense of rebellion, more people began having premarital sexual intercourse and even living with each other as part of a relationship. The birth control pill, which was approved for sale in Canada in 1961, was less of a factor, since under the Criminal Code it

A Japanese car, imported to North America in 1964.

remained illegal (although in practice the law was often ignored) to advertise or sell contraceptives until 1969, when Pierre Trudeau's government reversed the law. Legal or illegal, obtaining a prescription for the pill remained difficult for women, especially those who were single.

One other part of the boomer youth culture of the 1960s collided with the legal system. Young people increasingly experimented with illicit drugs in the 1960s. For some, such as future Prime Minister Kim Campbell, a student at the University of British Columbia in the first half of the 1960s, drug use involved a few puffs of a marijuana cigarette. For others, particularly as the decade progressed, more powerful drugs, predominantly the hallucinogenic LSD, became the non-liquid refreshment of choice. Whatever the drug involved, the state, for reasons that historically had little to do with health and much more to do with sexuality, racism, and class, continued to frown upon their consumption. Inquiries into the rise of drug use convened and various governments launched anti-narcotics educational campaigns. Police forces also expanded their efforts as drugs reached a wider segment of society. The result was a remarkable escalation in arrests for illegal drugs, rising in Canada from 516 charges in 1960 to over 8,500 ten years later.

In Quebec, young people also made their voices heard as in other parts of Canada. In many ways, they had even further to travel in terms of youth protest in a province where the Roman Catholic Church had long been a powerful institution. There was also a difference in the form of protest. Many young people turned toward the pursuit of Quebec nationhood [see the chapter on the Quiet Revolution].

Although many boomers continued to push for change into the 1960s, others, especially those who had remained outside of the social protests, began following the patterns of their parents by marrying and beginning families of their own. An economic downturn in the early 1970s and the end of the Vietnam War forced a reappraisal of the Cold War era priorities of the boomers, although their influence on the world around them continued unabated.

Radicalism in the 1960s and the Response of the State

A Hamilton "love-in" in the 1960s.

For Canada, the 1960s was a remarkable decade as a wide variety of Canadians openly challenged the founding tenets of the Cold War. Part of the originality of the period emanated simply from its contrast to the widespread dullness and conformity associated with the 1950s. Despite this reputation, however, the protest of the 1960s had its roots in the previous fifteen years. At its centre was the peace movement, which continued to gain strength as a variety of groups and individuals marched to oppose nuclear weapons in general, and specifically those weapons of mass destruction on Canadian soil. Between 1958 and 1962, the number of Canadians favouring a ban on American nuclear tests grew to nearly 50 percent. In 1961, the Canadian Committee to Control Radiation Hazards presented Prime Minister John Diefenbaker with a 141,000-signature petition rejecting the presence of nuclear weapons on Canadian soil.

Young people were particularly involved in the peace movement. The Combined Universities Campaign for Nuclear Disarmament (CUCND)

(above): A little girl at a Canadian
anti-nuclear protest, April 23, 1962.

(right): The police dragging a
protestor away at a demonstration at
the U.S. consulate, June 15, 1965.

A street protest, September 7, 1967.

formed in November 1959 and, a month later, its members held a silent vigil
at the War Memorial in Ottawa; they gathered again the following December
a few days before Christmas. Already in July of that year, forty-one university
students from Toronto, Montreal, and Ottawa, with the RCMP secretly in
attendance, had gathered in North Bay, Ontario, to picket a military base
containing Bomarc missiles, nuclear-equipped weapons designed to down
Soviet bombers.

Eventually, the CUCND presence on campuses gave way to the Student
Union for Peace Action, which established branches across the country in
1964. More importantly, it began publishing *Our Generation Against Nuclear
War*, which later in the 1960s, after shortening its name to *Our Generation*,
became a leading forum for protest that was labelled "new left" thought. It
was edited by Dimitrios Roussopoulos, who headed the CUCND in 1961,
and included contributions from university students.

Other American Cold War policies and influences inspired Canadian radicalism. One was the civil rights movement. Another of increasing
importance by the middle of the decade was American military involvement
in Southeast Asia. In November 1964, in an escalatory step, U.S. warplanes
began to bomb North Vietnam. According to opinion polls, the Canadian
public was divided on the matter. In 1966, a poll found that 35 percent of
Canadians approved of President Johnson's handling of Vietnam, while one
percent less disapproved. Others were less divided in their views. Some

within the New Democratic Party publicly criticized the United States while Canadian artists such as Neil Young and Joni Mitchell put their opposition to the war to music. Even the Canadian Broadcasting Corporation joined the chorus when "This Hour Has Seven Days" ran a program that was highly critical of American foreign policy.

More than American Cold War foreign policy inspired protest in Canada. In 1965, philosopher George Grant's *Lament for a Nation*, which played the funeral march for efforts to preserve an independent Canada, inspired many to fight back, especially against the Americanization of Canadian society.

Fuelled by growing domestic conflict in the United States and in Europe, particularly France, the level of social protest in Canada escalated in the latter half of the 1960s. For women, it was the beginning of the "second wave" of feminism, as many, especially the young and well educated, fundamentally challenged prevailing gender stereotypes throughout Canadian society. Part of the challenge was through activism involving sit-ins for better daycare facilities at the University of Toronto or public protests against the dripping-in-sexism Miss Teen B.C. Pageant. The activism took other forms. More subtly, women worked for the reproductive rights of women in a decade in which contraception and abortion remained illegal until near its end. Two women at McGill University produced and distributed thousands of copies of a brochure about birth control. Then, there were attempts at satire to gain attention, like the efforts of the Purple Penis Avengers and the Women's International Terrorist Conspiracy from Hell (WITCH).

The American Indian Movement and "Red Power" south of the border, which in turn were influenced by the U.S. civil rights movement, inspired many Native Canadians and their supporters to push for reform of the Indian Act and the alleviation of poverty on reserves. A similar pattern applied to the "Black Power" movement in the United States as, chiefly on university cam-

(above left): An anti-nuclear protest in front of a bomb shelter, August 5, 1960.

(above right): A sit-in at City Hall in Toronto.

Nuns march in support of Martin Luther King Jr. in Toronto, March 17, 1965.

Bob Dylan, 1965.

puses, expressions of Black pride and efforts at civil rights occurred. The Canadian government was particularly concerned that the tactics of the Black Panther Party would travel northward. The RCMP investigated heavily any expressions of anti-racism or so-called "Black militancy." It came to believe by the end of the decade that Black guerrilla camps had been established in southern Ontario in preparation for the launch of uprisings.

The year 1968 was key around the world. In the United States, both Martin Luther King, Jr. and Robert Kennedy were assassinated. In response to the first killing, riots — an increasingly recurrent event in the 1960s — erupted in several American cities. Then, in an event that shocked many Americans, students at Columbia University in New York City occupied the administration building and held it for several days, dipping into the liquor and cigars of the university president until the New York City police physically removed them, beating several. That occupation, part of a growing conflict on American campuses that involved the Students for a Democratic Society, had an undeniable influence in Canada. In November 1968, students at Simon Fraser University, labelled as the most "far out" university in Canada by one policeman, took control of the university administration. After a standoff, the RCMP moved in to peacefully end the occupation, arresting over one hundred students in the process.

Another university occupation, this one in February 1969 at Sir George Williams University, would end very differently. Charges of racism against a faculty member inspired protest gatherings. Then, an occupation of the computer centre ensued. It ended with a rumour that the police were on their way, a rumour that became prophecy when extensive vandalism prompted the police to be sent in for real. The entire event caused an enormous national uproar and led to open speculation as to who was behind the unrest among students.

In the Cold War, any sign of dissent inevitably led to suggestions of behind-the-scenes Communist machinations. The protest of the 1960s was no different. Throughout the decade, Canadian and American domestic intelligence services actively investigated student challengers of the status quo, and

An Ottawa civil rights march on March 14, 1965.

(above): A protestor throws a tear gas canister back at police at Kent State University in Ohio in 1970.
(below): An anti-Trudeau sign, August 15, 1969.

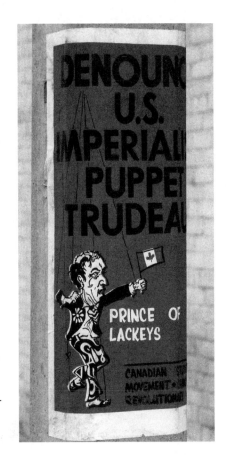

in the case of the FBI's Counter-Intelligence Program (COINTELPRO) attempted to destroy them. The authorities perceived the students as naive, misguided, and under the control of Communists who were furthering the strategic aims of the Soviet Union. The Johnson administration sought from the FBI evidence of the Communist role in campus anti-war demonstrations. J. Edgar Hoover, arch anti-Communist, was happy to comply.

The problem was that the evidence did not exist. The Central Intelligence Agency realized this in 1968 when it too explored youth protest, not only in the U.S. but also around the world. It could find no link to Communism, information that was unsatisfactory to the Nixon administration, which pushed for an even greater investigation of radicalism in search of a Communist link.

In Canada, the RCMP, which spent the 1960s spying on all forms of activism through its members, informants, and electronic surveillance, believed for most of the decade that Communist motivation was a given. That perception reflected its members' Cold War training. All of their work was geared toward dealing with Communist subversion in Canadian society. In the face of rising evidence in the middle of the 1960s that something new was afoot on campus, a diverse movement lumped together under the label of the "new left," the RCMP chose to interpret every incident of protest as Communist-inspired. Only by the end of the decade, and well after other countries had already recognized the reality, did Canadian state security come to accept that the social protest of the 1960s represented a new chapter in the Cold War era.

The Vietnam War and Vietnam War Resistors

In the 1960s, a war would appear on North American television screens for the first time. The location was Southeast Asia, specifically Vietnam but also including Cambodia and Laos, where the Cold War had once again become hot. As the decade wore on, American military intervention in what was essentially a Vietnamese civil war escalated. A particular turning point on the path to greater U.S. involvement was the August 1964 Gulf of Tonkin Resolution, named after an exaggerated clash between U.S. and North Vietnamese naval forces. In the resolution, Congress provided President Lyndon Johnson with a blank cheque with which to fight Communist North Vietnam. What followed was a rapid increase in American military presence in Southeast Asia, with 200,000 soldiers on the ground by 1965, and double that the following year.

Throughout North America, the escalation of the conflict fuelled a growth in opposition to the war, part of the general era of social protest already underway. The first teach-in on the war occurred at the University of Michigan in March 1965. Teach-ins soon followed at Canadian universities,

Paul Martin, Minister of Health and Welfare, being greeted by Vietnamese officials in Saigon during an Asian tour.

including Carleton University and the University of Manitoba. In turn, teach-ins gave way to campus marches, protests, anti-war conferences, "days of action," and sit-ins and occupations against continuing American involvement in Vietnam, and against any Canadian assistance to that effort.

Significant Canadian involvement in Vietnam actually predated that of the United States. In the early 1950s, the Canadian government (although without the knowledge of the prime minister) had shipped weapons and ammunition to Southeast Asia to aid the French in their war against Vietnamese nationalists. In 1954, France finally abandoned these efforts. A peace conference was organized and Vietnam was split into two zones with a demilitarized 17th parallel as the dividing point. Communists under Ho Chi Minh soon controlled the northern half of the entity, while in the south, Prime Minister Ngo Dinh Diem held power out of Saigon. To ensure a degree of stability, three special commissions were established to monitor compliance with ceasefires in Vietnam, Laos, and Cambodia. Three nations made up the commissions: India, Poland and Canada.

The Canadian commission members would find themselves caught up in the increasing U.S. interest in the defence of South Vietnam against a Communist guerrilla movement supported by North Vietnam. Filling the power vacuum left by the French, the Americans began contributing aid and instruction in an effort to shore up the South Vietnamese state. The Canadian element within the International Commission for Control and Supervision for Vietnam tended to accept potential American violations of pre-existing agree-

ments. Through the Canadian government, it also made a concerted effort to keep its ally informed of what it had learned through its role within the commission. In effect, Canada was an additional set of eyes for the burgeoning American juggernaut in Southeast Asia from the mid-1950s into the 1960s. The U.S. government even used a Canadian member of the commission, Blair Seaborn, as a secret errand boy to deliver messages to the North Vietnamese government.

Ironically, it would be Lester Pearson, Minister of External Affairs in the 1950s when Canada began playing its supplementary role to that of the United States in Vietnam, who would cause consternation in Washington over Vietnam while prime minister in the 1960s. At home, increasing numbers of Canadians had been demanding that their government do something about the growing war in Vietnam. One focus for demonstrations was industries with ties to the American military machine. In 1965, while speaking in the United States before an audience at Temple University, Pearson suggested that a pause in U.S. bombing of North Vietnam might be appropriate, angering the American administration, in particular President Lyndon Johnson [see chapter

Lyndon Johnson visiting US soldiers in Vietnam.

on Lester Pearson]. Ironically, the "Pentagon Papers" later revealed that at a secret meeting in May 1964, several months before the bombing campaign began, Pearson had given his approval to Johnson for a limited bombing campaign, with his only concern being the potential use of nuclear weapons.

Before long, Canadians would see their nation more directly affected by the impact of the war. Young American males, often accompanied by their wives and children, began to journey northward in increasing numbers as a means of avoiding being drafted into military service in Vietnam or to avoid retribution for having deserted the armed forces. Several organizations designed to assist the Americans formed, including the Toronto Anti-Draft Programme, which created and widely distributed a pamphlet to aid the war resistors. Many of those who came paid a heavy personal price. Marriages ended under the strain of exile, and children grew up separated from their grandparents.

Lester Pearson at a Liberal Party dinner, February 8, 1968.

Between 1965 and 1974, anywhere from 50,000 to 125,000 war resistors made the passage, numbers too significant to be ignored by either Canadians or their government. Despite (or maybe because of) the fact that an estimated 90 percent of those who came had some university education, a majority of citizens told pollsters that they should not be allowed into Canada. Because of their backgrounds, many of the newcomers took jobs along with other Americans at Canada's universities, which were rapidly expanding to handle the incoming baby boomers. In turn, this Americanization of Canadian universities inspired efforts at Canadianizing those same institutions.

The migration was not entirely one way. As many as 40,000 Canadians fought in Vietnam on behalf of the United States. Close to one hundred lost their lives in the process. Those who made it back found themselves in an even more difficult situation than American veterans since no support would be forthcoming from Ottawa, while getting help from Washington was virtually impossible.

The Canadian government responded contradictorily to the American influx. While seeking to avoid angering its neighbour, the government did not

American servicemen carrying their wounded off the battlefield in Vietnam.

find the entrance of the well educated objectionable, even though it did nothing to make the process easier. In 1968, it reminded border personnel that they had the discretion to bar the entrance of suspected military deserters.

Behind the scenes, the Royal Canadian Mounted Police took immediate interest in the war resisters, and also the individuals and organizations who assisted them, especially those already considered to be involved in social protest. In September 1969, for example, the RCMP in Toronto compiled a list of Americans active in southern Ontario who, because of their positions, the police suggested, "may be of influence." Selfishness only partially motivated the investigations. The RCMP supplied some of the information that it collected to the Central Intelligence Agency and the Federal Bureau of Investigation, both of which maintained a strong interest in the anti-war activities of American citizens.

The matter ultimately ended legally in January 1977, after the war itself had already concluded, when one day after being inaugurated as president, Jimmy Carter announced an amnesty for draft resisters and for those who had never registered. As for those who had deserted from the American military, Carter promised that their cases would be handled fairly on an individual basis. Despite these reassurances, for many Americans who had now established lives in their new country, there was no longer any question of going home.

Cold War Brainwashing: The CIA and the Allan Memorial Institute

The Allan Memorial Institute in Montreal.

D r. Ewen Cameron's name on page sixteen of the *New York Times* caught Canada's attention. In 1977, the newspaper revealed that at the height of the Cold War, the Central Intelligence Agency had secretly funded research into mind control. It was one part of a general CIA campaign that included extensive (and secret) financing for cultural and youth groups, collectively rationalized as an effort to remain one step ahead of the United States' Communist adversaries. Speculation that some American soldiers taken prisoner in the Korean War had experienced mind manipulation only heightened interest in comparable research.

The official opening of the Allan Memorial Institute, from left: G. Blair Gordon, Hospital President, Hon. Paul Martin, Minister of National Health and Welfare, Dr. Jean Gregoire, Deputy Minister for Quebec, and Dr. D. Ewen Cameron, Director.

Beginning in 1953 under the code name MKULTRA, the CIA funnelled hundreds of thousands of dollars in research assistance through a front organization, the Society for the Investigation of Human Ecology. The money was destined for those delving into topics of particular interest to American intelligence, including mind control or, in a term in vogue in the 1950s and 1960s, brainwashing.

The appearance of Cameron's name on the list of those receiving CIA funding quickly drew Canadian attention. The psychiatrist had conducted his research at the Allan Memorial Institute, on the campus of McGill University in Montreal. From there he had published widely, earning the respect of colleagues who elected him president of the American Psychiatric Association in 1953. A Scot by birth, roots that his accent betrayed, Cameron already received funding from the Canadian government. In the 1950s he successfully applied for a grant from the CIA front, and received $54,000 between 1957 and 1960. Evidence that he was aware of the original source of the funds does not exist, nor does it seem likely that he would have been aware, based on the CIA's perpetual desire for concealment. This desire for secrecy was heightened by the knowledge that the funding violated rules established between Canada and the United States, whereby government cross-border funding for research had to go through official channels.

What does exist is evidence of what Cameron did in his experiments. He made no secret of his approach to psychiatric work either in his scholarship or in his grant proposals. Indeed, it was the latter that drew the interest of the CIA. The McGill doctor intended to experiment on human subjects using sensory deprivation, sleep therapy, electroshock, LSD, and curare, all in an effort to break down minds and, once that was accomplished, implant new ideas. On the receiving end of his work were people who came to the doctor for help, such as a woman with postpartum depression, and another who had suffered a mental breakdown. In 1957 and 1958, he treated fifty-three patients with his de-programming techniques. Particularly brutal aspects of the treatment, such as the frequent resort to electric shock, occurred in "sleep rooms" that terrified his patients at the Allan Institute. Many of those who had sought help left with new wounds to heal.

In 1964, Cameron suddenly entered retirement. His clandestine benefactor had already ended its support due to a lack of results, and the doctor himself admitted failure. Three years later, he dropped dead after scaling a mountain. Nonetheless, the destructive nature

Dr. Ewen Cameron.

of his work lived on after him. With the revelations of his link to the CIA, victims of his research began to come forward. In 1980, Velma Orlikow, a victim and the wife of a Canadian Member of Parliament, launched a lawsuit against the CIA; eight other victims later joined her. Noises emanated out of Washington about an official apology, but the fear of litigation blocked any admittance of guilt. Assembling a case against the CIA proved difficult, in part because pertinent papers had gone to the paper shredder in the early 1970s. Wherever possible, the CIA blocked access to any remaining germane records on the grounds of protecting national security. In the end, nonetheless, the victims gained a measure of justice. Just before the trial in 1988, the CIA settled out of court, paying $750,000 in damages. In 1994, the Canadian government coughed up $7 million more in compensation. Money, however, could not soothe the pain of those victimized in the pursuit of Cold War supremacy.

Quebec's Quiet and Unquiet Revolutions

René Lévesque in Toronto, February 6, 1969.

In the early 1960s, the Cuban Missile Crisis, the Bomarc missile crisis, and the gathering storm in Vietnam continued to focus Canadians' attention on the Cold War. But in Quebec, cataclysmic events were taking place that would ultimately undermine the Cold War consensus that had gripped Canadian society since the late 1940s.

In 1959, the death of Quebec Premier Maurice Duplessis signalled the breaking of a log jam in Quebec society, culture, and politics. In 1960, the Quebec Liberals under Jean Lesage displaced Duplessis' conservative and corrupt Union Nationale in a provincial election. More than just a change of party, this unleashed profound changes, including the rapid modernization of Quebec. This soon became known as the Quiet Revolution, encompassing the secularization of what had been a church-dominated Catholic society, the emergence of an aggressive Quebec state, and the strong assertion of a powerful new nationalist consciousness. There were challenges to federal jurisdiction, demands for constitutional change, and an

French President Charles de Gaulle during his visit to Quebec, August 8, 1967.

insistent questioning of the basis of national unity, all of which deeply unsettled Canadians outside Quebec.

The Quiet Revolution undermined the Cold War consensus. The new thinking in Quebec quickly left behind the conservative Catholic anti-Communism of an earlier generation. In the late 1940s, the isolationist sentiment that had been so strong in Quebec during the war had been effectively set aside by a Cold War crusade that emphasized an anti-Communism with a strong appeal to the Catholic Church and conservative nationalists of the era. By the 1960s, anti-Communism had lost its grip, and Quebecers shifted to being among the most critical of American brinksmanship and the most supportive of moves toward nuclear disarmament.

Soon the Quiet Revolution turned distinctly unquiet. The demands of the Lesage government to become *maîtres chez nous* (masters in our own house) were paralleled by a separatist movement that wanted out of Canada altogether. The separatists tended to go two ways: into a democratic party, the Parti Québécois (PQ), and into a violent, terrorist wing. In 1963, bombs began going off in Quebec, set by a group that called itself the Front de libération du Québec (FLQ). There were police sweeps, arrests, and "political prisoners." In the late 1960s, the violence grew in scope, culminating in October 1970 when the FLQ abducted the British trade commissioner, James Cross, and abducted and later murdered the Quebec Minister of Labour,

Montreal mayor Jean Drapeau with French president Charles de Gaulle prior to his "Vive le Québec libre!" speech in 1967.

René Lévesque, May, 1963.

Pierre Laporte. An FLQ manifesto called for a Quebec that would not only be independent, but revolutionary socialist. The federal government, under a Quebecer, Pierre Elliott Trudeau, answered by invoking the draconian powers of the War Measures Act, citing an alleged and never proven "apprehended insurrection," detaining suspects without charges, legal counsel or habeas corpus, censoring the media, and sending the army into the streets of Montreal.

These traumatic events directly challenged the Cold War consensus. For years it had been conventional wisdom that threats to the security of Canada came from outside, from the Soviet bloc and from the Communists, who were merely the tools of Moscow. In 1970, Canada faced its worst security crisis ever, but it did not come from Moscow, or from anywhere else outside Canada. It arose out of a homegrown problem: the willingness of at least a few militant separatists in Quebec to challenge the Canadian state through bombing, kidnapping, and assassination.

The impact was particularly severe on the RCMP security service, Canada's front line of Cold War defence against Communism. When the Trudeau government was later taxed for overreacting to the FLQ crisis with the War Measures Act, there was a tendency on the part of government Ministers to deflect blame onto the RCMP. The Mounties were, it was alleged, an Anglo organization that had shown little understanding of Francophone Quebec, and had been so fixated on Communism that it had largely missed, or misunderstood, the domestic threat of violent separatism. Faced with the gravity of the crisis in 1970, and lacking good intelligence on the FLQ (so the argument went), the federal government had little choice but to invoke extreme emergency powers, round up all the usual suspects, and sort them out later. It was a seductive argument that let the Trudeau government off the hook. The only problem was that it wasn't really true.

At first, in the early 1960s, the Mounties did react to the emergence of the FLQ with Cold War reflexes. The new Quebec terrorists, they reasoned, were likely just a new front for the Communists, and Moscow. They soon abandoned this stereotyped analysis, however, and, by the late 1960s, were producing relatively good intelligence on the various Quebec separatist fac-

Lévesque speaking during the 1976 election.

tions, based on their own sources inside the groups. By the 1970 crisis, they had solid information on the identities of the FLQ militants, and indeed knew who had kidnapped Cross and Laporte. They were engaged in the careful, methodical police work necessary to locate where the hostages were being held. Then the Trudeau government decided on more dramatic measures, without asking for the RCMP's advice.

The consequences of the October Crisis were even more serious than the crisis itself. The Trudeau government was thoroughly alarmed at the apparent enormity of the threat posed by separatist terrorism. The RCMP were given new marching orders in the 1970s. Soviet Communism was no longer the main perceived internal menace, although the Soviet external threat did continue right up to the end of the Cold War in 1989–90. Ottawa had now determined that the most pressing threat to security came from Quebec separatism, and believed that the very foundations of the country were at stake.

The RCMP were given more or less a blank cheque to "counter" separatists by any and all means available, legal or illegal. Cabinet Ministers did not want to know the details, leaving themselves "plausible deniability," but they insisted upon results. Predictably, as is the case when police are given this degree of latitude, operations were neither restrained nor genteel. A police rampage ensued across Quebec, with break-ins, thefts, barn burnings, intimidation, agents provocateurs, dirty tricks, unauthorized mail opening, and a general disregard for civil liberties. And these methods did get results. The terrorist wing of separatism was broken, apparently definitively.

If the government was pleased with the results, they were not at all pleased when the cowboy cop methods became public scandals in the late 1970s. One by one, police scandals burst into the media. By 1976, the PQ had won office in Quebec under René Lévesque, and the PQ leaders were deeply suspicious that their federalist arch-rivals in the Trudeau Liberal government were using the RCMP to counter not just the FLQ (for whom they had no more use than the Liberals) but the PQ itself.

A Quebec nationalist.

Canadian troops on patrol during the October Crisis of 1970.

There is some truth in this, in that few distinctions were in fact drawn between lawful and unlawful separatists as subjects of surveillance. The PQ had been watched very closely by the Mounties from its inception. Indeed, what was not known publicly at the time of the first PQ government and the first referendum on sovereignty in 1980, was that the number two man in the PQ, the Minister of Intergovernmental Affairs and the architect of the PQ referendum strategy, Claude Morin, was and had been for some time a paid informant for the RCMP security service. So much for the idea that the RCMP had a tenuous reach into Francophone Quebec: the only figure of greater importance for the PQ government than Morin was René Lévesque himself.

On the other hand, the PQ respected democratic process, submitting both itself and its sovereignty project to the ratification of the voters. The Trudeau government in fact responded to the threat to national unity posed by the PQ quite differently than it did to the threat to national security posed by the FLQ. The latter it crushed by secret police action; the former it fought in public using the methods of democratic debate.

Nonetheless, the RCMP scandals in Quebec had serious effects on the legitimacy of the Mounties, and the federal government itself. The PQ government called a commission of inquiry to investigate illegal excesses of the police, both federal and provincial. The federal government was finally compelled to call its own commission, the McDonald Commission, to inquire into "certain activities of the RCMP." This was partly to pre-empt the Quebec inquiry (on the advice of senior RCMP brass). It was also to calm opinion in the rest of Canada — the RCMP had not confined its tactics to Quebec alone, but had gone after the "new left" outside Quebec as well. The McDonald Commission tiptoed gingerly around the question of ministerial responsibility, but it pulled few punches when it came to taking on RCMP wrongdoing. The commission's three weighty and very detailed volumes in 1981 represent a landmark in the public scrutiny of the secret state in Canada. Its recommendations were a turning point in public policy with regard to the control and accountability of the security service.

McDonald recommended the "civilianization" of the security service — that is, its removal from the RCMP, and the creation of a civilian, non-police agency with a clear legislative mandate from Parliament and institutionalized forms of accountability, review, and oversight. This was not the first time that the RCMP had been threatened with having the security service removed from its jurisdiction. In 1969, an earlier Royal Commission (Mackenzie) had called for a civilian agency to replace the Mounties in performing security and intelligence work. The Mackenzie Commission, however, reported in a Cold War context in which the security threat was seen as coming entirely from Communism. Its recommendations had little impact on the public, and the RCMP were able to easily weather the storm. This time they could not, and indeed the RCMP brass had decided that getting out of such a contentious area was probably in the best interests of the force. The decisive difference was that, while the political policing of an unpopular and marginal group such as the Communists did no harm and much good for the Mounties' image, the same could not be said for the controversial matter of the political policing of Quebec and of more mainstream protest movements. Separatism was not popular in the rest of Canada, but everyone could understand that, when legitimate democratic political parties such as the PQ could fall under the intrusive scrutiny of the secret police, the liberties of all Canadians were at some risk.

A Quebec nationalist demonstration during DeGaulle's visit, 1967.

In 1984, the Canadian Security Intelligence Service Act created the Canadian Security Intelligence Service as a civilian security intelligence agency with a mandate that states what it is empowered to do and what it is not to do. CSIS now states that it does not spy on parliamentary sovereignist parties such as the PQ and the Bloc Québécois, since they represent "lawful advocacy, protest, and dissent," which CSIS is specifically prohibited from investigating. Under the Progressive Conservative government of Brian Mulroney in the later 1980s, the War Measures Act was repealed and replaced by a new emergency powers act that is much more measured and proportional in its grant of extraordinary powers to meet emergencies.

The liberalization of security policy that finally resulted from the Mounties' ill-fated intervention in Quebec in the 1970s also had implications for Canada's Cold War. Even when a renewed Cold War was being promoted by the U.S. Reagan administration in the early and mid-1980s, there was no real renewal of the tough policing of the Communists and the left that had characterized North America in the early Cold War years of the 1940s and 1950s. When the McDonald Commission reported that the RCMP security service had amassed secret files on 800,000 individuals and organizations, there was general revulsion concerning the implications for liberal democracy. In 1986, the government ordered CSIS to shut down its Counter-Subversion branch, which it had inherited from the RCMP, get rid of its voluminous "subversive" files, and concentrate on terrorism and espionage as genuine (as opposed to ersatz), threats to the security of Canadians.

PART FOUR

The 1970s

The crew of the Soyuz 10 spacecraft, April 25, 1971.

The "Me decade" occupied a unique position in the Cold War era. It served as a period of brief respite between the tensions of the 1950s and 1960s and the increased confrontation that marked the first half of the 1980s. Rapprochement or, in the phraseology of the day, détente, was in.

Canada, in particular its prime minister, Pierre Trudeau, played a small but significant part in the defrosting of Communist-capitalist relations. Ahead of Washington, Ottawa made an effort to reach out to the Communists in Beijing, alienated from Moscow since the early 1960s. In October 1970, an agreement was reached on the official recognition of Communist China as the real China. The United States would eventually follow Canada's diplomatic lead. Where Washington feared to tread was in any diminution of its hatred for the Cuba of Fidel Castro. Again, it was Pierre Trudeau who symbolically thumbed his nose at the Cold Warriors in Washington when he visited the island and warmly embraced Fidel in 1976.

The warming trend extended to the relationship between the main protagonists. In 1972, a few more months before he would easily win re-election, Richard Nixon met Leonid Brezhnev in Moscow to sign a major arms control agreement. The sequel to the Strategic Arms Limitation Treaty (SALT) would be finalized during the Carter administration. The Vietnam War finally ended as well, after Nixon inflicted yet more misery on Southeast Asia before extracting American troops. Without American forces to bolster their side, South Vietnam proved to be easy pickings for the North, which captured Saigon in 1975, ending the conflagration and unifying the country in name but not necessarily in spirit. For many on both sides of the conflict, the war remained a controversial and painful event.

If Canada cheered the end of the violence in Southeast Asia, it was but half-hearted. The international scene, Trudeau's various foreign escapades, and even Canada's hockey triumph over the Soviet Union in 1972 (an event laden with Cold War symbolism) had failed to distract Canadians from problems on the home front. Tensions building in the 1960s erupted in October 1970 with the kidnapping of British diplomat James Cross by members of the Front de libération du Quebec (FLQ). A different FLQ cell then snatched Pierre Laporte, the Quebec Minister of Labour. The Trudeau government quickly invoked the War Measures Act, emergency legislation designed, as its name suggests, for wartime. Over four hundred people were arrested, many without being charged. Those holding Laporte promptly murdered him while Cross was eventually freed unharmed. Although damaged, the cause of Quebec nationalism remained vibrant. In 1976, the separatist Parti Québecois won the provincial election.

The anxiety of the period, however, would linger on during subsequent years as the federal government pressured the Royal Canadian Mounted Police security service into taking a more aggressive stance in Quebec. Several notorious incidents of RCMP wrongdoing subsequently ensued, including the infamous burning of a barn, and which led to public and media investigations into the actions of the police. The controversy would eventually lead to the elimination of the RCMP security service and the creation in 1984 of the

Canadian Security Intelligence Service.

Internal security agencies and the federal government geared up for extensive protest in the 1970s. Instead, there was a noticeable decline in the type of discontent that marked the previous decade. One factor in the shift, and an issue that plagued the Trudeau Liberals, was a major economic downturn in the early 1970s that left many with a sense of financial insecurity. Between 1971 and 1974, the rate of inflation more than tripled. Government red ink grew nearly as quickly. A $300 million budgetary surplus in 1970 had turned into a $5 billion deficit by 1976. The government responded with dramatic measures, in particular the introduction of wage and price controls.

Despite the reduction in Cold War tensions in the 1970s, they did not really disappear. By the end of the decade, signs abounded that the superpower grievances of old would soon re-emerge. In July 1979, the Sandinista guerrillas, after decades of struggle, finally toppled the Somoza family dynasty in Nicaragua. The new leaders of Nicaragua occupied the left side of the political spectrum, and this topic would dominate discussions in the centres of power in Washington by the early 1980s. Two days after Christmas in 1979, Soviet troops invaded Afghanistan in an attempt to quell growing instability in the nation. This volatility was directly encouraged by covert American funding in an effort to inflict a Vietnam-style problem on the Soviets. The final showdown in the Cold War was about to commence.

The Cold War and Ukrainian Canadians

A Ukrainian anti-Soviet protest in Canada during the 1960s.

The Cold War had particular meaning for Ukrainian Canadians. Ukrainians had first arrived in Canada in the nineteenth century. Experiencing considerable nativist sentiment from the dominant Anglo-Celtic society, the immigrants from Eastern Europe worked hard to maintain their distinctive identity. Many of those who arrived before the First World War were politically active, often on the radical left — a reflection of the nature of Russian society at the time. Along with other Eastern European activists, a small number became a dynamic and dominant force in the Communist Party of Canada through direct participation and the formation of organizations such as the Ukrainian Labour-Farmer Temple Association. Immigrants who arrived in the 1920s after the Bolshevik Revolution in Russia tended to have different politics, especially since elements had been involved in a failed effort to resist Soviet domination in a brief period of Ukrainian independence at the end of the First World War. In 1932, some of these Ukrainian nationalists created the Ukrainian National Federation, a preview of the Ukrainian Canadian Committee (UCC) that was created in 1940.

A Ukrainian celebration at the Canadian National Exhibition in Toronto in the late 1960s.

Ukrainian art at Casa Loma in Toronto, 1969.

The same was true for the approximately 32,000 Ukrainian immigrants who arrived, often as Displaced Persons (or DPs for short, a reference that quickly became derogatory) after the Second World War. Many opposed Communism and Stalinism, and some of those allowed in, in the face of opposition from other Ukrainians and Canada's Jewish community, had taken up arms on the side of the Nazis. Then, there was the pressure on the newcomers from the outside, as the federal government, social workers, and various other do-gooders such as the Imperial Order Daughters of the Empire collectively did their best to encourage rapid assimilation to the Anglo-Canadian norm, including conforming to traditional family and gender stereotypes. Each conversion to Canadianism represented by definition a victory in the perpetual struggle with the Soviet Union, while the state viewed with suspicion those who resisted.

Then there were the problems within. Although in theory a single "community," tremendous tension existed within this collective. The Cold War newcomers who had left the Stalinist Soviet Union had little tolerance for those Ukrainians who espoused Communism in Canada. An undercurrent of anti-Semitism appeared in some of the anti-Communist rhetoric. The resentment included threats against those on the radical left, the violent disruption of an Association of United Ukrainian Canadians' meeting (the new name for the Ukrainian Labour-Farmer Temple Association after November 1946), and the bombing of a Communist bookstore.

In the politics of the Cold War, however, those on the political left were automatically viewed with suspicion by the state and remained on the margins in terms of influence. More acceptable in the context of the post-1945 era were Ukrainian nationalists whose primary goal involved the liberation of Ukraine from Communism and the Soviet empire. The Canadian League for the Liberation of Ukraine had been created in the early Cold War for that very purpose. It and other nationalist organizations would later join the Ukrainian Canadian Committee, which became a central representative organization for those not on the left. In 1967, the UCC helped to form the World Congress of Free Ukrainians, an association of Ukrainians residing around the world.

A Ukrainian woman worshipping, 1967.

When it came to influencing Canadian foreign policy, however, the Ukrainian-Canadian nationalists could only look on in envy at the power of the Florida Cubans. As far back as 1919, a Ukrainian-Canadian organization had unsuccessfully lobbied the Canadian government to recognize the briefly sovereign Ukraine. Subsequently, Canadian governments repeatedly avoided advocating an independent Ukraine, since it represented both major implications for relations with the Soviet Union and an apparent impediment to the rapid assimilation of Ukrainian-Canadians. The federal government was certainly not soft on Communism. It took a more confrontational line when it came to Eastern European nations in the Soviet bloc. For example, there was the case of Hungary. Over 50,000 Hungarian immigrants had come to Canada in the first fifteen years of the Cold War, most arriving after the Soviet Union crushed an ill-fated revolution in 1956. Hungarian-Canadians displayed many of the same divisions as did the Ukrainians, yet the federal government, perhaps because the Hungarian uprising had occurred during the height of the Cold War, seemed less hesitant to advocate with the Soviets on their behalf.

Even the government of Prime Minister John Diefenbaker, that featured Canada's first Ukrainian-Canadian Cabinet Minister and relied on support from provinces with substantial Ukrainian-Canadian populations, failed to move beyond symbolism. In 1960, Diefenbaker taunted the Soviet Union before the United Nations General Assembly, focusing in particular on the continued Soviet control over Ukraine; he challenged Nikita Khrushchev to allow free elections. Yet nothing changed when it came to the official Canadian policy or recognizing Ukraine as a Soviet republic. Influence over Canadian foreign policy waned even further with the government of Pierre Trudeau. In a move that angered many Ukrainian-Canadians, Trudeau, while in Kiev on a May 1971 tour of the Soviet Union and with the recent October Crisis looming in the back of his mind, expressed a lack of sympathy for any person who violated the law "in order to assert his nationalism." Little would change until after the fall of the Soviet Union and the end of the Cold War, when both the Canadian government and Ukrainian-Canadians enthusiastically sought to foster ties with a newly independent Ukraine.

Alexei Kosygin's Stroll across Parliament Hill

E ven by the occasionally crazed standards of the Cold War, it was a strange and memorable encounter. After visiting the Soviet Union, Pierre Trudeau had invited Soviet Premier Alexei Kosygin, Nikita Khrushchev's successor in 1964, to make a return trip to Canada. In October 1971, the Soviet politician did so. Among the topics of discussion for the two leaders was the possibility of a series of hockey games between the best of both nations. Overall, the meeting was part of a series of steps designed to defuse Cold War tensions between the superpowers.

Of equal importance to many Canadians was the Soviet treatment of Ukrainian dissidents at home. Outcry had erupted after Trudeau had not raised the issue of human rights during his visit to the Soviet Union. When questioned about this neglect, the always controversial Canadian offered the

A Canadian delegation meeting with Kosygin at the Kremlin, 1966.

experience of the arrest of Front de Libération du Québec (FLQ) members and others in October 1970: "I didn't feel like bringing up any case which would have caused Mr. Kosygin or Mr. Brezhnev to say, 'Why should you put your revolutionaries in jail, and we not put ours?'"

Such comments further inflamed certain segments of the Canadian populace. Those with ties to Eastern Europe and ethnic minorities within the Soviet Union had witnessed the widespread suppression of rights by the Soviets. On October 18, 1971, one man decided to express his displeasure with the Soviet system in a new way.

It was a fine fall Ottawa kind of day. Trudeau and Kosygin were together at Parliament Hill for further meetings when they decided to enjoy the attractive weather first-hand by strolling the short distance across the lawn of Parliament Hill without the aid of the proverbial black limousines. The last-minute change of plans came as a surprise to the accompanying security detachment, which trailed along with Trudeau, his guest, and several reporters.

The Communist-capitalist procession quickly met a critic. "Russian pig, go home!" shouted Geza Matrai, a young Hungarian nationalist and immigrant to Canada. Then, to the amazement of onlookers, including the Royal Canadian Mounted Police and Soviet bodyguards, he vaulted onto the back of the Soviet premier. Kosygin, his arms entangled within his suit jacket, reacted with fear as Matrai attempted to drag him to the ground. Like a referee intervening in a hockey fight, Canada's prime minister moved to hold back the attacker long enough for some burly Mounties to slap on the handcuffs and haul him off.

Trudeau, in a bit of an understatement, described security as a "little lax," and an embarrassed Canadian government apologized to Kosygin. In January 1972, a court sentenced Matrai to three months in jail for the assault. A few months after that, Canadians would enthusiastically cheer even worse assaults on Soviets during the 1972 Summit Series for world hockey supremacy.

Cold War Hockey

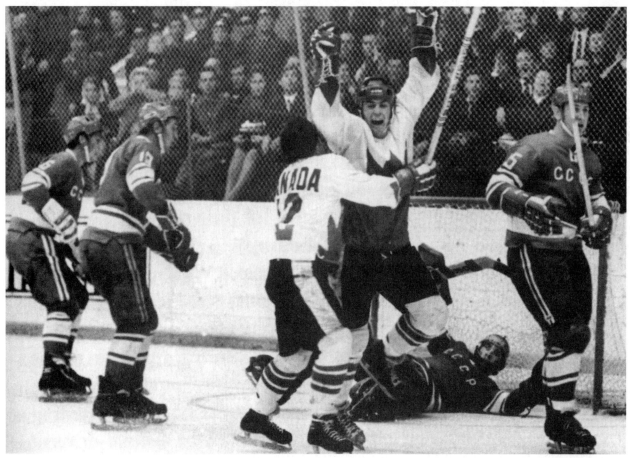

Paul Henderson scoring the famous goal that won the Canada-Russia hockey series in 1972.

It is one of the most famous images in Canadian history: Paul Henderson with his arms outstretched, surrounded by joyous teammates as they celebrated the winning goal in the remarkable 1972 hockey series between Canada and the Soviet Union. It is also an image of the Cold War, although not always interpreted as such, perhaps because Canada was more of a deputy to the American sheriff in the battle with the evil Soviet Union. The iconic American hockey moment versus the Soviets would come eight years later at the Winter Olympics in Lake Placid, New York, as the goaltender of the gold-medal-winning American hockey team draped himself in the stars and stripes.

For Canada it was 1972, and an eight-game hockey series with the Soviet Union that featured the best players in the world and led to unprecedented contact between the two Cold War adversaries. Organizing a hockey series between the two nations was no easy task, especially since the Soviet Union by definition did not have professional athletes and expressed a reluctance to face the professional stars of the National Hockey League.

The suspicions of the Cold War also mitigated against such contacts. Open hostility and suspicion characterized superpower relations into the 1960s. In such an atmosphere, triumphs were measured through the symbolic. Defections, for example, were a possibility whenever Communist athletes and artists travelled abroad, and any such episode caused hardship for the Soviet government in its propaganda efforts. Defeat in any head-to-head athletic competition, as well, would be interpreted as demonstrating the shortcomings of either the capitalist or Communist system, a factor of which the players involved were well aware.

A Russian delegation visiting Maple Leaf Gardens in 1956.

In turn, concern existed in the shadows of the intelligence world that the teams, specifically the entourages that accompanied them to the tournaments, could be used as cover for espionage efforts. Alexander Gresko, a Soviet official involved in planning the tournament and who accompanied the team in Canada, had previously been forced out of the United Kingdom after being accused of being a member of the KGB. In Canada, members of Canada's intelligence service, the Royal Canadian Mounted Police security service, closely monitored the Soviet team and those who accompanied it.

In general terms, a different phase of the Cold War, underway by the end of the 1960s, made the Canada-Russia series possible. Détente, as exemplified by the arms-control treaties between U.S. President Richard Nixon and Soviet Chairman Leonid Brezhnev, demonstrated that the chief protagonists could work together.

The year 1972 represented a beginning, but not in the sense of Canadian athletes competing against their Soviet counterparts. At an amateur level this had already occurred, although Canadian losses were shrugged off as the result of the Soviet best against inferior Canadian talent. The difference in 1972 was that Canada's best (widely viewed, especially in their home country, as the best in the world) would face, in the phrase of one writer, the "Red Machine." Moreover, it did not involve, the nation's greatest tiddlywink players, but the very masters of the sport that Canada treasured. In this context the series could not fail to be memorable.

The genesis of that magic dated from 1969 when the idea of a series between the top players of the two countries was first proposed and discussions began involving Alan Eagleson, the head of the National Hockey Players' Association, and representatives of the Soviet Ice Hockey

Federation. Difficult negotiations ensued, made more thorny by mutual suspicions. Even politicians sought to play a role. Prime Minister Pierre Trudeau's 1971 discussions with Soviet premier Alexei Kosygin involved mention of a hockey series as the Canadian government sought a better relationship with the Soviet Union in a time of détente, and a more sportsmanlike image in general abroad (Canadian hockey players were notorious in Europe for their "goon" tactics). Eventually, an eight-game format was agreed upon, with the first four games being played in four different Canadian cities, and the final four in Moscow.

The highly anticipated series (broadcasting rights went for $750,000 and over half of Canada's population watched some of the games) began in Montreal on September 2, 1972, the day after Trudeau announced the Liberal Party's election campaign. The anticipation in Canada was based on the widely held assumption that the home side players would clean the ice with their Communist opponents. Many media pundits predicted eight straight victories for the Maple Leaf-clad players. Only one was so bold as to suggest that it might be the other side that walked over the Canadians.

Overconfidence competed with stereotypes in the media build-up to September 2. The Soviet players, traditionally portrayed as "machines," now took on the appearance of "robots" with their methodical, relentless, and apparently unemotional approach to the game, characteristics that mirrored in Western minds the Communist approach to the world outside of sports. The helmets, not widely in use in Canada, which topped every single Soviet head, only contributed to the robotic reputation. A Canadian distiller ran an advertisement for its "capitalist vodka," adding, "If they can play hockey, we can make vodka." Even some of the Canadian players interpreted what was to follow as more of a battle between political systems than hockey teams. The Soviet invasion of Czechoslovakia in 1968 also directly affected the series. A Czech immigrant to Canada who had lost his automobile to a tank during the invasion had a judge award him the Soviet team's equipment for nonpayment of an award assessed when he sought damages for his car. To save the hockey

equipment and the series, Canadian organizers had to cough up the money.

The tension, anticipation, and excitement that preceded the series made the results of the first game even more shocking for Canadians. After scoring the first two goals of the game, Canada's professional stars found themselves under sustained Soviet playmaking that resulted in four straight pucks shot behind the goalie. After a Canadian score in reply, the team representing Communism finished the game with three more goals. Foster Hewitt, the legendary broad-

Pierre Trudeau receiving a Team Canada hockey jersey after Canada's 1972 series victory.

caster, repeatedly announced the final score of 7-3 for the Soviets so that there would be no doubt. A backlash across Canada quickly ensued as explanations were sought and blame attributed for what had occurred. Popular opinion deemed the Canadian players to have been overconfident while another segment wondered if, in reality, Canadian hockey was simply overrated. Tass, the official Soviet news agency, observed simply that "the myth of the invincibility of the best Canadian professional players is no more."

What was widely interpreted as a national disaster only increased the pressure on the Canadian players for game two in Toronto. The result reassured many, even some of the naysayers. Canada won the September 4 game 4-1 before an enthusiastic crowd, and at last, the media had a result over which to triumph. Two days later in Winnipeg, a similar result appeared in the making as Canada took a 3-1 lead into the third period and then held a 4-2 lead with just over six minutes to play. The Soviets, however, demonstrated that they would not roll over, striking back with two goals, including one with just over a minute left in the game, to tie Canada 4-4. With inflated expectations of Canadian success, a tie was as good as a loss, and a wave of media speculation about what was going wrong in a series that was now a best of five began anew.

On September 8, Vancouver hosted the final Canadian game of the series. The Soviets led 2-0 after the first period; 4-1 after the second, and held on to win 5-3. The frustration, even perhaps the sense of betrayal and humiliation that Canadian fans felt over another unexpected loss, emerged within the Vancouver arena: the fans booed the home side and some even tossed in equal measures garbage and obscenities at their departing heroes. Phil Esposito, one of Team Canada's more prominent players, made an impassioned plea after the game for Canadians to get behind the team as it faced having to win three out of four games in Moscow in order to capture the series.

As the scene shifted to the heartland of communism, the Cold War rhetoric escalated. It had an impact on the Canadian players and fans who journeyed by plane to Moscow. Once in the Soviet Union, the Canadian athletes needed little encouragement to see a KGB member behind every

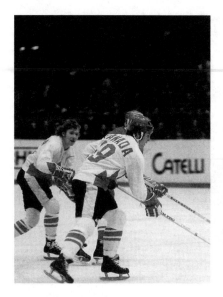

lamppost. An intercom system in each player's hotel room crackled mysteriously in the night and the telephone would ring with no one at the other end when it was lifted off the receiver. Then there were the bugs—hidden microphones, that is, not the real bugs that scurried under some beds —that several players fervently assumed lay concealed in their rooms. Wayne Cashman viewed his room's mirror as the likely hiding place, leading him to remove it, and forcing his wife to apply her makeup in another room. The most famous, and perhaps apocryphal, story is that of Frank Mahovlich frantically searching his Moscow hotel room for a microphone. At last he discovered a device hidden under the carpet on the floor and he invited a teammate to aid him in unscrewing it. Their efforts were rewarded with a loud bang from below as the chandelier that had just been released crashed to the floor.

The first game in Moscow initially offered new hope to Canada. With Brezhnev and Kosygin looking on in their perpetual grim-faced manner, the team wearing the Maple Leaf sweaters rallied and led 3-0 entering the third period when disaster struck. The Soviets scored five goals, including the last four of the game, to win 5-4. Team Canada had reached the point of no return. To win the series they were now required to win the final three games, all on the other team's home ice. A 3-2 win on September 24 began the climb. In its aftermath, fifty thousand Canadians dispatched telegrams of encouragement to the team. Game seven proved more difficult as Paul Henderson scored the winner in a 4-3 victory with just over two minutes remaining.

This left the final game to decide the winner of the already fabled series. As it was broadcast back to Canada in the morning and afternoon, viewing required huddling around televisions and radios in schools and workplaces from coast to coast to coast. A game that entered the second period as a tie quickly shifted in favour of the Soviets who led 5-3 as the final twenty minutes began. Canada scored quickly to the joy of two thousand Canadians in attendance and millions more back home. Ten minutes later, Yvan Cournoyer tied the game. Canada now pressed the Soviets relentlessly. With thirty-four seconds remaining, Paul Henderson picked the puck up off his own rebound and slid it past Vladislav Tretiak for the most famous goal in Canadian hockey history. In the words of one sportswriter, "Team Canada conquered Moscow."

Pierre Trudeau and ten thousand Canadians, many waving flags, greeted the conquering Cold War heroes at Montreal's Dorval airport. Phil Esposito kissed the ground as he embarked from the plane and all joined in an enthusiastic version of "O Canada." A few days later, eighty thousand people gathered in rainy conditions to cheer on the victors in Toronto. In a matter of weeks, the players had journeyed from being heroes to being figures of derision, and then back to being heroes, all of the waves magnified by the Cold War atmosphere and accompanying nationalism.

The 1972 series marked the beginning of a new era of hockey competition that would involve the best players of other nations performing against each other on a regular basis. It would end, in the aftermath of the Cold War, with a multinational National Hockey League that included players born in the old Soviet Union.

Cuba and China: Canada's Cold War Foreign Policy Balancing Act

Generally, Canada's Cold War foreign policy positions were thoroughly attached to those of the United States like a child connected to his or her mother by a short leash. Nonetheless, and perhaps in an effort to reassure itself that Ottawa could occasionally stand alone and out of a simple economic raison d'être, the Canadian government occasionally took stances that differed from those of the United States.

Cuba represented one example of this independent posture. Almost from the beginning of Fidel Castro's era on the island nation, Canada followed a different course. Economics made the choice easier. With the U.S. embargo of his country, Castro made it clear that he would look to Canada for replacement goods, a stance that the Progressive Conservative government of John Diefenbaker welcomed. Then came the Bay of Pigs debacle, which only encouraged deviation from the American norm, including an offer to act as a mediator between the two antagonists. Canadian advice that American policy actually pushed Castro further into the Soviet domain sparked an angry

Pierre and Margaret Trudeau meeting with Fidel Castro in Cuba in 1976.

Fidel Castro during Trudeau's 1976 visit to Cuba.

response from American Secretary of State Dean Rusk. In the fall of 1962, the Cuban Missile Crisis revealed for all the split and open animosity between Washington and Ottawa, much of the latter fuelled by Diefenbaker's well-documented dislike of his younger American contemporary.

The Diefenbaker government, however, began a trend toward Cuba that would continue with successive governments. Canada established particularly warm relations with Havana during Pierre Trudeau's tenure in office. In a 1976 state visit to the island, he gave his bearded host a warm embrace and, along with the gathered crowd, enthusiastically shouted "Vive Castro!" Their official relationship would translate into a personal friendship that continued after Trudeau left office and even after the former prime minister left this world—Castro attended his friend's 2000 funeral in Montreal where he hugged another Trudeau friend, Jimmy Carter. Economic ties expanded as Canadian businesses, including some owned by larger American corporations, smelled access to markets without fear of U.S. competition. Tourism at an affordable price brought many ordinary Canadians (along with the occasional American in violation of the travel embargo) and their much-desired money to the island.

In turn, these ties continued to anger right-wingers in the United States after the Cold War had ended and long after Cuba had ceased to be a flashpoint in the relations between the superpowers. One sworn enemy of Castro and Communism who took repeated verbal shots at the Canadian-Cuban relationship was a powerful senator from North Carolina, Jessie Helms. He and a Republican congressman from Indiana, Dan Burton, introduced the Helms-

Burton Bill designed to punish non-American companies that had economic interests in Cuba, in part by allowing American citizens who had lost property on the island to sue these companies for compensation. Coming into effect in 1996, the new legislation created friction between Washington and Ottawa, and President Bill Clinton moved to ensure that Canada was exempted from much of the law's recriminations. That was not good enough for two Canadian parliamentarians. In a successful effort to spoof the American law (which led to their appearance on the American news program "Sixty Minutes"), Liberal Members of Parliament (MPs) John Godfrey and Peter Milliken introduced a private member's bill. The Godfrey-Milliken bill granted the descendants of United Empire Loyalists, the two MPs among them, the right to seek compensation for land that was illegally seized from their families when they left the United States after the American Revolution.

Trudeau making a state visit to China, 1973.

It was not only its relationship with Cuba that afforded Canada a chance to step back from the shadow of its southern neighbour and offer it an occasional diplomatic poke in the ribs. An even more significant example involved Canada's relationship with the People's Republic of China (PRC). Traditionally, the Canadian government focused little on the region except when racism at home motivated efforts to block Asian immigration to Canada. Hostility replaced indifference with the victory of Mao Zedong and the Communists in 1949, as Canada followed the American lead by launching diplomatic and economic embargoes of the new regime, choosing instead to recognize the nationalists in Taiwan as the country's real government and possessor of China's membership in the United Nations.

In the context of the Cold War and with China's involvement in the Korean War on the opposite side from Canada, little impetus for a changed relationship existed despite occasional rumblings to the contrary and Beijing's interest in improving its position. Then, as with Cuba, economics entered the picture. The population of China represented a massive market for Canadian goods, and once again the government of John Diefenbaker moved to take advantage of American absence in the field. Agriculture proved an easy fit in this respect. Wheat farming in the Prairies, Dief's home turf, had never really recovered from the Great Depression, and this malaise extended through much of the 1950s. Then in 1960, the federal Minister of Agriculture, Alvin Hamilton from Saskatchewan, announced that the Canadian Wheat Board had successfully negotiated the first major wheat sale to China, worth $60 million in value. In 1957, Canada's entire exports to China had amounted to a measly $1.5 million. The value of trade between Canada and the Communist bloc as a whole jumped to $247 million in 1960 from $47 the year before. At the same time, Canadian wheat exports, some of which were now destined for the Soviet Union, increased by a whopping 250 percent between 1959 and 1965, and in the process, prairie wheat farming received a new life.

Despite Canada increasing its economic ties with China, diplomatically the world's most populous nation remained a pariah in the eyes of Western nations. Both the Diefenbaker and Pearson governments considered official recognition of the government in Beijing. However, in the context of the period, it was not possible to take such a dramatic leap forward. Instead, it fell to Pierre Trudeau, who, in campaigning for the leadership of the federal Liberal Party, pledged in 1968 to recognize the PRC "as soon as possible." He already had some familiarity with the nation. Before entering politics, the wealthy Quebecer had done some international travelling, including a 1960 stint in Red China, an adventure that he later recounted in a book.

In taking his stance toward recognizing China, Trudeau clearly stood at odds with a pro-Taiwan U.S. foreign policy and with his intelligence service at home, which recommended against recognition for security reasons. The diplomatic gambit, however, put the government in harmony with growing momentum from both within Canada — in particular the Department of External Affairs — and non–U.S. allies. After a series of difficult negotiations, a deal was worked out and announced in October 1970. Canada recognized the PRC as the real China while Taiwan lost that status and its diplomats departed Ottawa. Three years later, Pierre Trudeau returned to China, this time on an official trip as prime minister, a visit that included an audience with Chairman Mao.

Trudeau meeting with Chinese leader Deng Xiaoping in 1973.

Surprisingly, the Canadian position shift that led the way for other nations to do the same did not elicit a significant response from Washington. This was all the more curious since dislike for Trudeau ran through the administration all the way to the White House where, in private, President Richard Nixon had difficulty uttering the prime minister's last name without the adjective "asshole" preceding it. The muted response had more to do with similar plans being hatched behind the scenes by Henry Kissinger, who was preparing the way for Nixon's journey to China as the symbolic first step in the U.S. recognition of the PRC.

The Great Molehunt (Canada) Ltd. Or How the Mounties Got their Wrong Man

Jesus College at Cambridge.

A spectre haunted Western intelligence agencies throughout the Cold War — Kim Philby, master spy and arch-traitor. As head of the Soviet desk of the British Secret Intelligence Service, also known as MI6, Philby had been at the heart of the Western intelligence effort. In the late 1940s, Philby was in Washington, acting as a top-level intelligence liaison with the Americans. Few knew more Western secrets than Philby. And then in 1963, Philby turned up in Moscow as a newly minted Soviet citizen and member of the KGB. It turned out that he had been a Communist and a Soviet agent since the 1930s. Never had a "mole" (a deep-penetration agent), been planted more spectacularly, nor with such disastrous results for the country he had betrayed.

The story of Philby's treason is inextricably linked to the so-called "Cambridge Five," five privileged young Britons at Cambridge in the early 1930s who had converted to Communism and secretly set about penetrating the higher echelons of British government in the service of their adopted master, Stalin. Falling under suspicion, Guy Burgess and Donald Maclean, both of the Foreign Office, slipped out of Britain and defected to the USSR in 1951. Philby, a close friend of Burgess, was drawn into the web of suspicion, but brazened it out for another dozen years before joining his comrades in Moscow. It was learned much later that art historian Sir Anthony Blunt, by this time no less than Surveyor of the Queen's Pictures, was the fourth man (he was soon stripped of his knighthood and kept well away from Buckingham Palace), followed eventually by John Cairncross, who had worked for many years in the Treasury. Together the "Magnificent Five," as their KGB controllers were wont to fondly describe them, were a remarkable team of traitors. Philby stood out, however, even in this group, as the most strategically placed and the most damaging.

The spectre of Philby and the Cambridge Five continued for decades to haunt Western intelligence circles. The British were deeply embarrassed, and their American partners were self-righteous about how their colleagues had let down their side. (Many years later, after the end of the Cold War, the Americans were themselves embarrassed by a series of high-level Russian moles uncovered in the CIA and the FBI. But from the 1950s through the 1980s, it was Britain that had the traitors' donkey tail pinned on it.) What the story of the Cambridge Five told the counter-intelligence professionals was that the basis for treason was ideology. The Cambridge Five had sold out their country, despite their privileged position in British society, because of their faith in Communism and a higher loyalty to the Communist motherland, Soviet Russia. This confirmed the lesson of Igor Gouzenko's defection in Canada [see chapter on Gouzenko]. The Royal Commission that investigated the extent of the Soviet espionage network in Canada had insisted that sympathy with Communism and the USSR lay at the heart of why Canadian civil servants had betrayed their own country.

Western counter-intelligence soon set itself the task of uncovering more such Philby-like moles. Profiles were drawn up of what kind of people would be likely to fall prey to the seduction of Communist ideology. The stakes were high indeed: it was widely believed in the West that the Soviets had "stolen the secret" of the atomic bomb through their extensive espionage penetration of the Manhattan Project, based on nuclear physicists such as Klaus Fuchs who were sympathetic to Communism. Once both hostile blocs were armed with nuclear weapons and the intercontinental missiles to deliver them, the anxiety level surrounding security rose yet further. The year before Philby's public defection, the Cuban Missile Crisis had brought the world perilously close to the edge of nuclear Armageddon. What if there were more such traitors lurking in the highest ranks of Western governments?

To make matters worse, the Cambridge Five were only uncovered very slowly. After Philby, Anthony Blunt was publicly unmasked sixteen years later, in 1979. John Cairncross was fingered as late as 1990, at the very end of the Cold War. Meantime, the media enjoyed a decades-long carnival of speculation, and many eminently respectable Britons with long-forgotten left-wing pasts fell under public suspicion. What was not always known at the time was that behind the closed doors of the Western intelligence community, beginning in the late 1960s and peaking in the early 1970s, internal mole hunts had been launched that became increasingly manic and self-destructive. Intelligence agencies became divided camps, as long-standing officials fell under suspicion, and paranoia ran rampant. Two figures in particular stand out as mole hunters out of control: Peter Wright and James Jesus Angleton.

Cambridge winning a boat race,
March 28, 1970.

Wright, an officer in Britain's MI5 security service, was involved with a joint effort with MI6 to root out long and deeply buried moles in both agencies. This proved highly destructive of morale, but ultimately useless in actually uncovering verifiable moles. Eventually Wright, put out to pasture but aggrieved about the size of his pension, published a tell-all memoir called *Spycatcher* in 1987 that the British government tried ineptly and unsuccessfully to ban.

Angleton, head of counter-intelligence at the CIA, was a more influential, and ultimately more sinister, figure than Wright. Driven "half-mad," as one colleague recalled, by the perception that he had himself been compromised by Philby (when the latter served as intelligence liaison in Washington in the late 1940s, he and Angleton had many working — and liquid — lunches at a fashionable D.C. restaurant), Angleton became convinced that the CIA had been penetrated by myriad moles burying themselves deep within the agency's espionage operations. Many careers were blighted as a result of Angleton's paranoia. Finally, the CIA concluded that more damage was being done to the agency by Angleton than by the KGB, and the mad mole hunter was sacked.

Canada was not immune to the mole mania. An early target was diplomat Herbert Norman [see chapter on Norman], who fitted the profile of the ideological defector. Following Norman's suicide in 1957, his name was the first entry made into a special RCMP mole-hunting file called Feather Bed, that later became a scandal for the Mounties [see chapter on Operation Feather Bed].

The Mounties were right in one respect. There was a KGB mole operating in Canada, but he was in the RCMP security service itself. By the late 1960s, careful attention to counter-intelligence detail had revealed that someone with insider knowledge of the service's operations against the Soviets was tipping the adversary off. Too many operations had gone mysteriously awry, too many damaging coincidences had occurred, to be written off as mere accidents. The mole hunt was on, but the quarry was one of the Mounties' own. Therein lies a tangled tale of two Mounties, one a spy who might have been, but wasn't; and the other, a spy who should not have been, but was. In legend, the Mounties always get their man, but in reality, they caught the wrong mole and let the right one slip through their fingers.

Leslie James (Jim) Bennett was a man in the wrong place at the wrong time, or at least the man with the wrong profile. Bennett, the head of the Soviet desk at the security service, was a civilian member, which meant that he had never been a part of the Mountie mystique. He was in fact doubly an outsider, being a British immigrant to Canada. But to suspicious eyes schooled in ideological profiling, there were worse facts. Bennett had been born in a working-class family in the coal mining area of Wales. Like virtually everyone from that part of the world in the 1920s and 1930s, Bennett had grown up as a Labour Party supporter — a "left-wing" background that was a red flag to the mole hunters. During the war he had joined British military intelligence and then stayed on after the war as an employee of the signals intelligence agency (GCHQ). Might this not indicate someone who had sought to worm their way into a sensitive position? Then in 1947, Bennett had been posted to Istanbul as the ranking GCHQ man in the British embassy. His MI6 station equivalent was none other than Kim Philby himself. Bennett and Philby had been in contact with one another, the mole hunters noted, although this was hardly surprising, given their official duties in the same posting. (In fact, Philby, well-bred Oxbridge high flyer, had shown rather snobbish indifference to the working-class Bennett.) To complete the profile, it was then noted that Bennett had emigrated to Canada in the 1950s, found employment in the RCMP security service, and eventually become head of the Soviet desk, the equivalent to Philby's post in MI6. Moreover, it could be demonstrated that Bennett had been aware of each and every counter-espionage operation that had gone mysteriously wrong to the benefit of the KGB. Of course, as head of the Soviet desk, Bennett necessarily knew about all the anti-Soviet operations, but that was no defence to the mole hunters who convinced themselves that they were closing in for the kill.

Bennett's fate was further sealed when, at a private spies party in Washington, he had incautiously fallen into a heated argument with James Angleton on the subject of American McCarthyism, which Bennett, like many Canadians, found abhorrent. An aide to Angleton became so incensed at hearing such anti-American talk that he took a swing at Bennett. Angleton concluded that Bennett was a some kind of "pinko," and put the Canadian on a watch list, just as his own mole hunt was reaching its peak. The RCMP had to contend not only with their own doubts about Bennett, but with those of their closest ally as well.

Aware that he was under intense suspicion, Bennett was followed and bugged (even in his bedroom) by investigators. Finally, in 1972, he had his security clearance revoked and was taken to a safe house for five days of interrogation. There was nothing concrete against him, only circumstantial evidence. However, most of his interrogators' attention was focused on his past, pursuing the profile of a mole who might have been. It was impossible for Bennett to refute such suspicions. He was offered a "medical" discharge, on a miserly pension. With the break-up of his marriage occuring simultaneously, and his career in ruins, Bennett fled Canada, eventually winding up in faraway Perth, Australia, in penurious "retirement."

All this had been done behind closed doors. But the story of the alleged KGB mole who had been uncovered, a Canadian, Bennett, was too sexy to keep under wraps forever. In 1979, a journalist named Ian Adams published a novel called *S: Portrait of a Spy*, a fictionalized account of the mole hunt. "S" was never named, but the profile fit only Bennett. Angry that his reputation would now be publicly dragged through the mud, Bennett successfully sued

Adams. A subsequent paperback edition of the novel was forced to carry a curious notice at the front that "'S' is not Leslie James Bennett." In 1982, another journalist, John Sawatsky, published an excellent piece of investigative reporting, *For Services Rendered*, that probed deeply into the process of Bennett's identification as a KGB recruit and left the reader in little doubt that a serious miscarriage of justice had occurred.

If Bennett was not the mole, who was? That question was left hanging for many years until it came to an unexpected resolution. Enter here the mole who should not have been, but was.

Gilles Brunet was everything Jim Bennett was not. Not only was he a native-born Canadian and a regular Mountie, but the son of a Mountie. J.J. Brunet, his father, had even been the first head of the Security and Intelligence Directorate when it was established as a separate RCMP division in 1956, and ended his career as deputy commissioner. Holding all the right insider credentials, the young Brunet turned out to be a talented high flyer who achieved rapid promotion to the Russian desk, where he apparently excelled at counter-intelligence operations against the Soviets. Fluent in Russian, he charmed and impressed an internal performance assessment panel in 1972 that praised him as "well above average ... a solid member who is making a most valuable contribution." His future in the force seemed bright indeed.

But something funny happened on Gilles Brunet's apparently irresistible rise to the top. Brunet had a sidekick in the security service, Don McCleery, a tough guy from the wrong side of the tracks in Montreal, a cowboy operator never properly socialized into the respectable Mountie ethos. McCleery and Brunet had come, in the opinion of the RCMP brass, too close for comfort to shady Montreal underworld connections. Warned to back off, the pair refused, and in 1973 they were cashiered out of the RCMP.

Brunet's Mountie career had ended badly, but there was worse — much worse — to come. There were suspicions that he might have been involved with more than Montreal racketeers. His own wife had reported to his superiors that he was in possession of unexplainably large amounts of cash. Brunet was able to discredit this allegation by blaming it on his wife's jealousy, but he was kept under surveillance, even after his discharge, and was even seen meeting with a Soviet official. Brunet died young, of a heart attack in 1984, but the next year a KGB defector to the U.S. fingered Brunet as the KGB mole in the RCMP and identified the same Soviet official seen earlier with Brunet as his KGB handler.

In 1993, the Canadian government sent an emissary to Australia to offer Jim Bennett an unconditional apology and a lump sum of financial compensation. Eventually, there was official confirmation that the real mole had indeed been Gilles Brunet.

To the mole hunters, Jim Bennett had looked like the spy who should have been. He had the profile of the ideological traitor, the Canadian Kim Philby. To true believers, and nowhere were there more true believers than in the RCMP security service, the Cold War was a great ideological contest between freedom and Communism. Why else would foot soldiers in this great war betray their own side if not because they had defected to the forces of darkness, and having embraced evil? The Kim Philbys of the world, by their counter-faith in the devil, confirmed the true believers in their crusade for goodness. But what to make of a Gilles Brunet, who, it seemed, had no more faith in Communism than in freedom? What had driven such a privileged and promising young man to sell out his fellows and his country?

The answer to this question was most disappointing to those who would seek the high drama of the clash of great Cold War ideologies. Brunet was a greedy, self-indulgent hedonist who lived well above his means. The former head of foreign counter-intelligence for the KGB, General Oleg Kalugin, recalled that the Soviets had paid Brunet hundreds of thousands of dollars for his services. In spending his Soviet gold, Brunet showed a particular fondness for expensive and luxurious holiday jaunts to Mexico. His tombstone is adorned with a drawing of Acapulco and a Martini glass.

This might also serve as an epitaph for the high ideological drama of the early Cold War. It is now apparent that the spectre of the Kim Philby-like ideological traitor was almost entirely limited to the generation, such as the Cambridge Five, who were shaped by the Great Depression and the rise of Fascism in the 1930s, but before the great disillusionment set in against Stalinist tyranny. After this generation, the spies and traitors of the Cold War were much more likely to be motivated — on both sides of the Iron Curtain — by old-fashioned material greed. Gilles Brunet fits the actual profile of the later Cold War traitor, but ironically the counter-espionage professionals took their own rhetoric too seriously and went looking in all the wrong places. Jim Bennett paid the price, even if he did eventually receive some acknowledgement from Canada of how badly it had treated its loyal public servant.

Trinity College at Cambridge.

Operation Feather Bed

It began as a gleam in the eye of Terry Guernsey, the RCMP's crack anti-Communist investigator in the 1950s. It ended as a public scandal in the late 1970s, with the prime minister of Canada, Joe Clark, criticizing the RCMP for keeping "gossip, often of the most malicious kind, about virtually every senior public servant of prominence in Ottawa at a particular point in time." It was called the Feather Bed file. It was as close as the RCMP ever came to what J. Edgar Hoover did routinely in the U.S. — keep files on politicians and public servants containing information that could be used against them.

It began in the early 1950s with Guernsey, who was then in the B branch (Counter-Espionage) of the security service. Guernsey noted that Igor Gouzenko's revelations of Soviet espionage in 1945-46 had been limited to the networks established by the GRU military intelligence organization to which Gouzenko had been attached. Gouzenko knew that there were parallel networks operated by the NKVD (later the KGB), but had no details of names. Guernsey's bright idea was to identify KGB moles by starting with the known histories of those agents who had been already identified in Canada, the U.S., and Britain, and then finding similar patterns in the pasts of contemporary public servants. It was what a later generation would call the technique of "profiling."

Guernsey went to the RCMP brass with a proposal, but was turned down. The hierarchy immediately saw storm warnings about investigating the pasts of senior public servants on nothing more than vague suspicions. This had the potential to embarrass the force in the eyes of the government. As it turned out, their concern was justified, but Guernsey's idea did not die. He kept it alive with a slender file in his own drawer. Then, in 1957, Herbert Norman [see chapter on E. Herbert Norman] committed suicide in Cairo. Guernsey had interrogated Norman in 1951, and in his mind, the case was still open. He went back to his bosses, and this time received a green light. In early 1958, a file was opened on "suspect or known communist sympathizers employed by the Federal Government," and was given the name Feather Bed. Staff were ordered to identify profiles of civil servants that resembled the early career pattern of Herbert Norman.

By the early 1960s, a thousand personnel files had been reviewed and sixteen senior public servants identified in "positions of trust and influence who had in varying degrees communist affiliations or backgrounds of activity." By 1968, Feather Bed had mushroomed into a special section, sucking some of the best minds out of both the Counter-Espionage and Counter-Subversion branches. One of its directors was Jim Bennett, who was himself later to be wrongfully sacked as a Soviet mole [see chapter on The Great Mole Hunt (Canada) Ltd.].

Feather Bed was contemporaneous with the witch hunts for traitors that wracked the CIA and British intelligence in the late 1960s and early 1970s. While James Angleton in the CIA and Peter Wright in MI5 were riding high and sowing the seeds of suspicion and paranoia throughout their services, Feather Bed prospered in Canada. When Angleton and Wright were both finally sacked in the mid-1970s, and the internal damage that their reckless suspicions had caused began to be repaired, Feather Bed ran out of steam and legitimacy within the RCMP as well. By 1975, Feather Bed had become dormant, and its files had been returned to other sections.

Feather Bed might have been tucked away by the Mounties, but in the late 1970s, it came back to haunt the force and to confirm the wisdom of the senior officers who had vetoed Guernsey's original proposal back in the early 1950s. Rumours began to circulate about a Hoover-style file on prominent Ottawa figures, even including the then prime minister, Pierre Trudeau, and some of his Ministers. In the U.S. at this time, the Church committee of the US Senate was investigating the CIA as a "rogue elephant." In Canada, the RCMP scandals had led to the McDonald Commission, and concerns about wrongdoing by the secret police were running high. When the Conservatives came briefly to office in 1979, they insisted on looking into Feather Bed — and did not like what they saw.

J. Edgar Hoover had been very popular during his lifetime — and had assiduously used his position and the resources of the FBI to burnish his image. After his death in 1972, a darker side began to emerge when it was learned that he had in effect blackmailed successive generations of politicians, including presidents, with damaging information on them held in secret files. He had bugged the bedrooms of presidents, and gathered dirt on anyone who had the power to interfere with his plans for the FBI. He would finally be remembered, not as the patriotic crime buster and Red hunter he wanted to be, but as a gargoyle of repression who had fastened himself onto the body politic and fed on the weaknesses of the democratically elected representatives of the American people. It is an unenviable legacy. Does Feather Bed give any reason to think that the RCMP might have been contemplating using the information in its files to intimidate political leaders?

The thought may have occurred to the occasional Mountie on the Feather Bed detail. There is even a memo that survives from 1962 in which an unidentified Feather Bed staffer referred to the FBI's practice (then not widely known) of forcing the executive's hand on particular cases by feeding them to congressional committees, which then made them public. Might we not too, the writer inquired of the director of the security service, "go ahead using whatever means are available, to confirm or eliminate our suspicions?"

In fact, there is no evidence that the RCMP ever did follow the Hoover path. The Mountie brass, with very good reason, disliked the politicization of security issues that had occurred in the U.S. They were always very careful to keep their files close to their own vests, and not let their intelligence get into the hands of anyone they could not control — except, unfortunately, their FBI counterparts, who sometimes did abuse RCMP intelligence.

In any event, Feather Bed had always been an attempt to find Soviet moles and not to exert clandestine influence over politicians. On its own terms, it was a failure: not a single mole, or even a facsimile of one, was ever uncovered. The problem was in the design of the program. The cases that riveted the attention of counter-espionage in the 1950s through the 1970s answered to the profile of the ideological spy — such as the Cambridge traitors, Burgess, Maclean, Philby — or the Canadian spy who might have been, but wasn't, Herbert Norman. But this profile was off base for the next generation of traitors, who were much more likely to spy for greed rather than ideology. So Feather Bed became an obsession, with very nasty overtones of McCarthyism, that produced much suspicion, but no moles. And when notice of its existence did finally become public, it only contributed to a climate in Canada, both inside and outside of government, that grew sufficiently hostile to the Mounties' handling of security that in 1984 the entire security function was taken away from the RCMP and vested in the Canadian Security Intelligence Survey, a new civilian agency.

What of the rumours of a Feather Bed file on Pierre Trudeau? We know that the FBI had a file on Trudeau, as it did on Lester Pearson. It seems that there was a Trudeau file in Feather Bed, but we will not be allowed to see it until twenty years after Trudeau's death, which will be in 2020. One former security officer who claims to have seen the file is dismissive. "There is nothing in it," he says.

The Official Secrets Act

A central part of the legal armoury of the federal government in the Cold War was the Official Secrets Act. Passed on the eve of the Second World War in 1939, this statute was modeled closely on the British Act of the same name that dated back to 1911. It was an amalgam of two separate types of offence, espionage and "leakage." Espionage means the unauthorized disclosure of classified information to a foreign power; leakage means unauthorized disclosure to the press or public.

The Official Secrets Act was a draconian statute with many remarkable features. For the purposes of prosecution, it was irrelevant whether the disclosure of information was actually harmful to Canada, it need only be unauthorized. It was not necessary for the prosecution to show that the accused was guilty of "any particular act tending to show a purpose prejudicial to the safety or interests of the State." However, "he may be convicted if, from the circumstances of the case, his conduct or his known character as proved, it appears his purpose was a purpose prejudicial to the safety or interests of the State." The burden of proof was shifted from the Crown to the accused. Trials could be held in camera, with nothing made public other than the judgment.

The Official Secrets Act was first used extensively in the espionage prosecutions that arose out of Igor Gouzenko's 1945 defection. In the years since, only scattered prosecutions have been brought under the Official Secrets Act. Two high profile prosecutions under the leakage provisions were brought in the 1970s, one against a federal employee and the other against the *Toronto Sun* and its Cold Warrior journalist Peter Worthington for publishing a secret document detailing Soviet espionage in Canada. Both prosecutions failed, causing considerable embarrassment to the government that had brought the prosecutions.

For a variety of reasons, among them the entrenchment of the Charter of Rights and Freedoms, the Official Secrets Act had, by the 1980s, become pretty much a dead letter, as the Crown doubted its ability to secure convictions. As early as 1969, a Royal Commission on security had recommended an overhaul of the Act, but little was done to follow up. The British statute, on which the Canadian Act was modeled, was not subject to such problems in British courts, it was used with relative frequency in the post-war era, and almost always resulted in convictions. In one case, a Canadian who had spied for the Soviets, economics professor Hugh Hambleton, was never prosecuted in Canada. When he unwisely took a vacation in the United Kingdom, he was arrested upon entry, charged under the British Official Secrets Act, and convicted.

The British overhauled their statute in the late 1980s, but despite numerous demands for reform in Canada, including from the McDonald Commission who inquired into the RCMP, and a series of internal government task forces in the 1990s, the reform of the Official Secrets Act remained unfinished business. Finally, after the terrorist attacks of September 11, 2001, when the government passed the emergency Anti-Terrorist Act, it repealed the Official Secrets Act after a dubious 62-year lifespan and replaced it with a modernized Security of Information Act. Among other things, this new Act makes provision to exempt "whistleblowers" who release information in the public interest. It removes some of the other more contentious aspects of the old Act. It also adds new offences regarding terrorism and economic espionage.

Although it outlived the end of the Cold War by a decade, the Official Secrets Act was a monument to that era. It gave too much arbitrary power to the state, but became ensnared in its own contradictions and excesses, and ended ineffectual and discredited.

The "Boat People"

Fleeing in their rickety boats and congregating in decrepit camps, these refugees captured the attention of the world. Quickly known as the "boat people," they came mainly from the Socialist Republic of Vietnam and numbered in the hundreds of thousands. The long-term cause of their plight was the suffering of their nation in the war with the United States, a conflict that led to the deaths of nearly four million people. The immediate impetus for most to leave occurred in 1978 when Vietnam invaded Cambodia in a successful bid to topple the genocidal regime of Pol Pot. The People's Republic of China, an ally of Cambodia, was less pleased with the intervention and attacked the north of Vietnam in response. Many Vietnamese, especially in the north, were ethnically Chinese and soon found themselves at the wrong end of a backlash from their fellow citizens. Those who could fled to China. Others living in the South had no such option and instead took to the sea. Soon they were joined by other refugees, ranging from peasants to professionals, who left for their own reasons or because of a general unhappiness with the unified Vietnam of the Communist era.

What had been a regional issue soon became a world refugee crisis, particularly as the media began to broadcast images of the overladen boats around the world. Anywhere from 20,000 to 250,000 of those who left drowned before they could find dry land. Countries in the region, including Malaysia, where the deputy prime minister warned that refugees who came ashore would be "shot," wanted little to do with them. Those who did make it safely to shore found themselves living in horrendous conditions in refugee camps. The pressure on the rest of the world to act grew. In July 1979, a special international conference to address the problem convened in Switzerland.

One unlikely participant was Canada. Although it is a country built on immigration and by immigrants, the issue was perpetually controversial and frequently fuelled a backlash against both those who came, especially from Asia, and those

An overloaded Vietnamese refugee boat in the late 1970s.

who allowed them in. Another significant factor that seemed to mitigate against Canada offering assistance was the tiny Vietnamese community already present. Because of the prevalence of the French language, Canada, in particular Quebec, had been an attractive destination for Vietnamese students since the 1950s. Some of the students who came remained, but with the fall of Saigon and South Vietnam in 1975, the number of Vietnamese permanently residing in Canada was no more than 1500. Those numbers soon grew as Vietnamese students studying in Canada in 1975 were allowed to stay. Most of those who remained chose Quebec with its familiar language as their permanent destination, although a smaller number ended up in Ontario. The lack of numbers translated into little political influence and an equally negligible support network to assist large numbers of refugees.

Still, the Progressive Conservative government of Joe Clark pushed ahead, aware of the shame of Canada's failure to accept Jewish refugees from Nazi Germany in the 1930s. The immigrants from Southeast Asia, in addition, fit well with the Cold War game plan: they, like the Czechs and Hungarians in previous decades, were escaping Communism. In 1979, Canada accepted

more than 60,000 refugees, 58,000 from Vietnam and the remainder from Cambodia and Laos. As a overall ratio, Canada led the Western world by accepting one refugee per 324 persons. Australia came second at one per 332. Canada did not, however, accept the "boat people" without scrutiny. Immigrants were assessed to determine their suitability and adaptability.

Nor was it merely a top-down Canadian response to the crisis. At an almost unprecedented level, non-governmental organizations and ordinary citizens reached out to the newcomers. The federal government encouraged this enthusiasm by promising to match costs for everyone privately sponsored by either an organization or a minimum of five adults. Nearly 60 percent of the refugees were sponsored with the assistance of private citizens. Among those offering help, the Mennonite Central Committee aided four thousand "boat people," while a farm family and the local Mennonite congregation of Stratton, Ontario, sponsored twenty refugees between August 1979 and July 1982. Unlike previous newcomers from Southeast Asia, the newcomers were spread more widely across Canada, with 24 percent ending up on the Prairies and 5 percent in Atlantic Canada. Still, already existing

Vietnamese refugees in Canada in the late 1970s.

communities in Toronto and Montreal proved attractive destinations, and thousands more family members would later be allowed to immigrate to rejoin their loved ones.

Although the response to the refugees became a celebrated chapter in Canadians' continuing belief in their nation's perpetual tolerance toward outsiders, some opposition to the resettlement appeared. Newspaper ads warned that the move was just the beginning of a much greater influx of people. Famed radio broadcaster and professional curmudgeon, the late Gordon Sinclair, took to the airwaves of CFRB Radio in Toronto to declare that the refugees "belong[ed] in Asia." Moreover, although many private citizens stepped forward to offer aid, an opinion poll found that two-thirds of respondents expressed some negativity toward accepting the refugees.

Despite the grumbling and an undercurrent of prejudice, thousands arrived on Canada's shores. Life in the new land was not without hardship. Unlike earlier refugees from Southeast Asia, many lacked fluency in either French or English. Their arrival also coincided with a major economic downturn in the early 1980s. These factors contributed to the movement of many of the refugees to large urban centres where people of communities of similar backgrounds and languages already existed, making it easier for these Cold War migrants to establish firm roots.

PART FIVE
The 1980s

The funeral of Soviet President Leonid Brezhnev, 1982.

As the Cold War entered a new decade, there was no end in sight for a thirty-five-year struggle that had created two ideologically hostile camps, each armed with the potential to destroy human life on the planet several times over. While a lessening of tensions had occurred in the first half of the 1970s with détente, the end of the decade generated growing possibilities for direct conflict. In December 1979, the Soviet Union, with an ailing Leonid Brezhnev at its head, invaded neighbouring Afghanistan out of a fear that growing instability in the country, in part inspired by covert American funding for anti-Communist interests, could spread to neighbouring Soviet republics with large Islamic populations. The invasion sparked an enormous outcry in the West, and sanctions against the Soviet Union were introduced. President Jimmy Carter, in the final year of his administration and still facing the Iranian hostage crisis, announced that the United States would boycott the 1980 Summer Olympics in Moscow. Several other countries, including Canada, with Pierre Trudeau back in charge after the Liberals' defeat of the short-lived government of Joe Clark and the Progressive Conservatives in February 1980, quickly followed suit as tensions between the superpowers grew.

The climate of hostility served as a backdrop to the 1980 American presidential election. Carter sought another four years against the ultimate Cold Warrior, Ronald Reagan. Reagan, a former lifeguard, baseball announcer, actor, and governor of California for two terms, was ideologically committed, not just to a struggle with Communism and the Soviet Union, but to victory over them. This stance made him a magnet for ideologically committed fellow travellers who swarmed to his side.

The Republican challenger, acting the part of a leader, proved too much for the worn-out Carter, and swept into the White House and into formulating Cold War policy. A massive arms build up ensued, fuelled not only by ideology but also by inflated American intelligence estimates of Soviet economic capability. The U.S., through the Central Intelligence Agency, actively aided guerrilla movements in Afghanistan and Nicaragua. Republican rhetoric about winning a nuclear war and Reagan's labelling of the Soviet Union as an "evil empire" frightened people around the world. Opposition to American policy grew, especially among allied countries in Western Europe but also in Canada where protestors gathered on Parliament Hill to greet Reagan on his first presidential visit to Canada.

Although Pierre Trudeau attempted his own challenges to the Reagan doctrine, in general his government did little but follow the American foreign policy lead. This included making a controversial decision to allow the U.S. military to test the cruise missile over Canadian territory. Domestic issues generally dominated Ottawa's attention in the first half of the decade. In May 1980, the Parti Québécois government held a referendum seeking support for the negotiation of "sovereignty association" with Ottawa. After repelling the separatists, Pierre Trudeau's game plan involved amending and bringing back the British North America Act, Canada's constitution, from London in 1982. Economically, Canadians, largely because of Washington's fiscal policy, suffered from high unemployment, soaring inflation, and extraordinarily lofty interest rates. Before the end of the decade, the two countries would move toward even greater economic integration through the signing of a free trade agreement.

Internal affairs, however, were largely overshadowed by international events in 1983. On March 23, in a nationally televised speech, Reagan unveiled his administration's Strategic Defence Initiative, a space and ground anti-missile system that the media and the program's critics quickly labelled "Star Wars." On September 1, a Soviet aircraft mistakenly downed a Korean Airlines passenger airliner, killing all on board. The tiny island nation of Grenada found itself invaded by the American military in October. To the Kremlin, Reagan's rhetoric combined with a NATO military exercise in the fall heralded the real possibility that the U.S. and its allies were preparing a nuclear first strike against the Soviet Union. The Soviet leadership ordered intelligence operatives around the world to collect evidence of the impending attack.

In part, this fear reflected increasing instability at the top of the doddering Soviet regime. In 1982, Leonid Brezhnev permanently departed the workers' paradise. The health of his sixty-eight-year-old successor, Yuri Andropov, began to fail in 1983, and he died in early 1984. His replacement, the seventy-three-year-old Konstantin Chernenko, lasted until March 1985. Although little recognized initially, Chernenko's death led to the ascendancy of a new style of Soviet leader, the fifty-four-year-old Mikhail Gorbachev, the man ultimately responsible for bringing the Cold War to an end.

Gorbachev's efforts were initially greeted with suspicion by hardened Cold Warriors in the Reagan administration. The Soviet "expert" at the CIA labelled the new leader as a fraud, and predicted that the Soviet Union was working and as strong as ever. Gorbachev's appeals for Soviet internal reforms ("perestroika" and "glasnost") and repairs to the relationship between the superpowers eventually won him converts, including Ronald Reagan. The two met for the first time in 1985 and signed an agreement on intermediate weapons in 1988. By the following year, the reforms unleashed as part of the Gorbachev revolution began to tear apart his nation's empire. The Berlin Wall toppled and Eastern European nation after nation left the Soviet orbit and entered a world increasingly dominated by the remaining superpower. By 1991, Gorbachev had resigned and the Soviet Union and the Cold War had been consigned to the scrap heap of history.

As with any significant and lengthy historical era, the Cold War has a lengthy legacy, much of which remains pertinent to the present. For both Canada and the world, the list is indeed extensive. Its characteristics include paranoia, the triumph of the file, and American dominance and Canadian compliance. Then, there are the sweeping rationalizations, accusations, and scare mongering, billions of dollars wasted on intelligence services, militaries, and on weapons of mass destruction that continue to threaten the Earth, lives lost and others destroyed, and finally environmental degradation that lives on in the land and in the people exposed to uranium, PCBs, LSD, and other human contaminants. A collective psychosis is not easily healed.

The Cruise Missile

A Canadian student protesting Pierre Trudeau's decision to allow the United States to test cruise missiles in Canada in the early 1980s.

In April 1981, a polite letter arrived in Ottawa that represented a major dilemma for the government of Canada. It was a request from Caspar Weinberger, a California Republican and the secretary of defence in the two-and-a-half-month-old presidential administration of Ronald Reagan, to test a weapon system that had been in serious development since the 1970s, but that in form stretched back to the Second World War. Launched either from an airplane or a ship, the Boeing-built cruise missile was a 20-foot,

3,200-pound rocket code-named the "Tomahawk." On board it could carry either conventional explosives or a nuclear warhead. A built-in computer system allowed it to travel at 800 kilometres an hour at a low altitude and hone in on a pre-programmed target as far as 2,600 kilometres away. In the Cold War, the weapon was portrayed (to the disagreement of the peace movement, which in the post-Cold War was proven correct) as a defensive tool that would not be used as a first-strike weapon, a crucial issue in the Cold War era of tension between the Soviet Union and the United States.

Ordinarily the United States had little need for Canada, but in this case the system was still under development and testing was required. Seeking terrain similar to the Russia steppes and the Arctic, the American military looked no further than its northern neighbour. In particular, the U.S. military was interested in Canadian military weapons ranges in Alberta as possible sites to test the missile.

For the Canadian government, the request meant both opportunity and danger. Criticized by its partners in the North Atlantic Treaty Organization for reductions in commitments to the alliance, the request gave the government an expensive opportunity to prove itself to its allies. It offered the Canadian military the possibility of playing a more important role in its secondary relationship to the American military under the North American Air Defence command. Finally, for the defence industry in Canada, the testing promised money to be made in building components for the new missile, and its lobbyists pushed vigorously for Ottawa's approval.

Many within the government, however, dwelled on the drawbacks if Canada acquiesced to the American request. Before and after entering politics, Pierre Trudeau had been a determined foe of nuclear weapons, a goal only strengthened when he visited Hiroshima. Now he appeared ready to play the role of a hypocrite since, although the missile to be tested over northern Canada would not carry a real warhead, its ultimate purpose was to serve the American nuclear strategy. At a time of heightened tensions between the superpowers, the testing of the cruise missile would do nothing to improve the international situation; it had the potential for doing the opposite. There was a potential domestic political cost as well. Canadians had told pollsters of their increasing anxiety about international security. Within the government and the Liberal Party, there was a major constituency that was suspicious of American motivations, especially in the era of Ronald Reagan, and leaned in the direction of those actively working to rid the world of nuclear weapons.

With all of these existing factors in place, a simple and quick response to Weinberger's letter was not forthcoming. Instead, the government weighed its options as an institution. By December 1981, over a half a year after the American request arrived, Trudeau wrote Reagan to offer a qualified agreement to the testing. All of these machinations had occurred out of the public gaze, a luxury the government no longer enjoyed after the Canadian media reported the secret negotiations in March 1982. Now in the open, the government finally introduced the Canada-U.S. Testing and Evaluation Program (CANUSTEP) before the House of Commons on February 10, 1983.

Each government apparently had different interpretations as to what it was that Canada was agreeing to do. The Reagan administration believed a commitment to allow the testing had been made and applied pressure to make sure there was no retreat from this course. The Canadian government, specifically Pierre Trudeau, believed that more wiggle room still existed, an ambiguity that was about making Canada appear more as an American partner instead of a colony. As the legislation cleared the House of Commons, the Reagan administration increased its pressure in June 1983 when the American military attaché in Ottawa made the short trip to the headquarters of the Department of National Defence and presented a letter formally requesting permission to test the missile over Canada.

"So I said to Ronnie, nuclear payload or not, I understand these babies are supposed to seek out the Russians and get an immediate response from Andropov . . ."

In the build up to the Cabinet decision, efforts were made from both sides of the issue to sway public opinion and, more importantly, the federal Cabinet that would have the final say. Trudeau had publicly encouraged such campaigns by issuing a challenge: "Show me a consensus against testing, and I'll cancel it." Several Liberal backbenchers and former Cabinet Ministers announced their opposition to testing. The New Democratic Party introduced a motion into the House of Commons opposing the testing. The effort was defeated 213 to 34 with one Liberal and four Conservative Members of Parliament voting with the NDP. The Canadian Labour Congress publicly opposed the testing, as did several Canadian churches. Their collective efforts appeared to have an impact. A small majority of Canadians (52 percent according to Gallup) expressed opposition to testing the cruise, while 37 percent supported it.

Leading the charge was the peace movement. "Refuse the cruise" became the slogan of choice at rallies, including one involving fifteen thousand people in Ottawa in October 1982. Operation Dismantle, a leading peace group of the era, saw its membership increase dramatically. Activists even established a peace camp in the shadow of the Peace Tower on Parliament Hill.

Those in favour of testing the cruise fought back. In a crude and not terribly effective intervention, Paul Robinson, the U.S. ambassador to Canada, described testing opponents as "naive" and "misguided," and he hinted that a refusal by Canada could have dire implications for Canada's relationship with his country. Trudeau also expressed disdain for some within the peace movement. Within the bureaucracy, External Affairs and the Department of National Defence organized a public relations campaign to counter the peace movement's efforts at blocking cruise testing. A slide show and list of speakers was assembled to fan out and spread the positive word about the missile program.

The result was a heated debate within Trudeau's Cabinet as some, including Lloyd Axworthy and Donald Johnston, ideologically at opposite ends within the party, argued against allowing testing while others underlined that a commitment had been made and that Canada, especially in view of its allies, could not afford to shift direction. Trudeau was among those reluctant to allow testing. He made his feelings clear to Chancellor Helmut Schmidt, and it was the West German leader who pushed Trudeau back in the direction of allowing the testing. Schmidt emphasized that Canada was a member of NATO and, as such, had to make a contribution, just as West Germany was making a similar effort by accepting American nuclear weapons on its soil. The supporting NATO argument, which was frequently raised by Trudeau, lacked relevance because the form of the cruise missile destined for NATO was a version launched from the ground and not the air as was the model destined for testing in Canada. In the end, the cabinet voted to allow testing of the cruise missile, although those in the Cabinet minority stressed the need for further efforts at reducing the threat of nuclear war.

The testing went ahead but not without determined efforts by the peace movement to block it. Operation Dismantle and a number of other groups followed a legal course, using the recently adopted Charter of Rights and Freedoms to combat the Cabinet decision. Invoking Section 7 of the Charter, which guaranteed "life, liberty and security of the person and the right not be deprived thereof...," the argument was made that the Charter had supremacy over parliamentary decisions. The cruise policy, according to the peace movement, put Canadians at risk, specifically those in the testing zone, but also in general all Canadians because of the heightened international tension that the missile program fuelled. The peace groups won an initial victory, lost the second round, and then made an application to have the case heard by the Supreme Court of Canada. The nation's highest court agreed, and on Valentine's Day, 1984, it proceeded. The Supreme Court then reserved judgment, waiting until May 1985 to issue its verdict, which was that not enough evidence had been presented to support a violation of Section 7 of the Charter.

The tests, which had already been underway, continued in a zone that was 150 kilometres wide and stretched 2,600 kilometres from the Arctic down to the Primrose Lake air weapons range. Opposition continued as well. One novel attempt at thwarting the missile involved an Albertan who stretched a net across between two balloons, an effort he sent skyward at the time of testing. His approach failed. The testing continued until the missile was ready for action, not against the Soviet Union, but as a first-strike weapon against Iraq in the 1991 Gulf War.

The Squamish Five

Ann Hansen's memoirs.

At 11:31 p.m. on October 14, 1982, 550 pounds of explosives loaded into a stolen GMC van exploded against Plant No. 402 of Litton Systems of Canada on the outskirts of Toronto. The company, supported by financial assistance from the federal government, built the guidance components for the cruise missile. As such, it had long been a target for peaceful protests, particularly by the Cruise Missile Conversion Project, which, on a weekly basis, distributed flyers to Litton workers with the goal of converting them to the cause of peace and the factory itself to non-military production. The whole issue of the cruise missile and the American desire to test it over Canadian territory was saturated with controversy. Many in the peace movement rightly perceived of the cruise missile as a first-strike weapon, but their efforts to halt its development proved ineffective. Other cruise opponents decided to follow a different course.

Acting out of frustration over the course of the Cold War and Canada's seemingly perpetual subservience to the United States, a group of British Columbians targeted Litton Systems directly for attack. All had been involved in various anarchist and left-wing causes in the Vancouver area. Brent Taylor, the son of two university professors, had once hit Progressive Conservative Party Leader Joe Clark in the face with a pie. The other leading member of the five was Ann Hansen, who grew up just outside of Toronto. Before going off to university and becoming a member of a campus branch of the Communist Party of Canada (Marxist-Leninist), she had been a high school cheerleader and taught Sunday school. Litton was their second bombing of the year. Earlier in May they had played a role in the bombing of a hydro project on Vancouver Island.

Under the banner of "Direct Action" (the media would label them the "Squamish Five" after the town in B.C. near where they had stolen dynamite and trained), Taylor, Hansen, and another woman drove a truck loaded with explosives from Vancouver to Toronto. Having done reconnaissance work on previous visits to the city, they knew their target well. At 11:17 p.m. on the day selected for the attack, a van they had stolen was backed up against the factory. Three minutes later, a member of the cell made a warning call to the factory's security that the bomb would detonate in 25 minutes. Seeking to avoid casualties, the bombers left an elaborate warning along with a stick of dynamite. The latter, however, deterred the security from reading the warning and the bomb exploded twelve minutes early, possibly set off by the radios of approaching police cars. Ten people were wounded, including four who suffered permanent injuries. The explosion also caused $3 million in damage to the plant. Direct Action issued communiqués claiming responsibility for the attack and apologizing for the injuries it had caused.

The response in Canada's intelligence community was panic. An attack against a defence industry of particular importance to Canada's main ally had occurred right under the noses of Canadian authorities. A concerted and blanket campaign began to track down those responsible by pressuring any-one who might share the motivation behind the crime. The immediate targets were the "usual suspects," those who had a history of openly and non-vio-lently campaigning for peace and who were for the most part horrified at the bombing since it discredited their cause. A member of the Royal Canadian Mounted Police security service approached the head of Operation Dismantle for information. More dramatic tactics were used against Toronto-area peace groups and their members, who faced raids, electronic surveillance, and efforts to intimidate individual members into naming names and later into testifying against those facing charges.

Across the country, the RCMP in Vancouver had latched onto the prime suspects shortly after the Litton attack. The first break arrived from a Toronto newspaper reporter whose previous involvement in left-wing causes led him to link some of the rhetoric in Direct Action communiqués with a pamphlet published by Vancouver-area radicals. The pamphlet listed a mailing address in the city. That address belonged to an individual who the police knew was associated with Brent Taylor. In the minds of the local office of the RCMP security service, Taylor's past already made him a likely candidate for involvement. Ten members of the Watchers of the RCMP security service, a collection of nondescript women and men whose sole job was the surveillance of individuals, were put on the job starting on October 29, two weeks after the bombing. The Watchers produced enough evidence for the matter to be transferred to the criminal side of the RCMP in mid-November to finish the job. It employed electronic surveillance, as police officers secretly entered the home of the suspects to plant microphones, and a hidden camera was placed in a neighbouring house.

By January 1983, the police believed it had enough evidence to make arrests. Instead of surprising the five at home, a senior Mountie ordered that they be rounded up on a day when they were conducting shooting drills outside the city. That date was January 20. The Squamish Five, returning to Vancouver in their truck, encountered a road crew blocking traffic. When they reached the front of the line, the road crew, in reality police officers in disguise, pounced on them and dragged them off into custody. Their trials began one year later. Despite questions about the legality of important parts of the evidence, all five were found guilty, with Brent Taylor receiving a sentence of twenty-two years and Ann Hansen, life in prison. Before her sentencing Ann Hansen spoke to the court, acknowledging her guilt and apologizing for the injuries that her actions had caused. She added, however, that her regret extended only so far:

Ann Hansen.

> I will always live with the pain that I am responsible for, but these mistakes should never overshadow the incredible amount of pain and suffering that Litton contributes to every day and the potential for planetary extinction that the Cruise missile embodies.... I am not a terrorist. I am a person who feels a moral obligation to do all that is humanly possible to prevent the destruction of the earth.... I believe if there is any hope for the future, it lies in our struggle.

The Most Dangerous Films of the Cold War

Dr. Helen Caldicott during the 1980s.

In February 1983 the lights dimmed, the curtain drew back, and the image of a National Film Board of Canada (NFB) documentary began to flicker on the big screen. Then, courtesy of the administration of President Ronald Reagan, appeared a small addition. Added under the Foreign Agents Registration Act, a 1938 law aimed originally at Nazi sympathizers, a disclaimer warned that the film's producer was registered as a "foreign agent" and that in no respect did the registration represent "approval of the contents of this material by the U.S. government." The twenty-six minute piece of "propaganda" in the eyes of the Justice Department of President Ronald Reagan was "If You Love This Planet."

That film and the battle over it reflected the tension of the age. The election of Ronald Reagan in 1980 and his determination to be aggressive in fighting the Cold War, including dramatic increases in defence spending and talk of nuclear war being winnable, frightened people around the world including in Canada. Many of these signed on with existing peace groups like Operation Dismantle [see chapters on the cruise missile and Trudeau's peace mission]. Some were among the thousands who gathered in Ottawa to protest an appearance by Reagan on Parliament Hill in March 1981.

In turn, the Reagan administration had little time for critics. After having its domestic intelligence operations curtailed in the 1970s because of revelations of misconduct, the FBI renewed such work in the 1980s, targeting for surveillance critics of the Reagan administration's Latin American policy. And, in echoes of the treatment accorded "If You Love This Planet," the White House made a concerted effort to discredit a made for TV film, "The Day After," about a destructive nuclear attack on the U.S. The film aired in November 1983 and captured large audiences across North America.

It was not just films with an anti-nuclear theme that faced a backlash from the U.S. government. Two other Canadian films, "Acid Rain, Requiem or Recovery" and "Acid from Heaven," both addressing the environmental damage to Canada from pollution produced by its southern neighbour, also received the special treatment courtesy of the U.S. government. Besides the disclaimer, the law required the "foreign agent" to record a list of theatres and groups that showed the particular movie, the dates it was shown, and the number of people in attendance at the showings.

Of the three restricted documentaries, the selection of "If You Love This Planet" received the most attention. Consisting of a strong critique of the nuclear weapons policy of the Reagan administration, and of nuclear war in general, the film featured a lecture by Dr. Helen Caldicott, National President of Physicians for Social Responsibility and an outspoken Australian peace

activist. She spoke in explicit terms about the damage done by an atomic explosion and accompanying images ridiculed both Reagan and his administration, the former through a clip from one of his many forgettable film performances, "Jap Zero."

Allegations soon arose that the targeting of the films represented an effort by the Reagan administration to silence its critics. These were soon denied by the White House which said that the Justice Department's decision had been made by a career bureaucrat without political interference. The restrictions, according to one spokesperson, were "not unique," although the majority of the previous targets involved films designed to promote business opportunities in other nations. That a political motivation played a more direct role was divulged by the individual who actually attached the label to the NFB films. They were selected, according to the bureaucrat in question, because "we keep an eye on what issues are important as far as Congress is concerned. We know nuclear disarmament is an issue. We know acid rain is an issue." Even the head of the State Department, George Schultz weighed in. "Obviously, we must stand always for the principles of freedom of expression," he admitted. "But where that leads you in this particular case, I'm not ready to say."

Regardless of the motivation, the action triggered an immediate reaction on both sides of the border. Within days, the Canadian government politely (and ultimately unsuccessfully) asked Washington for first a clarification and then a reconsideration of its decision. In the American capital, Democratic politicians, sensing an opportunity to score political points, held special screenings of the film and Senator Edward Kennedy personally introduced Caldicott at a National Press Club speaking engagement. A colleague of Kennedy's had the films shown on the House of Representatives closed-circuit television system. The American Civil Liberties Union weighed in as well, filing a lawsuit in March 1983 in an effort to overturn the Justice Department's decision. That legal action proceeded through the American courts and four years later it reached the highest court in the land, the Supreme Court, which in a five to three decision upheld the power of the U.S. government to do just what it had done to the three Canadian films.

That, however, remained in the future. In 1983 a decision that smacked of censorship to many proved true once again the old adage that there is no such thing as bad publicity: the controversy expanded dramatically the film's audience. Special screenings in Washington, D.C., for example, attracted hundreds of people who would never have seen the films let alone heard of them had it not been for the heavy-handed action of the Reagan administration. Finally, and triumphantly for the National Film Board and the filmmaker Terre Nash, arrived April 11, 1983 and the annual Academy Awards ceremonies. That night before a world-wide audience in the hundreds of millions, Terre Nash paraded up onto the stage to accept her golden statue in recognition of the awarding of the Oscar for best documentary short to "If You Love This Planet." Eschewing a recent Oscar trend of overtly political acceptance speeches, she simply and in fine Canadian fashion thanked the U.S. Justice Department for its promotional efforts on behalf of her film.

Korean Airlines Flight 007 and Trudeau's Peace Mission

Ronald Reagan making a state visit to Ottawa in 1981.

Four words summed up the conclusion of 269 lives: "The target is destroyed." Major Gennadii N. Osipovich, a pilot in the Soviet air force, had just announced the result of his missile launch early on the morning of September 1, 1983. The target was not part of a drill, nor was it an enemy aircraft. Instead the pilot had just shot down Korean Airlines (KAL) Flight 007, a Boeing 747 carrying 269 passengers and crew, which had strayed into Soviet airspace.

Worldwide outrage was the response to the missile strike, which had occurred in a period of heightened Cold War tensions between the superpowers. Since its beginning, the presidential administration of Ronald Reagan had taken an aggressive tone with the Soviets, seeking to pressure them in a number of strategic areas, including through the Strategic Defence Initiative that Reagan had announced in March 1983. The program fit well with the president's earlier denunciation of the Soviet Union as an "evil empire."

The other side of the superpower divide suffered from the combination of nature and its geroncratic leadership. A state of flux existed at the top since the previous November when a decrepit Leonid Brezhnev had finally passed away.

"Nasty old bloodstains got you down, Yuri? Then try all-new Cold War Cool, with the miracle ingredient P.E.T. which turns murderous superpower confrontations into simple 'tragic accidents'...!"

His successor, former KGB head Yuri Andropov, also suffered from ill health and would be dead four and a half months after the missile strike.

Canada was among the nations that quickly responded to the event. Ten Canadians were among the dead, and Gérard Pelletier, the Trudeau government's ambassador to Washington, described the attack as "nothing short of murder." On September 5, Canada joined a number of countries in announcing sanctions against the Soviet Union. Many Canadians expressed outrage over the attack in stark anti-Communist rhetoric that matched the pronouncements of Ronald Reagan, who, in a speech to the United States and the world, bashed the Soviets over the attack, alleging that they had targeted the aircraft despite being well aware that it was a civilian airliner. In Southern Ontario, people were invited to retaliate against the attack by shouldering a sledgehammer and using it to smash a Lada, a Soviet-built automobile.

One who was not so quick to jump on the anti-Soviet bandwagon was Prime Minister Pierre Trudeau. He had long held qualms about the approach of the Reagan administration, and its use of the Flight 007 tragedy only escalated his concern. On September 25 and then on October 4, Trudeau publicly labelled the Soviet assault as an "unfortunate accident." In doing so, he invited attack from the opposition parties and from the Canadian media. Trudeau's critics, however, lacked one important fact. The Korean Airlines Flight 007 shoot down had indeed been an accident. Trudeau felt confident enough to label the incident an "accident" because he had viewed top secret intercepts of Soviet military communication that the National Security Agency had shared with Canada's Communications Security Establishment.

In correcting the line of the Reagan administration, the prime minister of Canada was in a sense returning to his roots. Before his political life, Trudeau had worried about the nuclear politics of the superpowers and had decried nuclear weapons in his writings. These views did not change once he entered politics, although he now had to act in a world of compromise, never more evident than when he and his government, after a lengthy debate, agreed to allow the United States to test unarmed cruise missiles over Canada. As his political career neared its end, he felt less bound by convention. He was also increasingly concerned about the anti-Communist and Cold War rhetoric coming from Washington. Earlier in 1983 at the G-7 summit in Williamsburg, Virginia,

Ronald Reagan in Ottawa, 1981.

Trudeau engaged in open conflict with Reagan and especially Reagan's soul-mate, Prime Minister Margaret Thatcher of the United Kingdom, who accused the Canadian of providing "solace" to the Soviets in his approach to the issue of disarmament. "Who does this asshole think he is?" pondered one outraged U.S. official aloud.

For his part, Trudeau found Thatcher rather doctrinaire and unnecessarily argumentative. He held considerably less respect for the former actor turned elderly president. "Reagan could be pleasant company for social conversation," he remembered, "but was not a man for thoughtful policy discussion."

Cumulatively, the KAL shoot down, his own past, and the policies of the Reagan administration inspired Trudeau to take a chance three years into his final period as prime minister. The course he would follow was more directly influenced by a meeting earlier in 1983 with anti-nuclear activist Dr. Helen Caldicott, featured in the National Film Board documentary "If You Love This Planet," a film banned as anti-American propaganda in the United States [see the chapter on the controversy]. Through ego stroking, Caldicott reinforced in him a desire to ensure a legacy for himself by steering the Soviet Union and the United States toward a path of peace.

The reaction of the Reagan administration to KAL 007 only reinforced Trudeau's chosen path. In late September, he met with bureaucrats from the Department of National Defence and External Affairs and announced his attention to pursue the cause of peace. Although the response to his announcement was decidedly unenthusiastic, a special panel of senior bureaucrats began mulling over a peace agenda for Trudeau to sell to the world. They received a scant deadline for their deliberations. The proposals needed to be ready for a speech the prime minister was to deliver at a conference on nuclear policy at the University of Guelph on October 27, 1983.

The panel set to work and quickly produced over two dozen peace proposals that were eventually reduced to five, including a ban on high altitude and space weapons, strengthening a non-proliferation treaty, and a conference of the five powers known to possess nuclear weapons. These would serve as the basis for

Trudeau's peace mission that he announced on October 27. The response to news of his peace mission ranged from mild interest, to general indifference, to open hostility. The issue he was tackling concerned Canadians. Thirty-eight percent listed international affairs as their main worry, a figure that was several times larger than anything found in previous polls dating back over the previous twenty years. The fear of nuclear war was heightened among the Canadian public in November when "The Day After," an American film that graphically depicted the effect of a nuclear conflict, appeared on television.

Far from enthusiastic about the mission were Canada's allies, who received but a brief warning of it by formal letter. In an effort to mollify his critics, Trudeau attempted to emphasize a two-track approach to the nuclear issue. Support would be forthcoming for future missile deployments, specifically of the Pershing II, the first of which was deployed in West Germany on November 23, but a renewed dialogue between the superpowers had to occur simultaneously.

The Canadian globetrotter began his mission in Europe, spending a week touring the capitals of several allies. One destination that did not appear on his initial itinerary was London, where Margaret Thatcher was not expected to offer a warm welcome. To Trudeau's surprise, however, she invited him to London for a discussion, although, as usual with the British prime minister, only one person did most of the talking. Stressing to her Commonwealth colleague the futility of his campaign, Thatcher added that nuclear war was not as bad as its critics made out. "[S]urely you know," she told a stunned Trudeau, "that one year after Hiroshima, grass was growing again."

From London, Trudeau returned to Canada before setting off on an Asian tour. While in India, the details on a trip to Beijing, China, were finalized. Suddenly the mission had a far higher profile, as Trudeau sat down with the leader of China, Deng Xiaoping, for an hour-long meeting on November 27. Again the prime minister of Canada found himself in the position of politely listening as the seventy-nine-year-old Deng droned on for nearly the entire meeting, catching his guest's attention when he decried the horrors of nuclear war but added: "Two billion people would be killed. But China would survive."

Regardless of his achievements, support back home for the mission remained strong. It was from Canada that Trudeau would embark on the most important leg of his mission, a trip to Washington. Little hope of converting Reagan to his cause existed. The president had found Trudeau condescending in previous meetings, and his advisors were no more charitably inclined. "Akin to pot-induced behaviour by an erratic leftist" was how one undersecretary at the State

Department described the mission, and he was considered to be sympathetic toward Canada. The criticism struck a nerve with Trudeau, who, in response to a question from an American reporter about critics of his peace efforts, decried such views as the ramblings of "Pentagon pipsqueaks."

The meeting with Reagan marked the high point of Trudeau's mission. Trudeau followed the advice of External Affairs to speak to Reagan on a personal basis — "Ron, I know you are a man of peace" was one such example — and this seemed to reach the president as he listened to Trudeau. In the end, however, Reagan made no commitment beyond wishing his Canadian colleague "Godspeed" on the remainder of his mission.

"Godspeed" did not take the would-be prince of peace very far. In January 1984, he travelled to Eastern Europe to meet with leaders of Romania, East Germany, and Czechoslovakia. His efforts to meet Reagan's rival, Yuri Andropov, proved futile because the Soviet's leader next major meeting was to be with a pine box. When he died, Trudeau flew to Moscow for the funeral and, in its aftermath, spoke with Andropov's successor, Konstantin Chernenko, who would die thirteen months later.

All that was left was a summary, first by Trudeau and then by the historians. The prime minister rose in the House of Commons on February 9, 1984, less than three weeks before he would take a fateful walk in a snowstorm and reach the decision to resign his office. Not surprisingly, he declared the mission a victory, pointing to ten principles on which the superpowers had found common ground, including the impossibility of winning a nuclear conflict. An Albert Einstein Peace Prize for his work soon followed.

But what had the prime minister's efforts actually accomplished? In his memoirs, he pointed to a significant reduction in Cold War rhetoric emanating from Washington after his visit. More significant to this cooling, however, was that the Reagan administration had learned through its intelligence services the seriousness of the possibility of conflict between the superpowers in the fall of 1983. NATO had launched a military exercise code-named "Abel Archer 83." The Soviet Union at the highest levels, believing in the aggressive language from Washington, became convinced that the military exercise represented subterfuge to the preparation for a first strike against the Soviet Union. KGB operatives around the globe were ordered to monitor the preparations for the strike. Only a relaxing of the American rhetoric and messages through diplomatic channels calmed the situation, and Pierre Trudeau did not factor into that.

Pierre Trudeau at the funeral of Leonid Brezhnev in 1984.

The Anti-Communism of Harold Ballard

In the Cold War year of 1985, for a change a hockey game at Maple Leaf Gardens sparked with excitement. That the match did not involve the Toronto Maple Leafs, a once glorious franchise that was now a North America-wide laughingstock because of its poor play, mediocre management, and crazed and cantankerous convicted criminal owner, may have accounted for some of the anticipation. The two teams that did play were not by any means top flight, and the game itself was merely an exhibition. Representing Canada was its Olympic team, largely composed of anonymous players in a non-Olympic year. The real significance of the event lay in the Canadian squad's opponents, the Moscow Dynamo, not so much because they were particularly good, but because they were a Soviet team playing at Maple Leaf Gardens.

An appearance of Soviets at Maple Leaf Gardens had not taken place in years, ever since the owner of the arena and the Maple Leafs, Harold Ballard, had banned Soviet players and even the Moscow circus from setting foot in his building. For the eighty-one-year-old owner, the conversion to anti-Communism had occurred rather late in the Cold War. During the 1972 Canada-Soviet hockey series, Ballard had spoken in glowing terms about

Soviet players, even suggesting that they had a place in the National Hockey League. That was then, however, and in the meantime his Maple Leafs had floundered, largely because of poor management handpicked by the owner, and made few inroads in developing European players.

Overnight, Ballard became an enemy of the Soviet Union, invoking Cold War rhetoric as the rationale behind his change of heart. He labelled the Soviet teams that came to Canada to play as "parasites," and added that they used the money earned on the tours to "buy bullets" back home to be used in future conflicts against the West. In one interview he suggested that his views had been no different during the 1972 hockey series: "Look, I hate Commies. When I was in Moscow for the '72 series, I slapped a Leaf sticker on that Commie Lenin's tomb. That's what I think of those jerks."

While initially ignoring the eccentricities of the Toronto owner, eventually the National Hockey League management, inspired by the desire to one day have Soviet players play in its league, forced Ballard to reopen his arena's doors to Soviet hockey teams. He did so unwillingly for the first time with the exhibition game between the Canadian Olympic team and the Moscow Dynamo. Ballard, however, was determined to have the last word on the matter while simultaneously capturing the spotlight for himself. As the end of the game approached, he ordered the arena's scoreboard operator to display a Cold War message: "Remember Korean Airlines Flight 007 shot down by the Russians. Don't cheer, just boo — Harold."

Harold Ballard promoting the Moscow Circus at Maple Leaf Gardens in 1983.

A Tale of Two Wheat Farms:

Gorbachev's 1983 tour of Canada and the End of the Cold War

Mikhail Gorbachev and Pierre Trudeau in Ottawa, 1983.

T wo Canadian wheat farms may have played a small role in bringing an end to the decades Cold War. The year was 1983 and a young (in relation to the gerontocratic leadership that ruled the Soviet Union) fifty-two-year-old Soviet secretary of agriculture had travelled to Canada for a ten-day tour. His name was Mikhail Gorbachev. Within two years he would be leader of the Soviet Union and within a decade his name would become synonymous with the end of the Cold War.

Arriving first in Ottawa, Gorbachev met with a variety of Canadian politi-

Reagan and Gorbachev at a summit in 1986.

cal figures including Prime Minister Pierre Trudeau with whom he had a friendly conversation. His discussions with other parliamentarians did not fare as well. When challenged as to why the Soviet Union stationed KGB personnel at its foreign embassies while advocating mutual trust, Gorbachev testily decried such "spy mania" blaming it on the rhetoric being generated out of the Communist-obsessed America of Ronald Reagan.

The real purpose of the Soviet agricultural secretary's visit was to examine the state of Canadian agriculture. Gorbachev's tour guide was Eugene (Gene) Whelan, Trudeau's bumptious minister of agriculture who was famous for wearing a green Stetson and for a style of speech that bordered on gibberish. Whelan had met his visitor two years earlier on a tour of Soviet farms and at the time had invited his compatriot to make the return voyage.

Although a fact-finding mission about agriculture, Cold War politics underlay the expedition. Whelan took great delight in displaying a supermarket flyer advertising discounted prices on a wide variety of food. "Gene," replied his guest, "you don't try to convert me to capitalism, and I won't try to convert you to Communism." When one discussion broached the subject of the Soviet invasion of Afghanistan, the unusual Soviet agriculture secretary amazed Whelan by labelling it as "a mistake." The two enjoyed themselves in each other's company to the point where they had dinner at an Ottawa steakhouse with a picture of their visit ending up on the restaurant's wall as a monument to the evening.

It was on a tour of two farms, one in Southern Ontario and the other in Alberta, that the course of international events were potentially influenced. Gorbachev could relate to farmers having grown up the son of a combine driver in an agricultural village where hard work was an inherent requirement of life. Now in Alberta, the better publicized incident of the two, he would have the opportunity of conversing with some real Canadian farmers.

Two distinct versions of his visit to a large mixed farm exist, each distorted

Mikhail Gorbachev and Eugene Whelan.

through the prism of the Cold War. Gorbachev met with its owners, a husband and wife, and in one account asked where the workers for such a large operation were. The farmer amazed the Soviet secretary when he replied that he and his wife ran the entire enterprise with only the occasional outside assistance. One of the translators heard the guest mutter "We are not going to see this [in the Soviet Union] for another 50 years" prompting some to suggest that the exchange represented a turning point in Gorbachev's thinking about the viability of the Soviet system.

In his memoirs Gorbachev offered his own version of the farm tour. He acknowledged asking the farmer how many workers he employed although no reference is made to his reaction to the farmer's answer. Then, according to Gorbachev, he asked the farmer about the amount of income from the farm. The farmer apparently hesitated before Whelan instructed him to answer the question: "To tell the truth, without subsidies and credit we wouldn't survive." A follow-up query about the length of vacation the farmer and his wife enjoyed elicited a similarly honest reply—they had virtually no vacation because of their responsibility for their farm. Gorbachev then asked his host why subsidies were required for such a productive farm. Whelan noted that all industrialized countries contributed heavy subsidies to their farming sector in order to keep agriculture viable.

Similarly conflicting interpretations of the other significant farm experience do not exist. The farm was Eugene Whelan's very own outside of Windsor, Ontario. Here Gorbachev and the long-time Soviet Ambassador to Canada, Alexander Yakovlev, joined Whelan for dinner. After the meal, the two Soviet guests asked to be excused and, without their accompany Soviet or Canadian security, wandered off into a neighbouring wheat field where they began a profound chat. The heart of that conversation, and both agreed on its significance, was that major change needed to come not only to Soviet agriculture but to the system as a whole that fared badly in relation to what the men had encountered in their Canadian travels.

History would soon demonstrate the significance of that stroll in the wheat field. After Konstantin Chernenko, General Secretary of the Soviet Union, breathed for the last time on March 10, 1985, the Politburo turned to a very different type of Soviet leader as his successor. Gorbachev, with Yakovlev now back in the Soviet Union as a senior advisor, quickly began a series of reforms that soon were recognized worldwide by their Russian names: *glasnost* (the opening up of Soviet society) and *perestroika* (the restructuring of Soviet society). Whether the end result, the toppling of the Communist Party from power and the dissolution of the Soviet Union, was Gorbachev's end goal remains the subject of debate. Regardless of intentions, his reforms unleashed forces that tore the Soviet Union apart and, in the process, ended the political career of the man who started the process. In September 1991 the Soviet Union officially dissolved, and on Christmas Day of the same year, Gorbachev resigned as the president of a nation that no longer existed in an era that had equally reached its conclusion.

Conclusion

I
t had seemed like it would go on forever. Those who had grown up in the shadow of the great global conflict between Communism and capitalism had known no other world. And then it came to a sudden, and largely unanticipated, end.

Cracks began to appear in Eastern Europe in the 1980s, but at first they were papered over. In Poland, the Solidarity movement caught the world's imagination, but was met by the imposition of military rule and more repression. It looked as if the old pattern of Hungary in 1956 and Czechoslovakia in 1968 was being replayed once again. Yet this time appearances were deceiving.

New forces came to the fore in the Soviet Union with Mikhail Gorbachev and his policies of *perestroika* (reform) and *glasnost* (openness). US President Ronald Reagan, who in his first term from 1981 to 1985 had pursued a new Cold War against what he called the 'Evil Empire', met with Gorbachev in 1986 at a summit in Reykjavik, appropriately enough, for old Cold Warriors, in Iceland. Astonishingly, they agreed between them to rid the world of nuclear weapons. Their respective military and political advisers quickly pulled the two leaders back from this leap of faith, but the pattern for further, if measured, cooperation between the superpowers had been set. Successful visits of Reagan to the USSR and Gorbachev to the US followed, as did some concrete progress on arms control.

Behind the façade of its 'superpower' status as an equal negotiating partner with the West, the Soviet Union, with its Warsaw Pact, was no longer a force that could boast, in Nikita Khrushchev's words from the 1950s, that it would 'bury' the capitalist West. Communism as an economic system had failed disastrously to provide both guns and butter, and now it increasingly could provide neither, and politically was losing its grip over a once cowed population. The house of cards came tumbling down in 1989, *annus mirabilis* for Eastern Europe.

The end came with astonishing rapidity. The world watched with amazement as one grim police state regime after another fell, usually without so much as a shot fired in defence. The tectonic shift was unforgettably dramatized by the sight of Germans, East and West, dancing on that ultimate symbol of the Cold War, the Berlin Wall. Within months, the German Democratic Republic, with its Orwellian Stasi secret police, had been consigned to the dustbin of history, and Germany was reunited once more, after four and a half decades of forced separation.

These events were possible because the USSR no longer had the means or the will to enforce its might upon its subject states. Soon the Soviet Union itself began to break up into several parts, divesting Russia of the vast empire it had ruled since the Revolution in 1917. Gorbachev, the agent of change, was himself pushed aside by Boris Yeltsin, and Russia was reconstituted as a non-Communist republic. The map of the world had been redrawn.

There was no victory parade to mark the end of this decades-long contest. There was some triumphalist chest-thumping by old Western Cold Warriors, but the new reality had barely been absorbed when new insecurities arose to take the place of the old. Some naively hoped for a 'peace dividend' following the end of the Cold War arms race, but this never materialized. New threats — terrorism, rogue states, regional ethnic conflagrations, nuclear proliferation, global criminal networks — reared their heads, and the same old Cold War players — the armed forces, the security and intelligence agencies — simply shifted targets and insisted that they needed even more resources to fight diverse, shadowy, and elusive new threats.

In former Communist states ugly ethnic conflicts, frozen in place for decades, erupted into bloody wars of secession. The former Yugoslavia disintegrated into successor states amid 'ethnic cleansing', and the most savage bloodletting Europe had seen since World War II. The rest of the world was even less safe. The Middle East, long a flashpoint for regional conflict, erupted again in 1990 when Iraq invaded Kuwait, and the US marshaled a large military coalition to repel the Iraqis in the first Gulf War. The region continued to boil, with the conflict between the Israelis and the Palestinians worsening over the decade, and another war with Iraq in 2003. India and Pakistan, both armed with nuclear weapons, were constantly at each other's throats, and the bizarre Cold War remnant of North Korea, its citizens starving by the millions, was nonetheless threatening its neighbours and the US with nuclear weapons and missiles to deliver them. The world of the twenty-first century is chaotic and frightening enough to make some yearn almost nostalgically for the lost stability and relative predictability of the Cold War.

During the Cold War, it felt like the West at least had the bad guys' home address. Campaigning in the 2000 Republican presidential primary election in Iowa, George W. Bush is reported to have said: "When I was coming up, it was a dangerous world, and you knew exactly who They were. It was Us vs. Them, and it was clear who Them was. Today, we are not so sure who the They are, but we know They're there." Half a year into his presidency, on September 11, 2001, terrorists struck with lethal fury at the World Trade Centre and the Pentagon. A decade after the end of the Cold War, it had once again become clear who the 'They' are, even if it has proven to be difficult to track them down. The world has entered into a new phase in international relations, a War on Terror. And once again, Canada is being enlisted by Washington for a global crusade against evil.

There are many eerie parallels today to the Cold War, especially in its early stages. Sometimes we can see where we are now headed by glancing into the rear view mirror, into the Cold War past. Then as now, we define ourselves in terms of the Other, the Enemy. Then it was Communism; now it is Terrorism. Then, it was personified in Stalin, Mao, and their successors.

Today it is Osama bin Laden and, less persuasively, Saddam Hussein. Then as now, the enemy posed both an external and an internal threat. Then, as now, the pursuit of the enemy without has grave implications for peace, while the pursuit of the enemy within is fraught with ugly consequences for civility, tolerance, and the fabric of civil liberties and liberal democracy. It is here that we can learn lessons from Canada's earlier experience of the Cold War.

There was a threat to the security of Canada during the Cold War. The USSR was a hostile foreign power that did challenge Western and Canadian interests at many points around the globe. The Communist Bloc states were oppressive police state regimes, with appalling human rights records. By the 1950s, the USSR was armed with nuclear weapons, and by the 1960s, it possessed intercontinental missiles that threatened to deliver these weapons of mass destruction to North America. The Soviets did spy on Canada, and they did persuade some Canadians with certain ideological views to betray their country. All these things were true, and Cold War critics risked discrediting themselves when they denied or rationalized these facts.

Nevertheless, over and over again, the West overreacted in its response to the USSR, and in this Canada was no exception. Especially in the early days of the Cold War, there were signs of panicked reactions, and excesses in pursuit of security that did liberal democracies like Canada no credit. Above all, there was often a failure to distinguish carefully between the actual threat posed and the alarmist exaggerations that were rife, and a failure to calculate coolly and rationally a measured and proportionate response.

Canada also faced constant pressures during the Cold War to import American notions of security into Canadian law and administrative practice. There was never any shortage of Canadians ready to urge just this kind of cooperation. Sometimes Canadian officials gave way to these pressures, sometimes they acted preemptively to avoid American criticism, and sometimes they persisted in doing things the Canadian way, but Canada rarely had the luxury of simply ignoring American pressures; almost always, it was reacting to US initiatives. Always, however, there was a dogged insistence on retaining at least some semblance of sovereignty. Despite the Cold War alliance, and the dependence of Canada on the American nuclear shield, and however much Canadians welcomed American movies, television, sports, and all forms of popular culture, they continued throughout the Cold war years to resist becoming part of the Republic to the south. As one Canadian politician once inelegantly put it, the Americans were our best friends, whether we liked it or not.

The War on Terrorism has brought many of the same pressures back to the forefront. American security concerns have focused on their northern border, and numerous unjustified criticisms have been made in the US about lax Canadian immigration security representing a threat to the US. Pressures to 'harmonize' Canadian policies within a North American security perimeter seriously challenge Canadian sovereignty. As in the Cold war, these pressures come not only from the US, but also from within Canada, and together they place great strains on the margin for autonomous action by the government of Canada. Once again, the government finds itself negotiating a precarious passage between reassuring the Americans on the one side, and protecting as much Canadian sovereignty as they can on the other.

The Cold War was an all-encompassing struggle that redefined the world to successive postwar generations. The Cold Warriors, convinced of the apocalyptic nature of the great contest between capitalism and Communism, between freedom and totalitarianism, a contest made even more portentous by the spectre of nuclear arsenals that could obliterate all life on the planet, tried to put every aspect of life through the Cold War filter: politics, economics, culture, religion, everything was grist for the Cold War mills. Yet one of the most striking observations about this era is that Canadians, except perhaps for a minority, never really bought this crusading vision. If Cold War ideology and Cold War obsessions dominated the media, and invaded even the thoughts and dreams of Canadians, they never did so exclusively. There was always, even from the very start, resistance. This resistance mounted with time, moving into the mainstream, so much so that it could be said that in many ways the Cold War was already over for Canadians well before the fall of the Berlin Wall.

The War on Terrorism reprises much of the evangelical zeal of the Cold War, especially in the eyes of the US. As George W. Bush declaimed in the wake of Sept. 11, you are either with us, or on the side of the terrorists. It has not taken long for resistance to this 'all-or-nothing' vision to rise in Canada, as it indeed has done in Europe and elsewhere around the globe. Canadians like to look for shadings, complexities, and seek the middle ground. Here perhaps is the final and most important lesson of the Cold War for Canada: Canada took sides in that conflict, and stayed loyal throughout to the cause of the West, but it insisted on doing this in a balanced, level-headed way. Canadians today abhor terrorism, and are willing to cooperate fully in doing their part. But they are already resisting pressures to see the world in stark terms of good vs. evil, and resisting pressures to follow the US in every foreign intervention it unilaterally declares. History teaches many lessons, and some are even learned.

Timeline

1945

September 5, 6: Igor Gouzenko defects from Soviet Embassy in Ottawa.

September 30: Prime Minister Mackenzie King discloses Gouzenko story to U.S. President Harry Truman in Washington.

October 6: Secret Order in Council authorizes the detention of espionage suspects in Gouzenko affair.

October 7: King arrives in London to consult with British Prime Minister Clement Attlee.

November 15: Canada-U.S.-United Kingdom secret agreement on handling Gouzenko affair.

1946

February 5: Taschereau-Kellock Royal Commission appointed to investigate Gouzenko.

February 15: Dawn raids sweep up twelve spy suspects for interrogation in Royal Canadian Mounted Police (RCMP) barracks.

March 5: Sir Winston Churchill delivers "Iron Curtain" speech in Fulton, Missouri.

April 16: Cabinet creates Security Panel to advise on internal security.

June 20: Only elected Communist Member of Parliament, Fred Rose, sentenced to six years for espionage.

1947

March 12: Truman doctrine announced, committing U.S. to combat Communist aggression worldwide.

June 5: U.S. offers Marshall Plan for European economic recovery.

1948

February: Quebec reactivates pre-war "Padlock Law" with raids on left-wing organizations.

March 5: Secret Cabinet directive on security screening of civil servants.

November 15 : Mackenzie King retires; Louis St. Laurent becomes prime minister.

November 20: Secret Cabinet directive on immigration screening.

1949

April 4: National Atlantic Treaty Organization (NATO) formed, and Canada becomes a member.

June: Trades and Labour Congress expels Communist-led unions.

September: Chinese Communists victorious in Chinese Civil War, and People's Republic of China proclaimed.

November: Purge of left-wingers in National Film Board; commissioner dismissed.

1950

June 25 - 27: War in Korea; United Nations (UN) Security Council calls on members to assist South Korea against Communist invasion from the North.

August 7: Canada sends forces to Korea.

October: Bruno Pontecorvo, atomic scientist at Chalk River nuclear plant, defects to the Soviet Union.

October-November: First investigation into the loyalty of Canadian diplomat Herbert Norman.

November: China enters the Korean War, driving UN forces back below 38th parallel.

1951

January 31: Canada sends land and air forces to Europe under NATO.

May 8, 27: British diplomats Guy Burgess and Donald Maclean defect to the USSR.

1952

January-February: Second investigation of Herbert Norman.

May 15: Cabinet considers but rejects laying treason charges against the Reverend James Endicott of the Canadian Peace Congress.

October-December: Efforts of Lester Pearson at UN to broker peace in Korea fail due to U.S. opposition.

1953

March 5: Death of Josef Stalin.

June 19: Juilius and Ethel Rosenberg executed in U.S. for atomic espionage despite worldwide protests.

July 27: Armistice in Korea.

November: Canada agrees to build Mid-Canada air warning line.

1954

April: French army defeated by Communists in Vietnam.

July: Canada joins International Control Commission in IndoChina.

November: Joint Canada-U.S. development of the Distant Early Warning (DEW) Line announced.

1955

February: Lester Pearson indicates to U.S. that Canada will not offer military assistance in the crisis over the straits of Taiwan.

1956

February: Krushchev's secret speech to the 20th Party Congress of the Communist Party of the Soviet Union.

October 23: Hungarian Revolt begins.

October 29-30: Britain, France, and Israel invade Egypt after Egyptian president nationalized Suez Canal in July.

November: U.N. negotiates withdrawal from Egypt and UN peacekeeping force; Pearson key diplomatic figure.

November 4: Red Army begins bloody repression of Hungarian Revolt.

December: 37,000 Hungarian refugees begin arriving in Canada.

1957

March 7: Supreme Court of Canada rules Quebec's Padlock Law unconstitutional.

April: Canadian Communist party in disarray; mass resignations.

April 4: Herbert Norman commits suicide in Cairo.

June 10: Liberals defeated; Conservative John Diefenbaker heads minority government.

August 1: Creation of North American Air Defence Treaty (NORAD) announced.

October 14: Pearson receives Nobel Prize for peace for his role in the Suez Crisis.

1958

March 31: Diefenbaker wins landslide majority in general election.

August 29: Canada-U.S. Defence Production Sharing Agreement.

1959

January 1: Fidel Castro's revolutionaries come to power in Cuba.

February 20: AVRO Arrow project for Canadian jet fighter cancelled.

1960

May 1: American U-2 spy plane shot down over the Soviet Union. The Soviet government later produces the pilot, Gary Powers, after Eisenhower administration denies the spy mission.

October 12: Nikita Khrushchev bangs his shoe on desk at the United Nations.

November 9: Democrat John F. Kennedy defeats Republican Richard Nixon to win U.S. presidency.

November: The split between Moscow and Beijing is made public.

1961

January 27: The Diefenbaker government finalizes Canada's first major wheat sale to Communist China. Larger deals would soon follow.

February 1: U.S. tests the Minuteman, an intercontinental ballistic missile.

April 17: CIA-sponsored Bay of Pigs invasion of Cuba fails.

May 16: Kennedy travels to Ottawa to meet with Diefenbaker.

August 13: Construction of the Berlin Wall begins.

1962

January 1962: Tim Buck steps down as leader of the Communist Party of Canada. Leslie Morris replaces him. After Morris's death, William Kashtan becomes the new leader.

June 18: In a federal election, the Diefenbaker government wins a minority government over Lester Pearson and the Liberals.

October 22: The Kennedy government announces its policy of quarantine in response to the discovery of the construction of a Soviet missile base on the island of Cuba. The crisis ends on October 28.

1963

February 4: Minister of Defence Douglas Harkness resigns from the federal Cabinet over the government's nuclear policy. The next day, the government loses two non-confidence votes. Five days later, two more Ministers quit the Cabinet.

April 8: Pearson and the Liberals defeat the Diefenbaker government, forming a minority government of their own.

November 22: President Kennedy is assassinated in Dallas. He is succeeded by Vice-President Lyndon Johnson.

1964

May: Lester Pearson meets secretly with Lyndon Johnson and raises no strenuous objections to U.S. proposal to bomb North Vietnam.

August 7: The Gulf of Tonkin Resolution provides the Johnson administration with the power to escalate American involvement in Vietnam.

October: Canada's former ambassador to the Soviet Union, John Watkins, dies of a heart attack during an interrogation by members of the RCMP security service on Thanksgiving weekend.

October: Senior party members force Nikita Khrushchev from power.

1965

March 2: Operation Rolling Thunder, an American bombing campaign against North Vietnam, begins. Shortly after the first teach-ins are held in the United States and Canada.

April 2: During a speech at Temple University, Pearson calls for a "pause" to U.S. bombing of North Vietnam.

November 8: Federal election returns a Liberal minority government.

1966

March 4: The name of Gerda Munsinger is raised in the House of Commons for the first time.

1967

July 25: French President Charles De Gaulle proclaims "Vive le Québec Libre" while on a state visit to Quebec.

1968

May 3: Thousands of students take to the streets of Paris in a month-long protest that would inspire young people around the world.

June 25: Pierre Trudeau and the Liberals win a majority government in the federal election.

August: Soviet and other Eastern European soldiers crush Czechoslovakia's "Prague Spring."

November 5: Republican Richard Nixon wins the U.S. presidential election.

November 21: Students occupy the administration building at Simon Fraser University. Two days later, the occupation ends peacefully.

1969

January 29: Students occupy the computer centre at Sir George Williams University in Montreal. On February 11, the occupation ends with vandalism and the arrest of ninety-one people.

July: Trudeau and federal Cabinet discuss the possibility of Canada withdrawing from NATO.

October: In October, the White House and the Kremlin announce the Strategic Arms Limitation Talks (SALT).

1970

October 5: British High Commissioner to Canada James Cross kidnapped by members of the FLQ, sparking the October Crisis that would lead to the invocation of the War Measures Act and the murder of Quebec Cabinet Minister Pierre Laporte.

1971

September 15: A boat named *Greenpeace* sails from Vancouver to protest against a U.S. nuclear test at Amchitka, Alaska.

1972

February 21: Nixon visits China.

March 13: The RCMP begin interrogating Leslie James Bennett, the former head of the Soviet desk in the security service, on the (incorrect) suspicion that he is a Soviet mole. In July, the RCMP would fire him. In 1993, the Canadian government would apologize to Bennett for the treatment he had received and pay him compensation.

May 22: SALT I signed in Moscow by Brezhnev and Nixon.

September 28: Paul Henderson's goal in Moscow in the final minute of the game gives Team Canada both a 6-5 triumph over Team USSR and victory in the eight-game series.

October 30: Pierre Trudeau's government squeaks through to a re-election victory by a margin of two seats. The NDP under David Lewis would play a significant role in maintaining the minority government.

November 7: Nixon wins re-election in a landslide over George McGovern.

1973

October 6: Egypt and Syria launch a surprise attack against Israel on the holiest day of the Jewish calendar. Oil embargoes would be used late in the 1970s as a weapon against the West's support of Israel.

October 10: Trudeau becomes the first Canadian Prime Minister to visit China. During the three-day visit, he meets with Chairman Mao.

1974

July 8: Trudeau and Liberals win a majority government.

August 9: Richard Nixon resigns as president; Gerald Ford becomes the thirty-eighth U.S. president.

1975

April 30: Saigon falls, and South Vietnam surrenders to North Vietnam.

1976

January: Trudeau visits Cuba and warmly embraces Fidel Castro. He proclaims, "Long live Prime Minister and Commander-in-Chief Fidel Castro. Long live Cuban-Canadian friendship."

June 16: Trudeau meets with President Ford in Washington and confirms Canada's commitment to NATO.

November 2: Democrat Jimmy Carter wins the presidential election over Ford.

1977

January 21: One day after his inauguration, Carter declares an amnesty for Vietnam draft resisters.

June 15: The provincial government of René Levesque, elected the previous year, appoints the Keable Commission to investigate RCMP activities. Less than a month later, the Trudeau government announces the creation of the Royal Commission to Investigate Certain Activities of the Royal Canadian Mounted Police (the McDonald Commission).

October 28: Trudeau informs House of Commons that in 1973 members of the RCMP security service entered offices of the Parti Quebecois to secretly copy party records.

1978

December 25: Vietnam invades Cambodia and eventually topples the genocidal government of Pol Pot.

1979

February 1: Ayatollah Ruhollah Khomeni returns to Iran as part of the Iranian Revolution.

May 22: Joe Clark and the Progressive Conservatives defeat Trudeau and the Liberals, winning a minority government.

June 18: Carter and Brezhnev sign the SALT II Treaty in Vienna.

July 1979: A special conference to address the tens of thousands of refugees from Southeast Asia (the "boat people") is convened in Geneva.

July 20: The Sandinistas topple the regime of Anastasio Somoza in Nicaragua.

December 24: The Soviet Union's invasion of Afghanistan begins.

1980

January 20: President Jimmy Carter announces U.S. will boycott the Summer Olympics in Moscow if Soviet troops are not withdrawn from Afghanistan. Forty-four other nations, including Canada, would follow the American lead and not send their athletes to Moscow.

February 18: Liberals under Pierre Trudeau defeat the Progressive Conservative government of Joe Clark.

November 4: Republican challenger Ronald Reagan defeats incumbent Jimmy Carter in U.S. presidential election.

1981

April: The Reagan administration requests Canada's permission to test the cruise missile over Canadian territory.

1982

February: Canada-U.S. Testing and Evaluation Program (CANUSTEP), the legislation to allow the testing of the cruise missile, is introduced in the House of Commons.

June 8: Reagan refers to the Soviet Union as an "evil empire."

October 14: Bomb explodes at Litton Systems of Canada, responsible for manufacturing a component in the U.S. cruise missile.

November 10: Brezhnev dies and is succeeded by Yuri Andropov.

1983

March 23: Reagan announces U.S. plans for the Strategic Defence Initiative or "Star Wars."

May: At the G-7 Summit in Williamsburg, Virginia, Pierre Trudeau repeatedly clashes with Reagan and the president's ideological soulmate British Prime Minister Margaret Thatcher over policy toward the Soviet Union.

May: Mikhail Gorbachev, a Soviet official, heads agricultural delegation to Canada.

September 1: Soviet fighter shoots down Korean Airlines (KAL) 007, killing 269 people.

September 5: Canada joins with other countries in announcing sanctions against the Soviet Union over the KAL attack.

September 25: Pierre Trudeau, reflecting secret intelligence information, labels the KAL 007 attack as an "unfortunate accident."

October 25: The U.S., without any advance warning to Canada, invades Grenada.

October 27: Trudeau announces his peace mission during a speech at the University of Guelph.

November 27: Trudeau, on his peace travels, meets with Deng Xiaoping in Beijing.

1984

January: Trudeau meets with several Eastern European leaders as part of his peace mission.

February 9: Yuri Andropov dies and is succeeded by Konstantin Chernenko.

February 29: Canada's prime minister announces his retirement.

July 16: The Canadian Security Intelligence Service replaces the RCMP security service.

September 4: The Conservatives under the leadership of Brian Mulroney win a majority government.

November 6: Reagan wins re-election in a landslide over Walter Mondale.

1985

March 10: Chernenko dies and is replaced by Mikhail Gorbachev.

March: Mulroney government and Reagan administration agree to a $7 billion overhaul of NORAD.

November: Reagan and Gorbachev meet in Geneva, Switzerland.

1986

October 12: Talks between Reagan and Gorbachev in Reykjavik, Iceland, end without an agreement.

1987

June 6: Reflecting hawkish attitudes in a time of lessening tensions, the Mulroney government introduces a White Paper on defence that proposes spending increases and the acquisition of ten to twelve nuclear-powered submarines. Due to the cost and public opposition, the plan is later scrapped.

December 8: In Washington, Reagan and Gorbachev sign an agreement to reduce nuclear stockpiles by ten percent and eliminate medium-range nuclear missiles.

1988

November 8: George Bush Sr., Reagan's vice-president, wins the U.S. election.

November 21: Brian Mulroney wins re-election as prime minister.

1989

February: The last Soviet soldiers depart Afghanistan.

November 10: The Berlin Wall falls.

December 29: Vaclav Havel, playwright and former dissident, is freely elected president of Czechoslovakia.

1990

October 3: Germany is reunified.

1991

December 31: The Soviet Union ceases to exist.

Additional Readings

Abella, Irving. *Nationalism, Communism, and Canadian Labour*. Toronto: UTP, 1973.

Adams, Ian. *Agent of Influence: A True Story*. Don Mills, ON: Stoddart Publishing, 1999.

Adams, Ian. *S: Portrait of a Spy*. Toronto: Gage Publishing, 1977.

Adams, Mary Louise. *The Trouble with Normal: Postwar Youth and the Making of Heterosexuality*. Toronto: UTP, 1997.

Avakumovic, Ivan. *The Communist Party in Canada: A History*. Toronto: McClelland and Stewart, 1975.

Barros, James. *No Sense of Evil: Espionage, the Case of Herbert Norman*. Toronto: Deneau, 1986.

Beeby, Dean. *Cargo of Lies: The True Story of a Nazi Double Agent in Canada*. Toronto: UTP, 1996.

Beeching, William, and Phyllis Clarke, eds. *Yours in the Struggle: Reminiscences of Time Buck*. Toronto: NC Press, 1977.

Bercuson, David. *Blood on the Hills: The Canadian Army in Korea*. Toronto: UTP, 1999.

Bothwell, Robert. *Eldorado: Canada's National Uranium Company*. Toronto: UTP 1984.

Bothwell, Robert. *The Big Chill: Canada and the Cold War*. Toronto: Canadian Institute of International Affairs, 1998.

Bothwell, Robert and J.L. Granatstein, eds., T*he Gouzenko Transcripts: The Evidence Presented to the Kellock-Taschereau Royal Commission of 1946*. Ottawa: Deneau, 1982.

Bowen, Roger. *Innocence is Not Enough: The Life and Death of Herbert Norman*. Vancouver: Douglas & McIntyre, 1986.

Callwood, June. *Emma: The True Story of Canada's Unlikely Spy*. Toronto: Stoddard, 1984.

Cleroux, Richard. *Official Secrets: The Story Behind the Canadian Security Intelligence Service*. Scarborough: McGraw-Hill, 1990.

Collins, Anne. *In the Sleep Room: The Story of the CIA Brainwashing Experiments in Canada*. Toronto: Lester & Orpen Dennys, 1988.

De Vault, Carole. *The Informer*. Toronto: Fleet Books, 1982.

Dion, Robert. *Crimes of the Secret Police*. Montreal: Black Rose Books, 1982.

Donaghy, Greg, ed. *Canada and the Early Cold War, 1943-1957*. Ottawa: DFAIT, 1998.

Donaghy, Greg, ed. *Uncertain Horizons: Canadians and their World in 1945*. Ottawa: Canadian Committee on the History of the Second World War, 1997.

Eayrs, James. *In defence of Canada*: 5 vols: Toronto: UTP, 1964-1983.

Eayrs, James. *The Commonwealth and Suez: A Documentary Survey*. London: OUP, 1964.

Endicott, Stephen. *James G. Endicott: Rebel Out of China*. Toronto: UTP, 1980.

English, John. *Shadow of Heaven: The Life of Lester Pearson, 1897-1948*. Toronto: Lester & Orpen Dennys, 1989.

English, John. *The Worldly Years: The Life of Lester Pearson, 1949-1972*. Toronto: Knopff Canada, 1992.

Evans, Gary. *In the National Interest: A Chronicle of the National Film Board of Canada from 1949 to 1989*. Toronto: UTP, 1991.

Evans, Gary. *The Politics of Wartime Propaganda: John Grierson and the National Film Board of Canada*. Toronto: UTP, 1984.

Finkel, Alvin. *Our Lives: Canada After 1945*. Toronto: Lorimer, 1997.

Frost, Mike (as told to Michel Gratton). *Spyworld: Inside the Canadian and American Intelligence Establishments*. Toronto: Doubleday, 1994.

Gonick, Cy. *A Very Red Life: The Story of Bill Walsh*. St. John's: CCLH, 2001.

Gouzenko, Igor. *Fall of a Titan*. New York: W. W. Norton & Co. 1954.

Gouzenko, Igor. *This was My Choice: Gouzenko's Story*. Toronto: J.M. Dent, 1948.

Granatstein, J.L. *Yankee Go Home? Canadians and*

Anti-Americanism. Toronto: HarperCollins, 1996.

Granatstein, J.L., and Norman Hillmer. *Empire to Umpire: Canada and the World to the 1990s*. Toronto: Copp Clark Ltd., 1994.

Granatstein, J.L. and David Stafford. *Spy Wars: Espionage and Canada from Gouzenko to Glasnost*. Toronto: Key Porter, 1990.

Green, Jim. *Against the Tide: The Story of the Canadian Seamen's Union*. Toronto: Progress, 1986.

Hannant, Larry. *The Infernal Machine: Investigating the Loyalty of Canada's Citizens*. Toronto: UTP, 1995.

Hansen, Ann. *Direct Action: Memoirs of an Urban Guerrilla*. Toronto: Between the Lines, 2001.

Heaps, Leo, *Hugh Hambleton, Spy: Thirty years with the KGB*. London: Methuen, 1983.

Hewitt, Steve. *Spying 101: The RCMP's Secret Activities at Canadian Universities, 1917-1997*. Toronto: UTP, 2002.

Horn , Michiel. *Academic Freedom in Canada: A History*. Toronto: UTP, 1999.

Infeld, Leopold. *Why I Left Canada: Reflections on Science and Politics*. Montreal: McGill-Queen's, 1978.

Kaplan, William. *Everything That Floats: Pat Sullivan, Hal Banks, and the Semen's Unions of Canada*. Toronto: UTP, 1987.

Kealey, Gregory S. and Whitaker, Reg (eds.):

The R.C.M.P. Security Bulletins The Early Years, 1919-29. St. John's: Canadian Committee on Labour History, 1994.

The R.C.M.P. Security Bulletins The Depression Years, Part 1, 1933-34. St. John's: Canadian Committee on Labour History, 1993.

The R.C.M.P. Security Bulletins The Depression Years, Part 2, 1935. St. John's: Canadian Committee on Labour History, 1995.

The R.C.M.P. Security Bulletins The Depression Years, Part 3, 1936. St. John's: Canadian Committee on Labour History, 1995.

The R.C.M.P. Security Bulletins The Depression Years, Part 4, 1937. St. John's: Canadian Committee on Labour History, 1997.

The R.C.M.P. Security Bulletins The Depression Years, Part 5, 1938-39. St. John's: Canadian Committee on Labour History, 1997.

The R.C.M.P. Security Bulletins The War Series, Part 1, 1939-1941. St. John's: Canadian Committee on Labour History, 1989.

The R.C.M.P. Security Bulletins The War Series, Part 2, 1942-45. St. John's: Canadian Committee on Labour History, 1992.

Kinsman, Gary, Buse, Dieter K., & Steedman, Mercedes, eds., *Whose National Security? Canadian State Surveillance and the Creation of Enemies*. Toronto: Between the Lines, 2000.

Lester, Normand. *Enquêtes sur les Services Secrets*. Montreal: Les Éditions De L'homme, 1998.

Lisée, Jean-François. *In the Eye of the Eagle: Secret Files Reveal Washington's Plans for Canada and Québec*. Toronto: Harper Collins Canada, 1990.

Littleton, James. *Target Nation: Canada and the Western Intelligence Network*. Toronto: Lester & Orpen Dennys, 1986.

Lunan, Gordon. *The Making of a Spy: A Political Odyssey*. Montreal: Robert Davies, 1995.

Lyon, Peyton V., *The Loyalties of E. Herbert Norman*. Ottawa: External Affairs and International Trade Canada, 1990. Reprinted in *Labour/le Travail* 28 (Fall 1991) 219-59.

Marks, John. *The Search for the "Manchurian Candidate": The CIA and Mind Control*. London: Allen Lane, 1979.

Mackenzie, David. *Canada's Red Scare: 1945-1957*. Translated by Fabien Saint-Jacques. Ottawa: Canadian Historical Association, 2001.

MacSkimming, Roy. *Cold War: The Amazing Canada-Soviet Hockey Series of 1972*. Toronto: Douglas & McIntyre, 1997.

Margolian, Howard. *Unauthorized Entry: The Truth about Nazi War Criminals in Canada, 1946-1956*. Toronto: UTP, 2000.

Mitrovica, Andrew. *Covert Entry: Spies, Lies and Crimes inside Canada's Secret Service*. Toronto: Random House of Canada, 2002.

Mount, Graeme S., *Canada's Enemies: Spies and Spying in the Peaceable Kingdom*. Toronto: Dundurn Press, 1993.

Owram, Douglas. *Born at the Right Time: A History of the Baby-Boom Generation*. Toronto: UTP, 1996.

Palmer, Bryan, ed. *A Communist Life: Jack Scott and the Canadian workers movement, 1927-1985*. St. John's: Canadian Committee on Labour History, 1988.

Penner, Norman. *Canadian Communism: The Stalin Years and Beyond*. Toronto: Methuen, 1988.

Pickles, Katie. *Female Imperialism and National Identity: Imperial Order Daughters of the Empire*. Manchester: Manchester University Press, 2002.

Ross, Douglas A., *In the Interests of Peace: Canada and Vietnam 1954-1973*. Toronto: UTP, 1984.

Sawatsky, John. *For Services Rendered: Leslie James Bennett and the RCMP Security Service*. Toronto: Doubleday, 1982.

Sawatsky, John. *Gouzenko: The Untold Story*. Toronto: Macmillan, 1984.

Sawatsky, John. *Men in the Shadows: The RCMP Security Service*. Toronto: Doubleday, 1980.

Scher, Len. *The Un-Canadians: True Stories of the Blacklist Era*. Toronto: Lester, 1992.

Smith, Doug. *Cold Warrior: C.S. Jackson and the United Electrical Workers*. St. John's: CCLH, 1997.

Smith, Denis. *Rogue Tory: The Life and Legend of John G. Diefenbaker*. Toronto: ?, 1995.

Stairs, Denis, *The Diplomacy of Constraint: Canada, the Korean War, and the United States*. Toronto: UTP, 1974.

Stanton, John. *Life and Death of the Canadian Seamen's Union*. Toronto: Steel Rail, 1978.

Stanton, John. *My Past is Now: Further Memoirs of a Labour Lawyer*. St. John's: Canadian Committee on Labour History, 1994.

Stark, James T. *Cold War Blues: The Operation Dismantle Story*. Hull: Voyageur, 1991.

Starnes, John. *Closely Guarded: a Life in Canadian Security and Intelligence*. Toronto: UTP, 1998.

Watkins, John, ed. Dean Beeby & William Kaplan. *Moscow Dispatches: Inside Cold War Russia*. Toronto: Lorimer, 1987.

Wesibord, Merrily. *The Strangest Dream: Canadian Communists, the Spy Trials, and the Cold War*. Toronto: Lester & Orpen Dennys, 1983.

Whitaker, Reg & Marcuse, Gary. *Cold War Canada: the Making of a National Insecurity State, 1945-1957*. Toronto: UTP, 1994.

Whitaker, Reg. *Double Standard: The Secret History of Canadian Immigration*. Toronto: Lester & Orpen Dennys, 1987.

Documentaries and Films

Brittain, Donald, dir. "Canada's Sweetheart: The Saga of Hal C. Banks." Canada: National Film Board of Canada, 1985.

Brittain, Donald, dir. "Grierson." Canada: National Film Board of Canada, 1973.

Brittain, Donald, dir. "On Guard For Thee, Part 1: The Most Dangerous Spy." Canada: National Film Board of Canada, 1981.

Brittain, Donald, dir. "On Guard For Thee, Part 2: A Blanket of Ice." Canada: National Film Board of Canada, 1981.

Brittain, Donald, dir. "On Guard For Thee, Part 3: Shadows of a Horseman." Canada: National Film Board of Canada, 1981.

Cobban, William, dir. "Mountie: Canada's Mightiest Myth." Canada: National Film Board of Canada, 1998.

Kramer, John, dir. "The Man Who Might Have Been: An Inquiry into the Life and Death of Herbert Norman." Canada: National Film Board of Canada, 1998.

Brenda Longfellow, dir. "Gerda". Canada: 1992.

Nash, Terre, dir. "If You Love This Planet." Canada: National Film Board of Canada, 1982.

Scher, Len, dir. "The UnCanadians." Canada: National Film Board of Canada, 1996.

Wellman, William A., dir. "The Iron Curtain." United States: Twentieth Century Fox, 1948.

Wheeler, Anne, dir. "The Sleep Room." Canadian Broadcasting Corporation, 1998.

Index

Photo Credits

Legend: Top — T; Centre — C; Bottom — B; Left — L; Right — R

All visuals provided by York University Archives except for those listed below:

Barris, Theodore. *Deadlock in Korea: Canadians at War, 1950-1953*. Toronto: Macmillan Canada, 1999: 70.

Beddoes, Dick. *Pal Hal: An Uninhibited, No-Holds Barred Account of the Life and Times of Harold Ballard*. Toronto: Macmillan, 1989: 234, 235.

Bowen, Roger W. ed. *E.H. Norman: His Life and Scholarship*. Toronto: University of Toronto Press, 1984: 80, 81, 82.

Canadian Public Health Association. *Uprooting, Loss and Adaptation: the Resettlement of Indochinese Refugees in Canada*. 1987: 214, 215T, 215B.

Communist Party of Canada. *Canada's Party of Socialism: History of the Communist Party of Canada 1921-1976*. Toronto: Progress Books, 1971: 18, 21. 32B, 33B, 34T, 108T.

Communist Party of Canada. *Power of the People: Fifty Years of Pictorial Highlights of the Communist Party of Canada 1921-1971*. Toronto: Progress Books, 1971: 34B.

The Diefenbunker, Canada's Cold War Museum, 3911 Carp Road, Ottawa, Ontario, Canada: 100, 119, 120TL, 123TL, 123TR, 123BL, 123BR, 125T, 127T.

Duberman, Martin Baum. *Paul Robeson*. Toronto: Alfred A. Knopf, 1989: 107B, 108B.

Les editions du Memorial (Quebec) Inc. *Le Memorial du Quebec*. 1979: 84, 85T, 85B, 86.

Edwards, Peter. *Waterfront Warlord: The Life and Violent Times of Hal C. Banks*. Toronto: Key Porter Books, 1987: 52T, 52B, 53T, 53B.

Grant, Bruce. *The Boat People*. Penguin, 1979: 212, 213.

Hansen, Ann. *Direct Action: Memoirs of an Urban Guerrilla*. Toronto: Between the Lines Press, 2001: 223, 225.

Haydon, Peter T. *The 1962 Cuban Missile Crisis: Canadian Involvement Reconsidered*. Canadian Institute of Strategic Studies: 1, 142, 143B, 144B.

Hitschmanova, Lotta. *The USC Story*. Toronto: Unitarian Services Committee of Canada, 1970: 55B, 56T, 57.

King, Al. *Red Bait! Struggles of a Mine Mill Local*. Kingbird Publishing, 1988: 91, 106.

Kingwell, Mark. *Canada: Our Century: 100 Voices, 500 Visions*. Toronto: Doubleday Canada, 1999: 181B, 182T, 219.

Look, April 24, 1962: 97.

Maclean's, March 25, 1985: 230B, 236.

McFarlane, Brian. *Team Canada: Where are they now?* Winding Stair Press, 2001: 194, 196.

Mollins, Carl. *Canada's Century*. Toronto: Key Porter Books, 2001: 155T, 181T, 182B.

National Archives of Canada: 29, 30, 79, 157, 171, 176, 191, 198B, 216, 231, 232, 233.

Newsweek, October 13, 1986: 237.

Peterson, Roy. *Drawn and Quartered: The Trudeau Years*. Toronto: Key Porter Books, 1984: 221, 230T.

Post, National et. al. *Trudeau*. Toronto: Key Porter Books, 2000: 197, 199.

Sawatsky, John. *Gouzenko: The Untold Story*. Toronto: Macmillan of Canada, 1984: 15TL, 15TR, 16T, 17.

Stewart, Walter. *MJ: The Life and Times of MJ Coldwell*. Toronto: Stoddart, 2000: 41, 42, 44B.

Strachan, Al, Duhatschek, Eric. *100 Years of Hockey*. Toronto: Key Porter Books, 1999: 192.

Time, November 3, 1980: 190.

Toronto Life, April, 1976: 156B.

Toronto Reference Library Picture Collection: 14TL, 16B, 28, 226, 227, 228.

Weiss, Stephen. *A War Remembered*. Boston: Boston Publishing Company, 1986: 169T, 172T, 173B, 174T.

Whelan, Eugene. *Whelan: The Man in the Green Stetson*. Toronto: Irwin Books, 1986: 238.

Whitaker, Reg. *Cold War Canada*. Toronto: University of Toronto Press, 1996: 47.